For Judy, Kimberly, and Christopher

CONTENTS

□□□□□□□□□□□□□□□□□□□□□□□□

PREFACE

□□□□□□□□□□□□□□□□□□□□□□□□

THIS brief work is a product of my frustration. For several years I have taught courses dealing with sociocultural change, and each year I find it necessary to describe the "evolutionary" approach, the "acculturation" approach, the "behavioral" approach, and so on—just to give the students the background to place their assigned readings and later classroom discussions into some sort of context. But what inevitably happens is that I spend so much time simply describing the approaches themselves that very little time is left to explore the readings critically with the class or to raise other issues of substance. By merely condensing this background material into a small, readable volume, I felt, the pedagogical problem would largely be solved.

Yet as I began to write I found that it would not do to characterize the approaches as completely isolated units. An essential part of the background, I became convinced, consisted of demonstrating that none of the efforts to analyze sociocultural change "just grew," that each represented in part a reaction to its predecessors. And I felt that a further, issues-oriented theme was also needed in the book. Such a theme, problems of documenting *processes* of change, readily suggested itself. But, even to offer a provisional definition of "process" that would not automatically exclude one or more of the approaches, I learned, takes some doing. And it proved a much more formidable challenge to carry this theme coherently through the several chapters. In short, by deciding to write the book I simply added another source of frustration.

A work of this kind is bound to overgeneralize, to be concerned more often with general similarities than with specific variations on a theme. In several instances I had to decide whether tracing the full range of variations within a single approach, such as the "historicist," would help or hinder a clear understanding of what the approach was all about. To keep the account short, my tendency was to avoid long-winded discussions of distinctions within each of the approaches and to concentrate on major distinctions and similarities between them. In other sections I have given very short shrift to issues that are important but somewhat tangential to the main thrust of my discussion. For example, in Chapter Two the role of "racial causation" in the evolutionism of some Victorian scholars is briefly discussed but by no means reflects the proportion of attention devoted to it in other works (cf. Stocking 1968; Harris 1968; Haller 1970). And, I have had to be very sketchy in my treatment of pre-Victorian approaches to change (cf. Harris 1968).

I intend to use this book in conjunction with a series of other readings. Likely anthologies include Bernard and Pelto 1972, The Kiste and Ogan Social Change Series in Anthropology (see Jacobson 1973; Kiste 1973; Miller 1973; Pelto 1973), Eisenstadt 1968 and 1970, and Bohannan and Plog 1967, among others mentioned in the Bibliography. In addition, Bobbs-Merrill has for years produced a large assortment of reprinted articles on sociocultural change. The point is that the book need not stand by itself, and it has in fact been produced in paperback so that instructors and students can feel free to incorporate other reading materials into their courses.

I wish to offer my gratitude to those who encouraged and helped me in writing the book. Charles Smith, Editor-in-Chief of The Free Press, has consistently given me free rein together with his encouragement. Professor Robert Kiste of the University of Minnesota has been a most valuable and patient reviewer of the manuscript, and I have found his suggestions very useful. Professors James Faris and Peter Newcomer of the University of Connecticut patiently read earlier drafts of Chapter Two, particularly the sections dealing with Marx and Engels. Professors Faris and Seth Leacock were generous in lending me materials for my research and in discussing specific issues of interpretation. Ms. Florence Dawson was a most efficient typist of the final draft.

A special debt of gratitude is owed to graduate and undergraduate students in my courses on sociocultural change at the University of Connecticut. They were early recipients of many of the perspectives and issues offered here, and their reactions always were in the back of my mind as the writing progressed.

R.L.B.

INTRODUCTION

▣▣▣▣▣▣▣▣▣▣▣▣▣▣▣▣▣▣▣▣▣▣▣▣▣

FOR A variety of reasons, twentieth-century Western man—perhaps in attempting to escape his predicament or perhaps in succumbing to mass-media advertising—has come to embrace a world view, a design for living, with its tenets rooted in the inevitability of change. Change is for him not only inevitable but desirable in the long run. For example, he *can*, he is assured by the mass media, solve some of his social or economic problems by changing brands of toothpaste, mouthwash, or detergent. "Today is the first day of the rest of your life" has become a byword and a design for living among those subscribing to a belief in the ultimate mutability of the *status quo*.

Perhaps it is not surprising that many Western anthropologists, among others who have been reared in this tradition, have directed their scholarly attention to the subject of change in human behavior, in some cases taking it for granted that change is a constant not only in Western lifeways, but everywhere and always (e.g., Herskovits 1945:143). It is worthwhile to ponder the possible states of present anthropological theorizing if anthropologists and other social scientists had been reared according to the view that the present life is essentially that of the past; that not only is there nothing new under the sun but that there *should* be nothing new under the sun. There are, of course, groups whose members have precisely this perspective on the nature of things, and their existence poses an interesting dilemma regarding the omnipresence of both change and persistence. But, again for many reasons, change (or the attempt to

1

evade it) is an important preoccupation of advertisers and anthropologists, progressives and conservatives. It deserves more exhaustive scholarly consideration than it has customarily received in college social studies curricula.

This brief book represents an attempt to summarize, compare, and contrast several of the major anthropological approaches to the study of sociocultural change. Immediately I must softpedal the "anthropological" adjective, however, because in the development of theory and methodology the traditional boundaries between the several social science disciplines have often (and inevitably) been breached. I have here opted for the relative strength of eclecticism at the possible risk of misclassifying some scholars whose contributions are not anthropological in the strictest sense.

The book is designed primarily for use in college undergraduate courses dealing with sociocultural change. I am interested in tracing the development of approaches to change in a way that is hopefully both coherent and interesting. To this end, the approximate chronological sequence in which each scheme was developed will determine the order in which it is presented here. Science becomes more sophisticated as basic assumptions are scrutinized, criticized, refined, and, in some cases, ultimately replaced. Scientific theories of sociocultural change have been handled in this fashion, although somewhat unfairly at times, I fear; scholars have not always been scholarly in their criticism of others' works, choosing to build straw men to attack or electing to wage warfare at the personal level for the added zest of stalking a living target. This, of course, is a necessary part of the impedimenta of increasing sophistication and deserves description in the pages to follow. But all too often *ad hominem* arguments, adherence to faddism, and an ignoring of analytic levels for the sake of an all-or-nothing repudiation have obscured similarity and continuity among approaches. This must also be considered here. The important point is that no one of these several approaches can be completely understood without some statement about its predecessors and the scholarly milieu in which it arose. Yet the discussion to follow aims only in part at being historical; this mode of presentation is not intended to obscure the substantive issues involved in the development of theory. I do not believe a "historical" mode is necessarily incompatible with an "issues-oriented" one.

This work has another basic task. From each of the approaches considered, it asks for answers to the question "*How* does change take place?" That is, what factors are involved in transforming human behavior patterns through time? What, in brief, are the *processes* of change as conceived by each approach? This theme takes its cues from recent statements by Fredrik Barth (1967:661) to the effect that much of the theory and methodology of change studies has not rigorously or consistently dealt with the problem of processes in change. Instead, "dynamic" theories have been tested by a series of very static ethnographic sketches at different points in time; or "dynamic" sequences turn out to be a series of static categories, ranked according to variations in a selected set of characteristics. Barth focused his comments specifically on the anthropologists' traditional preoccupation with changes in abstract forms of social arrangements, such as extended family groups or descent "rules," and argued that this focus may distort an understanding of changes in the behavior of individuals from which these forms supposedly are abstracted. But, again, I intend to push the point that analysis of change is possible from a variety of perspectives; I wish to inquire how adequately each analytical technique, on its own terms, is able to account for the processes by which change takes place.

"Process" is a very slippery term. It has been used repeatedly in the literature dealing with change (e.g., Herskovits 1945; Barth 1967) with little concern for defining it precisely or consistently, if at all. I am not sure the definition I propose here is any more precise than others, but it does state what my focus will be in the following chapters. "Process" refers to the interaction of causal factors so as to produce a given condition. By "change process," I mean *the interaction of causal factors so as to produce a transformation of one condition into another.* I will be using the concepts of "process" and "mechanism" interdependently.[1]

In other words, I intend to ask the question "Given *their* theory and *their* data, have the various approaches explained how sociocultural changes have taken place, in terms that are scientifically defensible?" Each of the approaches has conceived of the hows, the mechanisms or processes of change, somewhat differently. Mechanisms can be sought at several levels of abstraction, conceivably from that of the molecular to that of cosmic processes mentioned by one of the theorists to be discussed (White 1949b: 366–367). But whatever the level, the approach should be able to explain in some fashion how Condition A becomes Condition B with the passage of time. Lewis Henry Morgan's scheme of general evolution, for example, described a series of stages through which some cultures have progressed. I wish to inquire *how* a culture evolves from the stage of "Upper Savagery" to that of "Lower Barbarism": what are the mechanisms involved as Morgan himself conceived of them? I believe that the scholarly tasks involved in any study of change ought to include not only the documentation of the fact of change but also an explanation of how the transformation took place. The adequacy of the explanation can then be tested by applying it to other situations, thereby leading to its continued substantiation, to refinement, or to ultimate rejection.

A concern with process is a guiding preoccupation, a point

---

[1]This definition borrows from the insights provided by Harsanyi (1968:92; orig. 1960), who observed:

a dynamic theory of society will have to explain social development in terms of the basic causal laws governing the interaction among the various social and environmental variables. It will have to set up analytical models based on specific—and, if possible, quantitative—assumptions concerning the causal influence that each major social and environmental variable has on the other variables, and concerning the causal mechanisms which transmit this influence.

of departure for a critical consideration of the approaches discussed in the following chapters. It will be reviewed again in the final chapter, after the reader has had an opportunity to consider the various processual explanations emerging during the development of change theories. ("Processual" is my choice for the adjectival form of "process," cumbersome as it is when vocalized.)

However, at this point I should insert a qualification: I conceive of this focus on the processes of change as in some situations distinct from a search for the specific *reasons* for change. For certain purposes or at certain levels of analysis, it may be extremely difficult to find the specific reasons for this or that change in a very satisfactory fashion. To borrow a well-known example from natural science: paleontologists and paleoanthropologists may never be able to give specific reasons why *Australopithecus* was replaced over thousands of years by *Homo erectus* instead of by someone else; yet at a higher analytical level they are quite prepared to describe the evolutionary processes by which this transformation took place. So too, then, should anthropologists be in a position to comment on the mechanisms involved in the transformation of, say, a group of hunting bands into a series of more formally organized clans without being able to know the specifics of who did what and why. I am suggesting again a point made years ago by Melville Herskovits: often a search for the whys of a particular change is fruitless, because the events of change occurred too far in the past or cannot be unraveled from the observable data. I would add, however, that this should not deter us from attempting to understand the processes, the mechanisms, involved.

This is by no means a disavowal of the importance of studying specific reasons for change whenever we have information that allows us to do so; rather, it is a suggestion about the ordering of research priorities. As Julian Steward (1955:209; orig. 1949) suggested, we need not wait to find the whys before we begin a search for the hows.

I am interested in raising more problems than can be

solved in this volume. One of the intriguing aspects of the study of change is that there are so many loose ends, so many avenues of approach to the subject, so much yet to be learned, and such a gap between our theory-building and careful, consistent, protracted gathering of basic data to support these theoretical structures. I hope that the problems presented will not lead to a premature and cynical conclusion that theories of culture change have become lost in a series of mutually exclusive mazes.

CHAPTER ONE

SOME FACETS OF THE STUDY OF CHANGE

□□□□□□□□□□□□□□□□□□□□□□□□□□□□□

I WANT to confront the reader initially with some of the facets involved in the study of sociocultural change, beginning with the important one of definitions of terms such as "social structure" and "culture." This chapter is intended as a résumé, not as an exhaustive discussion: I wish to call attention to the existence of these facets, to identify them sketchily, and to indicate their importance in any study of sociocultural change. I will not leave them hanging at the end of the chapter, never to reappear; after this brief introduction, they will be used to focus the discussion of the approaches to follow. By the time the book is read, the student should have a much more thorough understanding of their nature and importance.

Problems of Definition

"Culture" and "social structure" are two of the hoariest terms in the lexicon of anthropologists. One might think that in the long period of their maturation as concepts they have been refined to the point at which they are used consistently in the literature. Indeed, that impression is strengthened by thumbing through introductory texts in anthropology or by sitting in introductory lectures: after such experiences we all "know" what is culture and what is not. We are able, with varying success, to write examination essays on the relationship between culture and social structure. Yet when we read further and hear more, we find that scholars, while agreeing on broad definitions of the two concepts, still feel it necessary to preface many of their theoretical discussions with a line of demarcation between them, usually drawn with statements such as "*culture* here considered will consist of . . ., while *social structure* refers to . . . ." In fact, then, a considerable inconsistency in application has been the reward of old age for the two terms, both in their definition and in the relationship thought to exist between them.

In some of these postulated relationships either the social or the cultural aspects assume a dominant, active role in group life while the others become subordinate, passive, or perhaps even nonexistent. Yet most anthropologists would probably agree with A. L. Kroeber's (1948:9) characterization of the relationship as that of "two intimately intertwined aspects of a complex of phenomena that regularly occur only in association," although they probably would haggle about which, society or culture, is the more important. (Kroeber, in fact, in the same volume [p. 10 n.] went on to declare that "Specific human societies are more determined by culture than the reverse, even though some kind of social life is a precondition of culture. And therewith social forms become part of culture!")

I must hedge in offering definitions of culture or social structure because of the different meanings attached to these terms by scholars whose works are discussed in the following chapters. It would only add confusion to present yet another definition at this point. I offer instead the following observation, by no means uniquely mine: human behavior is the raw data of social scientific inquiry, and, for this inquiry, it can be conceived as including both cultural and social structural aspects, plus one more, the "psychological" aspect.

The three aspects can be considered interrelated yet analytically separable (cf. Geertz 1957:33–34). If the objective is to understand changes in human group behavior, it is ultimately imperative that changes in all of these aspects be understood—whether one is considered "part" of another, all are "abstract," all are "real," or what have you. Perhaps the neatest, most rigorous studies methodologically are those that focus on changes in only one or two of the three, holding the other(s) constant or given. While this may be perfectly defensible scientifically, scholars ought to continue to push toward a complete, integrated understanding of change processes.

There is a second and perhaps more fundamental observation that needs to be made at this point: all the preoccupation with definitions is not a game to boggle students' minds. *The way in which a given writer defines "society" or "culture" and how he characterizes their relationship often indicate his basic approach to studies of changes in human group behavior.* For example, we will see that some theorists conceive of culture as an analyzable entity in and of itself that includes the aspect of social structure within it and that for analysis requires no specific reference to the psychological nature of its human bearers. Others wonder if the whole concept of culture has gotten completely out of hand, being changed from its original nature as a useful abstraction into something that grows, dies, spreads, and engages in all sorts of other activities. Some of this latter group of scholars advocate a study of individual mental processes as the basis of "culture" change. And for still others culture consists of traits, such as the bow and arrow, metallurgy, *patolli* and pachisi, and patterns of kinship (social) structure—and it is traits that receive the focus of attention.

Additional problems arise in the attempt to find a workable definition of "change." If the aim is to be as inclusive as possible, one of Webster's dictionary definitions seems adequate: "change denotes a making or becoming distinctly different, and implies either a radical transmutation of character or replacement with something else." Clear enough, perhaps—until one is forced to decide whether or not a certain act or series of acts does or does not represent a "change." It is under such circumstances that one must look more closely at the adjectives in definitions like Webster's and determine to his own satisfaction *how* different "distinctly" different is and to whom it must appear thus. Or just *how* radical a "radical transmutation" must be before it may be considered "change." The problem involves in part a selection of what sorts of sociocultural phenomena one should focus on as representative of change. And this, in turn, is partly determined by the degree of inclusiveness or breadth of scope one selects in a study of change.

Let me illustrate the point with some examples. In a famous study of changes in women's fashions, Jane Richardson and A. L. Kroeber (Richardson and Kroeber 1940; Kroeber 1948:332–333) examined much of the available literature on western European and American "high fashion," going back some three hundred years. Inevitably, their study revealed that fashions did change almost yearly: necklines plunged and then became prudishly unrevealing; hemlines rose one year, rose higher the next, then went back down the third year. (So far as I know, they encountered nothing quite so brief as the miniskirt or "hot pants" during the entire period.) But in a larger perspective, the authors were able to demonstrate that in reality women's fashions during the three-hundred-year interval were cyclical in their patterns, ranging between points of maximum exposure and maximum cover at roughly fifty-year periods. Part of the researchers' intention was to prove that even though individuals thought fashions changed in accordance with personal whims and desires, in fact the alterations from year to year and the trends over a decade or more were merely variations on a basic Western culture pattern with respect to clothing, a pattern that remained basically *unchanged* throughout the entire period. In Western cultures, the feminine pattern was essentially a loose-fitting skirt, with the portion of the dress from the waist up fitted closely to the contours of the body. At the level of inclusiveness or abstraction that these authors were using (in this case, the "general cultural pattern"), there was no change, although at a more specific level, that of the yearly fluctuations, change was very apparent, although not always drastic.

Another example is that in an admirable study of the political systems of highland Burma. E. R. Leach (1965; orig. 1954) demonstrated that Kachin groups radically shifted their political structures back and forth between two types: one hierarchical, with a system of graded ranks; the other fundamentally egalitarian, with a system of lineages existing on a par with each other. Certainly this is an example of change at one level; yet at a different, more inclusive level, as Leach pointed out, these two types both constituted part of a persistent pattern of life in the Kachin Hills.

And finally, consider the case of an individual's passage through the various stages of life: infancy, adolescence, marriage, senescence, and death. Is this sequence to be considered a social or a cultural change—or change at all? The individual himself would heartily assert that there was change involved; others, with a broader, more abstract perspective, would be much more cautious. Godfrey and Monica Wilson (1945:58–59), for example, wrote explicitly about this situation. They drew a distinction between what they called social "circulation" and social "change." Social "circulation" was used with reference to routine progressions through the life cycle of an individual, or normal fissions and fusions of groups of kinsmen. Social "change" was conceived as change in the various statuses of a given group, such as the disappearance of the office of "chief," rather than as a simple change in personnel forced by the facts of old age and senility. (However, even here a consistent distinction may be difficult to make in a series of specific cases, because, as Evon Vogt [1960] and others have implied, a series of minor, perhaps initially undetected aberrations in the circulation process could cumulatively result in significant change.)

Again, what one conceives as change is partly dependent upon the phenomena and level of abstraction chosen for study (more on this later on). It makes little sense at this point to select one of the existing definitions in the anthropological literature and claim that it has some sort of advantage over all others; Webster, with qualifications, will suffice for now.

Change, Persistence, and Equilibrium

Change, wrote Melville Herskovits (1966:40; orig. 1955), is a constant. It is taking place at varying rates and degrees everywhere and always. Yet he and others posed a dilemma, for they observed that there is also a tendency toward the maintenance of the *status quo*, a trend of persistence, in the patterned behavior of human groups. For some scholars this presents an intriguing problem: how does one account for persistence, given the constancy of change? Why is it, for example, that the Manus of the Admiralty Islands, who almost literally dumped their old way of life into the sea and welcomed a far-reaching new order with open arms (Mead 1956), nonetheless allowed some of the old ways to survive (albeit somewhat surreptitiously)? And why do some sophisticated members of the Potawatomi Indian tribe of Kansas still pull their window shades or check around outside their doorways before discussing the subject of witchcraft with anthropologists?

Various explanations for persistence exist in the literature, explanations ranging from the psychological to the social and cultural. Edward Bruner (1956), for example, in his "early learning hypothesis" suggested that behavior patterns learned early in an individual's life cycle seem more resistant to change than those learned in later years. John Kunkel

(1970) stated that persistence has something to do with the manner in which new behavior patterns are introduced to recipients. Fredrik Barth (1967) argued that persistence may be explained by social and cultural constraints (or limiting factors) operating upon a given set of behavior patterns. I will describe these and other ideas more fully in subsequent chapters.

Yet there is a real danger of distortion in presenting the problem as a dilemma of change versus persistence, of conceiving of the dynamics of group behavior as an either-or situation and then trying to sort out which pattern is an example of which condition. The actual conditions of human existence for most purposes could perhaps more accurately be conceived as an infinite series of adjustments between tendencies toward both change and persistence. A layman's knowledge of human behavior tells us that people do not often or voluntarily toss the cultural accumulation of countless generations into the Pacific Ocean; nor are they able to resist the attraction of the new or the improved forever. It is possible to apply here some of the notions of scholars of "functionalist" or "integrationist" persuasion (see Chapter Five), according to which a group's way of life is considered a social and cultural system whose components influence each other in such a way that a change in one may have some effect on the others. If the system is to continue to operate optimally, the components or subsystems (e.g., kinship, economics, religion, and politics) must fit together, must be integrated, without persistent and radical contradictions. The stimuli for sociocultural change are constantly operating to alter the pre-existing elements in the system; but insofar as the system, the general pattern of life, is considered worthy of preservation by its members, they will (consciously or unconsciously) take action aimed at insuring that change does not suddenly obliterate all or even most of the stabilizing links with the past. It could be argued that even some radical social movements represent an effort to keep old traditions alive, so as to re-establish a measure of stability that they perceive as missing because elements of the present system no longer mesh with each other (cf. Wallace 1956). There is thus a constant adjustment process that attempts to keep the system alive and adaptive. In short, one could say that there is a trend toward stabilization (Harding 1960:45–68) or equilibrium apparent at the systems level of analysis.

Yet, because change is constant, one cannot read into such words as "stabilization" or "equilibrium" the implication of a perfect and unchanging balance or integration of components (cf. Gluckman 1968:222). The equilibrium or stability are tendencies that are almost always present yet always relative. Contradictions and incompatibilities between patterns seem to be the rule rather than the exception. And how, after all, is one able to judge when a sociocultural system is at rest (cf. Harding 1960:54)? or when a system has achieved equilibrium? Surely, these conditions can only be relative to other systems or past time periods and be detectable only at a circumscribed level of analysis at a single point in time.

Given the fact that change is constant, what appears as persistence at a particular point in time might most accurately be conceived as change occurring at a relatively slow rate. As I will show later, this conceptualization of sociocultural dynamics does no violence to the traditional positions of either the "functionalist" or the "evolutionist" scholars on this particular point; in spite of the argumentation of both sides, their thinking on this seems quite compatible, even though their methodology is apparently distinct.

Variables of Methodology in the Study of Change

It is one thing to sketch in overview fashion the dynamics of group life but quite another to describe how these dynamics might best be studied. It is on this issue that the views of the functionalists, evolutionists, and other ists come into their most apparent disagreement. The following roster of variables is not specific to any particular methodological approach. It is actually comprised of a series of questions that each analyst of change attempts to answer in his overall research design. In any actual situation they are not completely separable; the manner in which one of the variables is methodologically handled may be determined by decisions already made in handling others. This is, then, decidedly not a suggested sequence for the development of research designs.

The roster also provides a way of examining the various approaches to sociocultural change in the following chapters. Each of the approaches deals in some fashion with most, if not all, of the variables briefly described here, and the reader may well wish to consider how differently, for example, evolutionary and decision-making approaches each cope with them.

TIME

Change is a process in time. And time can be a crucial factor in a determination of what is changing, and to what degree, as well as how rapidly this change is taking place. Let me return for a moment to the example of Richardson and Kroeber's study of changes in women's fashion. Had they selected a time period of only five years, instead of three hundred, in their analysis, their perception of the degree of change and the pattern it assumed would have been markedly different. Conceivably, they may have tuned in on the hemline level as it was in the process of an upward movement and during their hypothetical five-year time span may have determined that no cycle was involved. In the absence of data to the contrary, they then might have concluded that the pattern indicated a continuing upward trend, with an ultimate morality crisis looming in the not-too-distant future. Instead, their broader time span enabled them to perceive the cyclical nature of this and other changes, as well as to describe an overall pattern with quite different characteristics.

Ideally, of course, each analyst chooses a time period that he feels is adequate to encompass the magnitude and kind of change he is particularly interested in. Actually, the time-period boundaries may be limited by factors over which he has no control, such as the extent of reliable data regarding past conditions. This is a notable limitation in studies of nonliterate peoples whose lives have been spared close monitoring by a colonial power. Or, the analyst may find that the time period originally selected was too broad to permit a highly detailed analysis, and he is thus forced to narrow the range.

These comments so far have been limited to what has been called "historical time," and patterns like those emerging from the fashion study could be said to have a *historical duration.*

There is at least one other type of time-reckoning that can be crucial in the analysis of change. This is "structural time," and it is possible to speak of *structural,* rather than historical, *duration* (Gluckman 1968:220 ff.). This generally refers to the time scale "built into" a given social structural component, such as a family or other kinship group or, to use one of Max Gluckman's own examples, a legislative assembly. Each social component, it is argued, has its own built-in cycle of existence, and it is essential to know something of the complete cycle before making conclusions about whether or not change has occurred. For the individual, his family has a cycle, a structural duration, with a beginning and an end, and this cycle has no consistent correlation with elapsed historical time. He is born into the family (the beginning); he becomes an adult, marries, has children, becomes a grandfather, and dies (which may or may not be the end of the structural duration of a "typical" family in his group). So, too, the analyst studying the family structure at a given point in historical time must be able to relate it to the cyclical pattern of most families in that society if he is to make a judgment about the presence or absence of change. The cyclical pattern in most family structures requires four generations to run its course (although in some societies the cycles may be longer; and in any one instance the cycle may be broken by death, divorce, or other factors [Gluckman 1968:222]). Structural time and duration are calculated usually from the patterned behavior of the groups being studied. Thus the "three election" structural duration of the British House of Commons is determined by "the rules and customs which organize it" (Gluckman 1968:223), just as is the "four generation" structural duration of the family—although in the latter case the duration or cycle is linked not only to the existing cultural patterns but to the facts of biology as well.

The increments of time may thus be "generations" or "elections" or "age sets" or whatever other units may be relevant to a given group of people. But the point again is to determine what goes on during the progression of a social form between the beginning of a cycle and the point at which it can be said the cycle begins to repeat itself. Families can go on for generation after generation, just as Houses of Commons endure election after election. But the family seems to be back where it started from in its cycle after about four generations, and the House of Commons after three elections.

"Time" is thus a relative consideration—relative to the task the analyst wishes to accomplish; yet, whether its measured units are "historical," "structural," or even "ecological" (Evans-Pritchard 1940:94–108), it is a necessary consideration in any study of change.

CHANGE FROM WHOSE PERSPECTIVE?
"EMIC" VERSUS "ETIC" ANALYSIS

The notion of "structural time" was used by E. E. Evans-Pritchard (1940) to refer to means by which one group, the Nuer of Africa, themselves reckoned the order of occurrences (as well as closeness of relationships among kinsmen). This introduces us to the problem of deciding from whose perspective—the analyst's or his human subjects'—the detection and description of change will be conducted. Usually, unless we are informed to the contrary, it is taken for granted that the observer is being "objective," and that therefore what he is describing as change is objectively change, whether the people living under the given set of conditions perceive change or not. Occasionally, the discrepancy between what the people themselves characterize as happening and what the analyst views as taking place is a focus of the analysis (as in Leach's study of highland Burma mentioned earlier). And, it is entirely possible that the analyst may base his analysis entirely on his subjects' conceptions of what is changing and what is not. Certain scholars lumped here into the "decision-making" approach have adopted this latter perspective in large part.

Marvin Harris, borrowing concepts originally developed by the linguist Kenneth Pike, has used the terms "etic" and "emic" to refer to the distinct perspectives: "emic" approaches are those in which the *subjects' own* perceptions, motivations, and so forth become the basis for analytical conclusions. "Etic" approaches, on the other hand, depend on the *analyst's* perception of conditions, relationships, and so on. The etic conclusion that change has occurred is not based on subjects' perceptions but upon his own—ultimately verifiable through observations by his fellow scientists rather than by his informants in the culture he is studying (Harris 1968:568–585). (Incidentally, practitioners of the emic approach may be in for some frustrating times when trying to determine from a collection of subjects' opinions whether a given condition is change or not!)

DEGREE OR MAGNITUDE OF CHANGE

Is the analyst looking for gaudy, sweeping change, such as occurred among the Manus, or among the Japanese after they opted for Occidental industrialization? Or are his goals less spectacular, aimed at documenting changes in basketry techniques or pottery designs? Perhaps the most ambitious undertaking has been the attempt to study the vast panorama of all major changes among all the peoples of the world since the time of the earliest hominids.

It is necessary to repeat a cautionary point about distinguishing between major and minor changes: what appear to be "minor" changes during a rather brief time span may in a broader perspective culminate in an alteration that could only be described as "major" in its proportions. The point is illustrated by one agent of directed culture change who in the past ordered the installation of latrines in a village in highland India. Within a short time, the "innocuous" introduction radically diminished the power of the local priests, caused the village to be moved to a new location, and created a serious factional dispute among the villagers (Mandelbaum 1941:24–25).

BOUNDARIES

Many analysts are interested in tracing the sources or stimuli of change and often classify the stimuli as being external or internal to the group being considered. Such statements imply that the analytical boundaries of the group have already been established. It is of utmost importance that the boundaries be clearly and consistently drawn; otherwise, there is persistent confusion about what in fact is changing and how pervasive the change might be. A case in point is the study of change in American Indian reserva-tion communities. Often it is misleading to use "tribe" and "reservation" interchangeably, because characteristically not all tribal members live on the reservation and hence are not always included in its changing patterns. If the "reservation" is the social boundary, then are officials of the U.S. govern-ment who have their offices on reservation land to be included or excluded? If the agents are included, what about the higher offices and policies they represent? And, back for a moment to the emic-etic distinction mentioned earlier, how do the Indians themselves sketch their social boundaries (cf. Barth 1969)? Sometimes the boundaries of the system suggest themselves in fairly clear-cut fashion. Sometimes, too, the analyst must be somewhat arbitrary in specifying the limits, consistent with the other analytical decisions he has made. This brief paragraph does not reflect the considerable interest anthropologists have shown in the detection of social boundaries (see, e.g., Barth 1969, Cohen 1969, and Naroll 1964). Again, however, the issue is a complex one and is crucial if we are to understand *what* is changing.

DETECTION AND DOCUMENTATION

Although other alternatives exist (e.g., Barth 1967), by far the majority of the studies of change have detected and documented change by analyzing conditions at two or more points in time, then extrapolating from these analyses the processes by which the change from one point to another took place. I have already discussed the problem of constancy of change; I must now for the moment reverse the thrust of that argument to make a general methodological point: if the objective of a particular approach is to study changes in a system over an extensive time period, it is necessary (with few exceptions) to regard that system *as if* it were static—frozen in time—at some point or points in its history (keeping in mind the importance of the structural duration, which is not inconsistent with such an "as if" set of conditions). If this were not done, it would be most difficult to understand how the elements of the system interrelate, and it would be impossible to detect changes in this interrelationship.

This method has its problems. The first is the accuracy with which conditions in past time periods can be reconstructed. Some members of the anthropological community have voiced considerable contempt for what they call "studies of memory culture," in part as a justification for observation of only what is presently observable. "Memory culture" refers to the ethnographic reconstruction of past conditions using only the recollection of key informants, and in some preliterate societies of the recent past this was the only way of getting a notion of bygone conditions not detectable in the archeological record. Informants' memories are nonetheless a valuable source of information about the past and are characteristically used with the understanding that the more remote the time period the more hazy the memory is liable to be. But other sources of information must be used as well. Colonial administrators' reports, travelers' accounts, and other written historical documents, as well as archeological evidence, all must be fully utilized whenever they exist to supplement informants' memories. The absence of supporting information usually forces limits on the time period to be encompassed in the study, as I mentioned earlier. And there is still the question of how much evidence of this reconstructed sort is enough to allow unqualified conclusions.

One way around this problem of accuracy of reconstruction is the popular "restudy" technique, in which the analyst conducts a thorough ethnographic study of a system as he observes it at one point in time, then he (or others using his materials) returns to the same system years later to determine what sorts of changes have taken place in the interval. Insofar as the accuracy and completeness of the initial observation can be trusted, the reconstruction problem is largely solved. Raymond Firth's work on the Pacific island of Tikopia (1936 and 1959) and Margaret Mead's Manus study (1956) are examples of this technique.

But the restudy method introduces a second and related problem. Assume that between the time of the first study (T_1) and the restudy (T_2) a pattern of organization—say, political organization—has apparently changed. A logical inference would be that the T_2 pattern *developed out of* the T_1 pattern; after all, both patterns are political patterns, each serving the same function. The naive analyst would be content with the conclusion, perhaps. But, how does he *know* the T_1 and T_2 political patterns are in such a relationship? The burden of proof is on him, and the development is liable to be taken for granted when it should not be. For the sake of argument, assume that the T_1 pattern was that of consensual decision-making and diffuse leadership; the T_2 pattern is one of hierarchical decision-making and authoritarian leadership. The similarity of function in the two patterns could cause the analyst to focus on the T_2 pattern without recognizing that the T_1 pattern had in fact persisted into the present. Under such conditions, the assumption that T_2 had developed from T_1 would be very difficult to substantiate. In brief, then, the restudy is able to reduce the perils of reconstruction, but it does not necessarily solve the problem of accurately documenting the daily and yearly flow of events between T_1 and T_2.

The restudy technique for this reason may be inadequate for an understanding of the processes by which the perceived change took place, because such an understanding must still be based on extrapolation from two or more known points. Perhaps the best means of avoiding inference is to junk the restudy concept entirely and embark on one continuous long-term research task, with investigators present in the society constantly (see Vogt 1960:29). However, without major research funding and some general direction to the continuing investigation, this ideal is almost impossible to achieve.

Alternatively, an analyst could play it safe and decide to conduct his inquiry at a level of abstraction in which the danger of inference would not be as threatening. Such a decision may well take him from the frying pan to the fire, because the problem of inference or extrapolation is usually present to some degree at any level.

So, again, the realistic alternative seems to be that of collecting large quantities of data, utilizing the widest possible net, to fill in the information gap existing between time periods. In dealing with this staggering amount of detail, the analyst must be wary of falling prey to the "can't see the forest for the trees" syndrome, in which he discovers a process or series of processes that is so specific that comparison with other cases of change becomes extremely difficult. Or, the opposite might occur: in order to account for the exceptions, the resulting conclusions may be so general that they can be applied to any situation without achieving any usable insights. In the latter case, critics may be justified in observing, "That's perfectly true, but *so what?*"

LEVEL OF ABSTRACTION

Careless handling of different levels of abstraction, in my opinion, has generated much of the heat of scholarly debate among adherents of various theoretical predispositions. I intend to make my case more adequately in the chapters to follow. For now, let me say that another of the key decisions in the analysis concerns the degree or level of abstraction (or generalization) to be used; in other words, how far is the focus of the study removed from the raw data level of individual behavior in group contexts? There are no sets of preestablished levels that all social scientists would agree upon; even if there were, there would probably be squabbles about terminology. The levels might be rankings of units of social or political structure, perhaps beginning with the individual and extending to the global, through intermediate steps of family, neighborhood, town, district, state, nation, and so on. The hypothetical analyst has to decide at which of these levels he intends to study change.

For the purposes of this text, I have chosen to conceive approaches to the study of change as lying at or between two extremes of abstract levels, the most inclusive being the large-scale, multisociety comparative analysis. The other extreme is the analysis of individual mental processes. My choice is intended more as a means of lending some coherence to my presentation than as yet another typology to be rigorously imposed and vigorously defended. Study at any of the levels, however they may be conceived, involves some degree of generalization or abstraction from the raw data, of course. The point I wish to stress is that usually *the questions asked at one level are different from those asked at another level, the focus is brought to bear on different degrees of inclusiveness of behavior patterns, and, as a result, the techniques of analysis at each level are different.* It should be obvious that a scholar wishing to analyze changes in the international market system would not want to spend all his time investigating changes in the behavior of feather merchants in Tegucigalpa.

A scholar need not be confined to a single level of abstraction in his study. On the contrary, the value of a study that begins at one level and carries the analysis successfully to other levels would be great. Less valuable are studies that claim a continuity between levels but fail to demonstrate the nature of this continuity, or studies that apply the techniques and insights from one level to make conclusions about patterns at a different level without demonstrating that the transfer is possible or relevant.

My intention in raising this issue of levels is to make the reader aware that a considerable amount of the debate over which theory or approach is best often leaves the concept of levels of abstraction out of account and that the debate is therefore somewhat unproductive. For example, some of the criticisms of general evolutionary approaches were, as I interpret them, designed to discount these approaches in favor of others that focus on the analytical level of the individual. The reader may conclude from the attacks that the general evolutionists are feeble theorists indeed, because they do not cope with the issue of individual diversity. When, however, the argument is seen as one involving two different levels of abstraction from human behavior, the positions are not necessarily contradictory and may even complement each other in some analyses. In short, I wish to alert the reader to the possibility that scholars may be talking past one another in the criticism of each other's approach.

Yet this discussion of levels of abstraction should not be allowed to obscure the fact that significant differences often exist between approaches at essentially the *same* level of analysis. For example, the "historicist," or "diffusion," approach and the "acculturation" approach operate at the same analytical level: the relationship between two or more autonomous sociocultural systems. Yet whereas the historicists are (or were) primarily interested in the transmission of traits between cultures (what was transmitted and when), the acculturation approach stresses not only the transmission itself but how the transmitted traits are fitted into the pre-existing system of the recipients. So, too, with the fashion study by Richardson and Kroeber and the Burmese highlands study by Leach. Although both were speaking of whole societies and even clusters of societies rather than of individual behavior, Leach was interested in what he called the "underlying structural pattern," whereas Richardson and Kroeber concerned themselves with the "general cultural pattern." Such differences in emphasis must not be minimized when lumping them into the same gross level of abstraction.

And another qualification: I do not wish to imply that all the methodological variables mentioned so far can be collapsed into the single one of levels of abstraction. Time and boundary variables may be short or long, narrow or broad, respectively; we may also distinguish between micro and macro change. But none of these are the same as levels of abstraction: diffusion between two sociocultural systems can be broken into intervals of five, fifty, or two hundred years for analysis and can focus on basketry patterns or techniques for harnessing nuclear energy; but the level of abstraction remains the same.

* * *

This chapter, then, has presented a bare outline of some

of the most important methodological issues sooner or later to be confronted by anyone eager to study sociocultural change. Please keep in mind that they are almost always interdependent: the time period one wishes to cover, for example, is influenced by the availability of data, level of abstraction, degree of change, and so forth. We will be examining theories of change partially on the basis of how they deal with time, detection and documentation, and the other variables; so, by becoming aware of these variables through this somewhat didactic introduction, the reader should be in a much better position to think critically about the following theories and what they have or have not accomplished.

CHAPTER TWO

SOCIOCULTURAL EVOLUTION: THE EARLY PROTAGONISTS

◻◻◻◻◻◻◻◻◻◻◻◻◻◻◻◻◻◻◻◻◻◻◻◻◻◻◻

FOR OVER two thousand years, men have been interested in stages of sociocultural evolution, although it has been a major scientific preoccupation of social thinkers for a mere two centuries or so. Because of the sheer volume of published materials, the diversity of intellectual viewpoints on the subject, and the fervor of their allegiances, this is perhaps the most difficult approach to summarize neatly.

I want to sketch the evolutionary contributions of five important men of the nineteenth century: Karl Marx, Friedrich Engels, Herbert Spencer, E. B. Tylor, and Lewis Henry Morgan. But I can do so only by ignoring some of their major contributions and many of the intellectual issues of the times. For the most part, their works are far from being irrelevant antiques—from them modern theories of sociocultural evolution trace most of their basic elements.

First, however, it is necessary to offer some glimpses of the intellectual legacy to which they themselves became heirs and of the currents against which they launched their ideas.

The Intellectual Background

European intellectuals in the eighteenth century, when not preoccupied with revolutions, thought a great deal about the relationship between God, man, nature, and the state. And they were confronted by an apparent dilemma. On the one hand, there was God the omnipotent—creating, causing, and, more than occasionally, punishing. On the other hand stood the works of men like Sir Isaac Newton and Sir Francis Bacon, whose results indicated more and more strongly that certain sorts of conditions could be explained through the application of scientific principles and that there existed in the universe a set of "natural laws" that regulated relationships between matter. To understand cause and effect, it was necessary to discover through rational inquiry what sorts of natural laws may be operating in a given situation. There were those, in short, who were not buying "God's will" as a satisfactory cause of the fall of fruits, feathers, or stones.

Some, less certain about the hand of God in human affairs (yet not always willing to deny its influence), were convinced that man was a part of nature and thus that human existence was ultimately understandable through rational searching for the natural laws governing its characteristics. The task for these scholars became one of knowing more about their fellow humans, past and present, with one of the objectives being to understand the linkages between the life-ways of benighted savages (if there were any) and those of enlightened Europe.

In this task they already had something upon which to build—notions persisting since the time of classical Greece and Rome that recognized the historical development of civilization from precivilized beginnings and that acknowledged the possibility of dividing this development up into stages or periods for closer scrutiny. The stage concept reemerged during the Enlightenment (with Vico in 1725; Montesquieu in 1748; Turgot in 1750; Ferguson in 1767; and Condorcet in 1795).[1] The aim was in part reconstruc-

[1]Marvin Harris (1968) has written in detail about these several contributions.

tion, so as better to understand the natural laws operating in human affairs. There was also a concern with the factors involved in this development—with what accounted for the change from lower stages to higher ones. There was, for example, the precocious effort of William Robertson (1812; orig. 1777) that foreshadowed Lewis Henry Morgan's three-part evolutionary sequence (using identical terms). He also noted that sociocultural similarities in widely separated parts of the world could be explained by the presence of similar conditions, including similar subsistence patterns (Harris 1968:33–34; Hoebel 1960:648). In other words, it was not necessary to argue the world-wide spread of culture traits from a single source in order to account for similarities between groups.

Other portions of the Enlightenment legacy were passed on to the nineteenth-century scholars by Condorcet (1795), including the notion not only that the development of the human intellect proceeded in orderly fashion but also that it tended in the direction of progress. Progress was understood in thoroughly moral terms; that is, it was *good* that men strove toward increasing freedom of the intellect and increasingly spectacular technological accomplishments. To be sure, not all of Condorcet's enlightened contemporaries shared his optimistic view of man's rise and future perfectibility. For example, Thomas Malthus's pronouncement that population growth would eventually outstrip the available food supply was hardly calculated to inspire confidence among future generations. Yet, however qualified, the notion of general progress was clearly present in Enlightenment thought (cf. E. Wilson 1953:5; orig. 1940; Harris 1968:40).

The post-Enlightenment scholars of the early nineteenth century were thus able to tap, if they wished, a considerable intellectual and methodological reservoir in creating their own evolutionary schemes: the notions that human existence was as subject to natural laws as other components of the universe and that these laws might be discovered through the rigorous application of scientific principles; that human life-ways developed through time and in response to a variety of stimuli; that there was a possibility of subdividing this development into stages or periods for more intensive investigation; and that the course of development could be more or less satisfactorily described as progress.

Two brief examples of early post-Enlightenment philosophy can help trace the development of the evolutionary argument to the mid-nineteenth century. One is that of a Frenchman, Auguste Comte; the other, that of the German G. W. F. Hegel.

Foreshadowing Herbert Spencer, Comte was able to see the importance of *material* factors, such as population increase, as stimuli for social and mental evolution; population pressure presented new problems of survival and thereby forced a division of labor and hence a more rapid development through specialization. Yet in the end *mental* factors dominated material ones in causal importance:

To complete my long and difficult demonstration, I have only . . . to show that material development, as a whole, must follow a course, not only analogous, but perfectly correspondent with that of intellectual development, which, as we have seen, *governs every other* [Comte 1961:1339; orig. 1830–1842; italics added].

The relative importance of material over mental factors in evolution, we will see, has persisted as a heated issue since Comte's time.

Hegel wrote shortly after the optimist Condorcet died in a French prison and before the period of Comte's early popularity. Like Comte and his contemporaries, Hegel was preoccupied with tracing the development of man's rational potential—that is, with the emergence of reason, or "mind." The ultimate goal of this development was, he believed, the "Absolute Idea," the "flawless truth" purged of the "dross of existence" (Marcuse 1960:164). Philosophically, however, Comte and Hegel were poles apart. I want to empha-size only one difference here: Hegel's use of what he called "the dialectic" as a model for describing the way in which the development unfolded.

Material factors, such as systems of labor, were simply vehicles used by man in pursuit of the Absolute Idea. As systems of labor became more complex, man was brought closer to the freedom for realization of the Idea. But the development was by no means placid. It was beset with conflicts and contradictions. In fact, Hegel argued, progress could unfold *only* through the conflict generated by contra-dictions. For example, a given system of labor, such as that of the early Industrial Revolution, contained the seeds of its own destruction: it operated well enough initially for the satisfaction of human needs, but then profit-taking and wealth differences led to "the utmost dismemberment of will, inner rebellion and hatred" (quoted in Marcuse 1960:81). The system had thus come to produce the situa-tion it was originally designed to avoid; and, for Hegel, progress could come only through its replacement by a state-regulated system operating according to legal contract. This, then, was the dynamic of the dialectic. Let me restate it in more formal terms: every sociocultural system (thesis) tends to generate its own internal contradictions (antithesis); this leads to conflict, which can only be resolved by the altera-tion of the given system (synthesis). The new system then becomes the thesis, and the process continues.

After Hegel's death a group of young philosophers in Berlin began an assault upon aspects of his philosophy. The group included Ludwig Feuerbach and Karl Marx. Remem-ber that for Hegel, as for many of his Enlightenment prede-cessors, the "Idea" or the "mind" was what was evolving; the material factors of existence were mere vehicles for the realization of this process. Feuerbach did not cast the first stone, but he did offer a direct contradiction to this notion by arguing that man's existence under the influence of material factors was the reality: ideas were *products* of this existence, instead of the other way around (Engels in Feuer 1959:205, 211; orig. 1888). The observation was simple yet profound, as Karl Marx realized full well. (But Marx later took Feuerbach to task for his failure to carry the materialist argument far enough.) In the 1840's then, armed with a critical Hegelianism heavily influenced by materialist philosophers and British classical economists, Karl Marx began a career as a radical newspaper columnist and met Friedrich Engels. (Comte continued his social philosophical writings during Marx's and Engels' early careers, but his influence was much more profound on Spencer's and Tylor's works. Because of this, I want to leave him for brief mention later in the chapter.)

Marx and Engels on Sociocultural Change

Marx and Engels' focus was as much on the future as on the past, because change for them was above all revolutionary change. To determine the dynamic processes of society was much more than an intellectual exercise: it furnished evidence for the inevitability of the decline of capitalism. Socialism and, ultimately, communism, they hoped, would rise after capitalism's fall. This latter development could be hastened by men like themselves, who worked to aid events in that direction. Social science, to their thinking, could not therefore be divorced from the politics of social revolution.

For Marx, man was a social animal whose consciousness was first and foremost shaped by relations with other men. Some social relations were much more influential than others, however, and Marx singled out what he called the "relations of production" as the most basic: those relationships created between men in their production of goods from raw materials and between workers and those who controlled their productive efforts. "Relations of production" were

the real foundation, on which rise legal and political superstructures and to which correspond definite forms of social consciousness. The mode of production in material life determines the general character of the social, political, and spiritual processes of life [Marx in Feuer 1959:43; orig. 1859].

Marx and Engels devoted much of their scholarly lives to the application of this materialist approach to an analysis of capitalism, describing in detail the effect of the factory system on the relations among industrial laborers (proletarians), how effective political power went along with wealth among the upper classes, how the "ideology of the times" (or of any time) was merely the ideology of the ruling classes, and how a preoccupation with wealth turned honest men away from a concern with developing their "human" qualities and toward a belief that acquisition of consumer goods was in fact the supreme fulfillment. The material base was, in other words, the determinant of other elements in human societies.

THEIR HISTORICAL-EVOLUTIONARY MODEL

There were three major statements about general cultural evolution, the earliest being Marx and Engels' *The German Ideology* (1970; orig. 1846). Marx refined the scheme later in his *Pre-Capitalist Economic Formations* (1965; orig. 1857–1858) and briefly in his *Introduction to a Critique of Political Economy* (1970; orig. 1857). Then Engels, using Marx's notes, wrote the final form in his *Origin of the Family, Private Property, and the State* (1972; orig. 1884).

Like their Enlightenment predecessors, Marx and Engels divided the evolution of society into a series of stages, which were determined on the basis of different forms of *property:*

The various stages of development in the division of labour are just so many different forms of property; i.e., the stage reached in the division of labour also determines the relations of individuals to one another with respect to the materials, instruments and products of labour [Marx and Engels in Bottomore 1964:115; orig. 1845–1846].

The first stage, or first *form,* was that of *tribal property,* found among small groups whose subsistence was based on hunting, fishing, herding, and, later, agriculture. This was followed, depending on locality, by either the *oriental form* or the *communal and state property of antiquity* (the *ancient form*), and, later, the *Germanic form.* From the latter emerged feudalism, which was eventually surpassed by capitalism. In the future, socialism, then communism, would overwhelm capitalism.

Something of Marx and Engels' account of the transition between the various stages can be gathered from the following brief outline of the emergence of capitalism from feudalism, the two periods for which they had their best documentation.

New world markets created by European expansion during feudalism increased the demands for finished products. These demands, in turn, forced changes in Europe from a handicraft mode of production to a manufacturing mode. The guild masters of handicrafts in feudal towns were displaced by groups of middle-class manufacturers, who successfully converted spinners and weavers from rural households into factory wage-laborers (Marx 1965:115; orig. 1857–1858). Expanding markets continued to increase the wealth and thus the power of the manufacturers, which in turn placed them in a position to dictate the reduction of both the rents and the wages they paid. "In other words, to the extent that the landowners and workers, the feudal lords and the common people, fell, so the capitalist class, the bourgeoisie, rose" (Marx in Bottomore 1964:128; orig. 1847). In time, the land itself became a form of capital, and the feudal lord vanished as a social status distinct from that of the capitalist. The position of the rural serfs had been increasingly precarious for some time; they were "driven from the land by the conversion of fields into pastures, and by the progress of agriculture which reduced the number of hands needed for cultivation" (Marx in Bottomore 1964:134–135; orig. 1867). Ever larger numbers of serfs moved into the cities to become wage laborers—the proletarians. In time, the post-handicraft manufacturing processes were themselves inadequate to cope with increasing demands for commodities, and the mode of production thereby became "industrial," based on "steam and machinery." For Marx, the capitalist stage began in the sixteenth century (Marx in Bottomore 1964:134–135; orig. 1867).

The rise of capitalism brought Marx up to the time of his own harsh existence in nineteenth-century Europe; and as the Marx-Engels descriptions covered events ever closer to that time, they became increasingly detailed. The groundwork for the next evolutionary stage was already being prepared in Marx's Europe, he believed. There would come a time when the oppressed proletariat would overwhelm the oppressor capitalists and, after the conflict, establish an order based on the abolition of private property and, eventually, social classes.

Marx conceived the stage sequence as in part a catalog of ideal types; each stage set forth a series of ideal conditions, all of which may not have been found in a specific group. He warned repeatedly in *Pre-Capitalist Economic Formations*, for example, that the oriental form could vary from group to group, depending on a host of local factors, including "geography" and "climate."[2] So, too, could his

[2]Apparently, Marx never traced in detail the impact of natural environmental features on social systems. He could not be labeled a "cultural ecologist."

Germanic form vary, although this title is perhaps misleading.

There were some obvious and tantalizing gaps, as well as outright errors, in the evolutionary sequence, particularly in the accounts of earlier forms. Part of this could perhaps be explained by a lack of information. But it is also possible that these gaps, seen better in retrospect, were not considered important to them at the time or at least were less important than other aspects of the sequence. Marx and Engels here and there seemed more concerned with the internal dynamics of a given form (like that of feudalism) than with a detailed tracing of the ways in which it became transformed into its successor. This is a problem common to other evolutionary schemes as well, as will be seen.

MARX AND ENGELS ON DYNAMIC PROCESSES

The two men shared with the earlier Enlightenment scholars the notion of progress toward a future, desirable state of society, but the road was obviously not a smooth one. Only when men reached the classless stage, Marx believed, would they be truly free to develop their "human" potential for brotherly love and intellectual and esthetic achievement. The evolutionary path as charted was not unilineal in the sense that one form led inevitably to one, and only one, other. And retrogression, such as occurred in the ancient form following the fall of Rome, could be a condition of historical evolution.

Their conception of the structure of society is summarized in the following diagram.[3] The labels for each of the components are those used by the two scholars:

[3]The specific nature of the interrelationship of the components and their appropriate contents is still a subject for debate among Marxist scholars; this must therefore be understood as a pedagogical device designed to simplify rather than to offer a final pronouncement. The contents and relationship among components in egalitarian or pre-class societies may differ to some extent from those diagrammed here, for example. The position of Modes of Production on the chart is also moot.

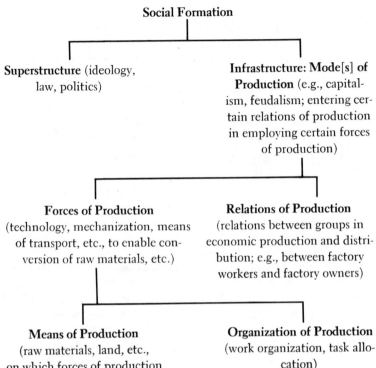

Although all components are in a dynamic interaction, limiting or facilitating each other's development, the evolutionarily significant interaction is that of *conflict*. A fundamental conflict always exists between the forces and the relations of production; it usually is expressed by conflict between the "haves" and the "have-nots"—that is, between groups controlling the means of production and others who must work as producers. There is thus a perpetual conflict between social classes: one trying to gain ascendancy, the other trying to maintain it. Eventually, the old arrangements of property and control of production are destroyed and replaced by a new order (Marx in Feuer 1959:43; orig. 1859); this continues until, finally classes are abolished and there can be no more conflict between the producer and those who control his production.

Marx and Engels utilized Hegel's concept of the dialectic to describe the general pattern that this process followed. But, aided by Feuerbach's reinterpretation (mentioned above), they changed the dialectic from a vehicle for the development of "the Idea" into a dynamic model for the development of material reality. Material factors after all, they argued, govern social consciousness. Thus, in their scheme each succeeding type of production developed *within itself* the contradictory elements that would eventually destroy (or "negate") it and thus surpass it. In the evolutionary sequence just outlined, for example, the ancient form arose as a consequence of the need to maintain control of rural areas, yet in time became antagonistic to rural interests. In the feudal form, the Germanic rural household economics became the seed of capitalist manufacture, which eventually grew to destroy (or "negate") the household system. And the proletarians, originally an integral part of the capitalist system, would grow to destroy that system and create something different.

Marx and Engels' basic assumption, then, was that social systems are inherently dynamic, not static, even though some may be more dynamic than others. This, Marx shrewdly observed, was in spite of the fact that human beings in control of production try to keep things as they are, try to keep them static by "reproducing" the same mode of production generation after generation.

But this reproduction is at the same time necessarily new production and the destruction of the old form.
For instance, where each individual is supposed to possess so many acres of land, the mere increase in population constitutes an obstacle. If this is to be overcome, colonization will develop and this necessitates wars of conquest. This leads to slavery, etc., also, e.g., the enlargement of the *ager publicus* [common lands], and hence to the rise of the Patricians, who represent the community, etc. [Marx 1965:92–93; orig. 1857–1858].

This, of course, was expressed dialectically; but it was also an astute observation about the apparent dilemma of change versus persistence in human societies. Yet some social structures did manage to persist even though they became mere parts of the new order and even though they underwent some alteration in the process. For example, there was not an abrupt break between feudalism and capitalism; some of the older Germanic elements were to be found in both forms, but they no longer constituted the basic structures of the subsequent periods. Marx made this more explicit in his *Introduction to a Critique of Political Economy* (1970:145; orig. 1857):

[In studying bourgeois economics one can see] the structure and the relations of production of all formerly existing social formations the ruins and component elements of which were used in the creation of bourgeois society. Some of these unassimilated remains are still carried on within bourgeois society, others however, which previously existed only in rudimentary form have been further developed and have attained their full significance.

The thrust of his argument here is that social forms are products of historical development and that history is both change and persistence.

DETECTION AND DOCUMENTATION OF CHANGE: MATERIALISM AND DIALECTICS

Marx and Engels' pronouncements on the prime mover of sociocultural change sounded blatantly deterministic and therefore scientifically suspect. It is clear in their evolutionary scheme that modes of production were certainly prime movers of change. Materialism was not very respectable in scholarly circles in the latter part of the nineteenth century (Stocking 1968:102), and many anthropology texts today still repeat the antigeographical and antieconomic determinist catechism developed by anthropologists in the early twentieth century. Marx and Engels' contributions deserve better. Their approach to the study of history, with its emphasis on material factors, was at least researchable, an "eminently empirical issue, not to be answered by logic alone" (Harris 1968:232). Certainly the emphasis on productive modes was a giant step away from the vagueness of "Reason" or the "Absolute Idea." If Marx and Engels were at times unconvincing in their tracing of material factors of change in the transition from ancient to feudal forms, at least others who used the same theory but better data could prove or disprove the theory itself.

Marx's later writings (e.g., *Introduction to a Critique of Political Economy*) softened the determinist bite of the earlier pronouncements, and Engels tried to set the record straight near the end of his own life:

According to the materialist conception of history, the *ultimately* determining element in history is the production and reproduction of real life. More than this neither Marx nor I has ever asserted. Hence if somebody twists this into saying that the economic element is the *only* determining one he transforms that proposition into a meaningless, abstract, senseless phrase. The economic situation is the basis, but the various elements of the superstructure [i.e., law, politics, ideology] . . . also exercise their influence upon the course of the historical struggles and in many cases preponderate in determining their *form*. There is an interaction of all these elements in which, amidst all the endless host of accidents (that is, of things and events whose inner interconnection is so remote or so impossible of proof that we can regard it as non-existent, as negligible), the economic movement finally asserts itself as necessary [Engels in Feuer 1959:397–398; orig. 1890].

Implicitly in this passage and more explicitly in other portions of the long letter from which it is taken, Engels advised that the analysis of causal elements and their interrelationships can best come inductively, from the analysis of data of a given historical situation—although the materialist framework would always be the point of departure for the analysis. The infrastructure was always the most basic, but external or superstructural factors could intervene to produce a specific condition. The determinism of the preaching thus seemed to fade somewhat in the practice.

The Marxian analytical level usually shifted between that of all human society and that of a single society, although, as already mentioned, Marx and Engels were often pre-occupied with the economic and political aspects within a single social system. There was to them no question that the abolishment of social class and private property would come, hastened by a world-wide movement, and thus they operated at times at a general level. Yet their most masterful analyses were at the level of a single social system operating in a somewhat restricted period of time (e.g., Marx's *The Eighteenth Brumaire of Louis Bonaparte* [1963; orig. 1852]) or were of a single aspect of several coexisting social systems (Marx's *Capital* [1967; orig. 1867]). It is at these two levels that their concern with historical context as well as with the causal role assigned other than material factors in socio-cultural change became most apparent.

At its worst, the Marxian dialectic was mere mysticism, as for example Engels' infamous discourse on the dialectic of the growth of a stalk of grain (1947:201–202; orig. 1888; as quoted in Harris 1968:59). For some modern Marxists, on the other hand, dialectical contradictions are a constant in the natural and social world and are only waiting to be discovered by more-sophisticated methodology (e.g., Mao Tse-tung 1967). Certainly in the abstract there was (and is) a vagueness about the notion that makes it difficult to handle.

Yet, as a methodological concept, as an *approach*, it can be very useful. Social conflict is unquestionably a dynamic factor in social life and is unquestionably a product of contradictions generated within a given system. The dialectical framework suggests what to look for and serves as a way of ordering empirical data into a statement about dynamic processes. For example, it offers an understanding of *how* the feudal form of property changed into the capitalist form.

But, again, some cautions and drawbacks: it must be used with scientific discretion—the data must reveal its presence, or else it is sheer dogma. And, in the abstract, it does not in itself suggest where the boundaries of systems should be drawn. That is, Marx and Engels discussed the dialectical process primarily as it took place in the productive systems of societies. Does it work in the superstructures as well? Does a particular art style include within it the elements of its own extinction? In many groups, there are both political systems and philosophical systems. Does a contradiction between the two mean that there will be a change in the political system, or the philosophical system, or both? One of these outcomes is likely. But must the analyst by some hocus-pocus create a new "politicophilosophical system" in order to apply the dialectic, that is, to show the contradictions to be within a *single* system?

And must conflict always be resolved by open confrontation and revolution? Resolution could come as readily by a gradual elimination or modification of the sources of conflict (cf. Harris 1968:69); it depends on the particular context in which the conflict arises (see also Boulding 1970).

Marx and Engels' evolutionary scheme was not new in its basic outline, nor was it entirely unique in emphasizing the importance of material conditions. The major scientific contribution of both it and their other, more detailed studies was toward developing a materialist methodology for the study of the mechanism of sociocultural change. The causal priority of man's material relations could be scientifically investigated and on that basis proved, disproved, or modified. The omnipresence of conflict and its resolution as a source of dynamics could also be treated to scientific investigation. Critics could claim that conflict played much too pervasive a role in the Marxian scheme; but historical proof, not simply logic or rhetoric, was required to make the criticism stand.

Herbert Spencer

Spencer continued the tradition of the Enlightenment in his attempts to show that the evolution of culture revealed the operation of natural laws that could be formulated according to scientific, not purely philosophical, principles. It is no coincidence, then, that much of what he wrote about *cultural* evolution had its analog in *biological* evolution, where the operation of natural laws was becoming increasingly apparent.

EVOLUTION: BIOLOGICAL AND CULTURAL

Many of the elements of Charles Darwin's theory of biological evolution had been anticipated in both the biological and cultural realms years before *The Origin of Species* went to press in 1859. It is possible to argue, in fact, that Darwin's work was based on a sociocultural model, rather than the other way around (Harris 1968:128 ff.). Some of the most coherent of these pre-Darwinian statements were written by Spencer himself (Carneiro 1967:xvi; Greene 1963:84).[4] Unquestionably, Darwin's work in turn had an impact on Spencer's later writing. (Marx, incidentally, wanted to dedicate the first volume of *Capital* to Darwin in acknowledgment of the latter's achievement.) Spencer's *Principles of Sociology* (1876–1896) was rife with analogies between biological and social evolution,[5] but it was the single Darwinian principle of natural selection that loomed largest in his work and in the works of other cultural evolutionists. For Spencer this principle meant "survival of the fittest," and he argued repeatedly that societies best

[4]However, Spencer adapted ideas of men like Charles Lyell, Gustav Klemm, and Thomas Malthus. From the latter came the notion of "survival of the fittest," which both Spencer and Darwin utilized (Coser 1971:100; Harris 1968:128).

[5]However, Spencer clearly stated the limitations of the analogy between biological and social evolution.

equipped to win conflicts with others were best fit to survive
(e.g., Spencer in Carneiro 1967:33; orig. 1876–1882).
This idea gave impetus to a distinct Victorian chauvinism
that came to be known as "Social Darwinism." Perhaps the
attitude should really be billed as "Social Spencerism,"
because it was essentially Spencer's (and Malthus's) "survival of the fittest" plastered onto the achievements of
western Europe and America during the Industrial Revolution (Harris 1968:134). Social Darwinism, quite simply,
included the conviction that England and her allies were
obviously most fit to survive because they had become the
most prosperous of nations. It was only proper that these
most "fit" countries should expand into the more barbaric
portions of the globe to uplift the local populations. In
economics, "survival of the fittest" became the watchword
of laissez-faire capitalism, an economic structure far from
being the anathema to Spencer that it was to Marx and
Engels. And Social Darwinism carried with it racist beliefs
in the inherent superiority of whites as the contemporary
bearers of this most "fit" way of life.

SPENCER ON EVOLUTIONARY PROCESS

For Spencer, cultural evolution involved the operation of
a series of interrelated factors. One was *population increase,*
which was in turn linked to *local food supply* and *natural
habitat:*

Where a fruitful soil affords much food, and where a more
settled life, leading to agriculture, again increases the supply of
food, we meet with larger social aggregates. . . . Here a hundred
or two, here several thousands, here many thousands, are held
together more or less completely as one mass. And then in the
highest societies, instead of partially aggregated thousands, we
have completely aggregated millions [Spencer in Carneiro
1967:10; orig. 1876].

His statement refers not only to a rise in population but
to an integration ("aggregation") of population elements

or groups as well, emphasizing his point that development meant change in both the size and the interrelationship of elements. While an increase in food supply led to larger groupings, other factors had to be present to keep the aggregates functioning together—there had to be control and organization. And this control stemmed primarily from the need to wage effective offensive or defensive warfare (Spencer in Carneiro 1967:15, 33; orig. 1876). Control was necessary for success in combat, of course; but in the temporary absence of war the militant leadership could still function as controlling elements in the organization of society.

There were thus two basic systems in the earlier stages of evolution: one for control or regulation and one for sustenance (providing the members with food, commodities, etc.). Each of these systems became increasingly complex to the point where a third, intermediate system, the distribution system (merchants, communications, roads), was needed to transfer products and influences from element to element in the society as a whole if it was to survive.

Military success (implying military-administrative control), combined with an adequate subsistence base, made large aggregates possible and kept them growing. Growth in turn created heavier demands for goods within the group, demands that could only be met by a steadily more efficient organization of productive groups and an increasing effectiveness of technology. And the greater the population and amounts of goods produced, the greater the importance of the distribution system.

Spencer distinguished between "militant" and "industrial" societies as types according to which of the two basic systems—control or sustenance—predominated in group activities. He noted that the typology could not be very specific, because the ratios between the two systems "admit of all gradations" (Spencer in Carneiro 1967:62; orig. 1876). Yet the preponderance of the sustenance-industrial system clearly represented an evolutionary advance from the more militant

types, because with it emerged the freedom of the individual. Militant societies were characterized by oppressive authoritarian control; industrial societies by decentralized,
voluntary controls and free institutions. Again the Enlightenment concern with "progress" and again the chauvinism: England of Spencer's time was the acme of industrial
society, he felt. How different the perspectives of Marx and
Spencer, living in the same country at the same time and
focusing on much the same sorts of social activities![6]

In addition to this basic industrial-militant dichotomy,
and not entirely consistent with it, Spencer constructed a
system of four evolutionary stages, beginning with "simple
societies" and culminating in "trebly compound societies."
Societies from around the world could be fitted into the
stage sequence on the basis of the complexity of their internal organization and the extent to which their component
groups were consolidated into a single aggregate. Most
Eskimos, for example, were representatives of simple societies; England was trebly compound if not higher (Spencer
in Carneiro 1967:48–53; orig. 1876).

Yet Spencer, as Marx and Engels, seemed much less concerned with classification than he was with tracing the
dynamics of the interrelationship among components of culture. True to his biological analogies, he emphasized that
changes in form inevitably implied changes in function. As
societies became more complex, the functions of the component elements became increasingly specialized yet essential
to the satisfactory operation of the societies as wholes
(Spencer in Carneiro 1967:214; orig. 1876). The bulk of
his massive *Principles of Sociology* (1876–1896) was a detailed discussion of these basic evolutionary principles
applied not only to entire groups but also to the mechanisms
of political evolution, the evolution of legal systems, property, and revenue. Whether a particular society was in fact
doubly compound or trebly compound was not a topic of

---

[6]Spencer in fact was disgusted with the collectivist drift in English
mercantile relations. See Coser 1971:125.

lengthy discussion. What was discussed was *how* a society *could* become trebly compound and the functional interrelationships involved in such a shift. He was talking about processes.

MATERIALISM VERSUS IDEALISM

In his use of biological analogies, Spencer laid a good deal of stress on the relationship between the social system and its local environment (e.g., Spencer in Carneiro 1967:10; orig. 1876). He underlined the importance of agriculture for cultural development but cautioned that agriculture required a favorable environment. And groups living in isolated mountain valleys were more likely to consolidate into a series of small independent states rather than a single far-flung kingdom, he believed, because of the natural barriers to communication and coordination of activities (Spencer in Carneiro 1967:Chapter 14; orig. 1882).

In anticipation of important twentieth-century theories of cultural evolution, he suggested that energy and man's capacity to harness it were basic to man's social existence: "Whatever takes place in a society results either from the undirected physical energies around, from these energies as directed by men, or from the energies of men themselves" (as quoted in Carneiro 1967:xxxv; orig. 1862). However, this was not a dominant theme in his later work.

At times he made statements strikingly similar to those made earlier by Marx and Engels, although to my knowledge he was not familiar with their work. For example, he emphasized that the division of labor was crucial and inevitable in the growth of societies (Spencer in Carneiro 1967:5; orig. 1876) and, as mentioned earlier, stressed the effects of warfare on the consolidation of savage groups and the eventual rise of private property (e.g., Spencer in Carneiro 1967:87–88; orig. 1882). He wrote a great deal about distinctions between social classes and about oppressors and the oppressed. But his emphasis was not on the internal conflict generated by such factors. External conflict between societies was for him the driving force of evolution.

For Spencer, the evolution of ideas derived from the evolution of material factors. He firmly believed in the ultimate morality of individualism and noted that it accompanied the evolution of the industrial society; but it was not a motivating influence in his scheme—man was not constantly pushing toward some final realization of his ideal state. This could come only after appropriate material conditions had been met. Spencer made his stand on the side of materialism very explicit in the following comparison of his ideas with those of Comte:

Comte proposes to describe the necessary, and the actual, filiation of *ideas*. I propose to describe the necessary, and the actual, filiation of *things*. Comte professes to interpret the genesis of our *knowledge of nature*. My aim is to interpret . . . the genesis of the *phenomena which constitute nature*. The one is subjective. The other is objective [1904, II:570; as quoted in Coser 1971:89].

So Spencer was a materialist—even though he did not wish to be known as one (Carneiro 1967:xxxv)! In Marxian terms, his focus was on the modes and means of production as these developed in a series of geographical settings. This was a researchable perspective. For example, if he erred in laying too much stress on the evolutionary importance of warfare, other scholars could gather data to point out the error.

Lewis H. Morgan and Edward B. Tylor

Lewis H. Morgan and Edward B. Tylor were near-contemporaries of Spencer, Marx, and Engels, although their major intellectual contributions were made somewhat later in the nineteenth century. Morgan, an American Presbyterian and lawyer, and Tylor, a British educator, proposed schemes of cultural evolution that were similar enough to warrant their joint description here, although they differed markedly in some of the particulars of their evolutionary approaches and although each was interested in separate problems that transcended those of cultural change.

Their goal in evolutionary studies was to reconstruct man's past to better understand his present condition. Like Marx, Engels, and Spencer, they were concerned with injecting science into their efforts, although, just as the others, they never completely isolated themselves from social philosophy. And, as Marx and Engels, their schemes were designed in part as a refutation of opposing views prevalent among intellectuals of the time. One important source of opposition was the theological doctrine of degeneration.

PROGRESS OR DEGENERATION?

Darwin's work had added fuel to a long-standing controversy between social evolutionists and theologians over whether the differences between civilized and savage life were to be explained by the progress of the former or the degeneration of the latter. Arguing on theological grounds, the opponents of the idea of progress in human history declared that the savage peoples of the earth had fallen from God's grace; they had once enjoyed a much higher stage of existence but had been forced backward culturally as a consequence of divine wrath. Ironically, it was an argument that could be used to support the same Victorian chauvinism that Spencer, Tylor, and Morgan all shared, in spite of the fact that the analogy between social and biological evolution, if allowed, would favor the progressivist view.

Tylor in particular was concerned with documenting the progressivist position, and much of the analysis in the first volume of his *Primitive Culture* (1874; orig. 1871) was devoted explicitly to a destruction of the degeneration argument. He wrote that cultures develop "by processes still in regular operation as of old, the result showing that on the whole, progress has far prevailed over relapse" (1874, I:32; orig. 1871). Morgan agreed, declaring that the concept of degeneration "was never a scientific proposition supported by facts. It is refuted by the connected series of inventions and discoveries, by the progressive development of the social system, and by the successive forms of the family" (1877:506). Yet neither Tylor nor Morgan was so naive as to insist that *no* degeneration had occurred in evolution. On this point they chose to distinguish two analytical levels: (1) the totality of culture through time and (2) individual cultures at given historical points. This enabled them to cite cases of decline in a specific culture such as that of the Mayas of Middle America (although Tylor considered this a poor example because the decline was apparently caused by invasion by outsiders). Culture as a whole, however, had progressed rather than degenerated, and it was the progress of culture that they were determined to trace in their reconstructions.

MORGAN'S EVOLUTIONARY SCHEME

Morgan and Tylor both saw fit to subdivide the continuum of socio-cultural evolution into a series of periods or stages. Morgan's is perhaps the best known and simplest of the sequences presented in this chapter; Tylor used similar terms but apparently did not become so involved in the specific ramifications.

Morgan recognized that evolution could be traced by using two different sets of data: (1) *social structural forms,* such as kinship, family, property management, and politics, and (2) "inventions and discoveries," that is, *material items* such as pottery, the bow and arrow, and metallurgy. It was the latter set that he chose to characterize the different strata of his evolutionary model. He assumed that these material "tests of progress" furnished a somewhat rough but sufficient indication of the social structural forms in each stratum. However, he was not particularly pleased with using material traits alone; patterns of subsistence would have been better tests of progress "from the great influence they must have exercised on the condition of mankind . . ." (1877:9). But he felt he lacked the evidence to use the subsistence criterion with certainty.

He divided evolutionary development into three major strata or "ethnical periods": Savagery, Barbarism, and Civilization. The first two of these strata each included three substrata (1877:9–18):

I.   *Lower Status of Savagery*
     Human beginnings, including development of language, "fruits and nuts" subsistence, ending with development of fishing subsistence and knowledge of the use of fire. (No living examples of this stratum.)

II. *Middle Status of Savagery*
     Beginning with fishing subsistence and use of fire and ending with invention of the bow and arrow. During this period mankind expanded to cover "the greater portion of the earth's surface." (Examples are Australians and Polynesians at the time of first contact with Europeans.)

III. *Upper Status of Savagery*
     Beginning with the invention of the bow and arrow and ending with the invention of pottery. (Examples include American Indians of the western sub-Arctic, Columbia River valley tribes, and "certain coast tribes of North and South America" at the time of first contact with Europeans.)

IV. *Lower Status of Barbarism*
     Beginning with the invention of pottery "whether by original invention or by adoption" and ending in the eastern hemisphere with the invention of

animal domestication and in the western hemisphere with the cultivation of plants by irrigation and use of adobe-brick and stone in house construction. The dichotomy was forced by what Morgan perceived as "the unequal endowments of the two hemispheres"—differences in domesticable flora and fauna; the new world had few domesticable animals and only one grain: maize (1877:22). (Examples include American Indian tribes east of the Missouri River, and tribes of Europe and Asia who had pottery but no domesticated animals.)

V. *Middle Status of Barbarism*
Beginning with animal domestication in the Old World and with plant cultivation with irrigation and adobe-brick and stone houses in the New World and ending in the invention of iron-ore smelting. (Examples include Pueblo Indians of the American Southwest, village-dwelling Indians of Mexico, Central America, and Peru, and tribes in the Eastern Hemisphere practicing animal domestication but lacking the knowledge of iron-ore smelting. Ancient Britons knew about iron metallurgy through contact with other cultures, but Morgan placed them in this stage because of their less advanced social structure.)

VI. *Upper Status of Barbarism*
Beginning with the smelting of iron and ending with the invention of the phonetic alphabet and use of written literature. (Examples include Grecian tribes of the Homeric Age, Italian tribes before the founding of Rome, and the Germanic tribes of Julius Caesar's time.)

VII. *Status of Civilization*
Beginning with the use of the phonetic alphabet and literary writing. Hieroglyphic writing on

stone tablets is an equivalent. (Examples can be divided into *Ancient* and *Modern*, the former including classical Greece and Rome, the latter including Great Britain and the United States.) Note that Morgan, as Marx before him, conceived the scheme as both a classificatory device and a model of sequential development—hence the alternative use of the terms "status" and "ethnical period."

After outlining this general evolutionary sequence, Morgan (1877) proceeded to reconstruct the evolutionary sequence of development of government, the family, and property. It is clear that social structural and ideological patterns were his major preoccupation; artifacts were important as means of classification and as implications for the degree of social structural and ideological complexity of groups. Whether or not he was concerned with processes as much as he was with patterns is an important issue to be considered below.

MORGAN ᷝAND TYLOR ON EVOLUTIONARY PROCESSES

For Morgan and Tylor there were two logical explanations for the development of cultures along similar paths; either the major patterns were independently reinvented time after time by different peoples or the patterns had diffused from group to group as a result of intercultural communication. But what could cause the similarity in two patterns that had been independently invented? Their answer in essence was that there existed a basic psychic unity among all mankind. Morgan reasoned that all men possessed certain "germ ideas" that served as the basis for the parallel development of sociocultural patterns;[7] these germ ideas had been part

[7]"Psychic unity" was a term applied by *others* to describe Morgan's and Tylor's concepts, apparently (Harris 1968:15). Even though neither man used the term explicitly, it is certainly implied in the writings of both, especially in Morgan's concept of "germ ideas."

of mankind's mental equipment from the lowest period of savagery:

> The human mind, specifically the same in all individuals and in all the tribes and nations of mankind, and limited in the range of its powers, works and must work, in the same uniform channels, and within narrow limits of variations. Its results in disconnected regions of space, and in widely separated ages of time, articulate in a logically connected chain of common experiences. In the grand aggregate may still be recognized the few primary germs of thought, working upon primary human necessities, which, through the natural process of development, have produced such vast results [1877:255].

Tylor agreed, noting that the mental processes of men everywhere were essentially similar and that there were basic similarities of life-ways among savages that were not due to diffusion (1874, I:6; orig. 1871).

In the abstract, both explanations—psychic unity and independent invention—were allowable. The rub came when trying to decide which of the two adequately explained the specific similarities between diverse groups. When it was discovered that a given culture trait—such as a specific family form, a game such as the Indian pachisi, or metallurgy—was found among widely separated peoples, could the co-occurrence be due to widespread transmission from a single original source, or was it the result of a series of independent inventions in each of the groups?

There were profound implications riding on which of the two alternative processual explanations was finally to be selected, and again the issue of progress versus degeneration was involved (Stocking 1968:71). One prominent writer had observed that "degenerate" savage groups could progress only under the influence of more-advanced peoples (i.e., diffusion). If Tylor were to combat this notion, he would have to push the independent invention alternative. This he apparently did in *Primitive Culture* (1874; orig. 1871), to the limits his empirically oriented conscience would allow. Diffusion, on the other hand, could have made the evidence for the universality of certain mental processes much more questionable, because there would have been the dilemma of whether the similarities were not actually due to widespread transmission of traits.

In fact, neither Morgan nor Tylor ever argued exclusively for one of the two alternatives. There were simply too many obvious instances of diffusion to be ignored for the sake of psychic unity. Their conclusions about which of the two explanations accounted for a given similarity were drawn on the basis of evidence as they saw fit to use it. Tylor was perhaps the more cautious of the two, often presenting the dilemma and then withdrawing to wait for more evidence to accumulate. Morgan, in a logical contradiction to his germ-idea concept, suggested a world-wide diffusion of a given type of kinship group (the "gens") from a single origin and suggested other world-wide dispersals of specific family forms, based mainly on the argument that the forms were too complex to have been invented more than once (1877:379, 386).

There was still a sticky processual issue to be resolved, however: if psychic unity and diffusion were both operative, how could the simultaneous, nineteenth-century existence of both "civilized" and "savage" groups be explained? Why had some groups evolved faster or more radically than others? On this score, Tylor and Morgan (and Spencer as well) sometimes became tangled in a confusion of racial and sociocultural factors as "causes" of evolutionary process, and the relative clarity of the psychic unity/diffusion alternatives became frustratingly muddled.

BIOLOGICAL AND CULTURAL EVOLUTIONARY PROCESSES

In brief, Morgan, Tylor, and Spencer resorted at times to racist explanations for the unsynchronized evolutionary development among the world's peoples (Harris 1968:138 ff.). Morgan, for example, in noting the widespread dispersion of what he called the "Ganowanian" family type, went beyond mere diffusion as an explanation and argued that this form was "transmitted with the blood" (1870:274). The mind of the American Indian, he believed, never experienced what could be called a "profit motive," and this was "doubtless the great reason for his continuance in the hunter state" (Morgan 1851:139; as quoted in Harris 1968:138). Tylor, in his *Anthropology* (1897:407; orig. 1881), compared "civilized" morality with that of savages and barbarians: "Moreover, there is this plain difference between low and high races of men, that the dull-minded barbarian has not power of thought enough to come up to the civilized man's best moral standard."

But how can these explanations be fitted with the notion of psychic unity? The anthropologist Marvin Harris (1968:139–140) offered this interpretation of Morgan's ideas:

As the races evolve, they pass through similar biocultural stages. At any particular stage, the innate mental condition of the descendants of any branch of the human species tends to be essentially similar. They thus tend to react to similar conditions in similar ways and to move in parallel fashion from savagery to civilization. However, they certainly do not move in tandem, all at the same time.

Thus there were "superior" and "inferior" races as indicated by their level of cultural evolution; and of all the racial groups, only white men had achieved the arbitrary standards of "civilization" by the mid-nineteenth century.

Harris's interpretation does not resolve the apparent contradiction satisfactorily. Obviously, Morgan, for one, did not consistently argue that the innate mental conditions of all races were essentially similar at a given stage of evolution (American Indians, *unlike whites*, lacked a profit motive). I believe these statements about innate mental similarity as opposed to racial differences in mentality must remain contradictory even in hindsight. Either Morgan and Tylor did not see the problem or they simply ignored it; they did not clearly resolve it. To make the confusion still more profound, both writers seemed at times to use the terms "races" and "cultures" interchangeably.

But just as they did not stick solely to either psychic unity or diffusion as explanations for cultural similarities, they did not resort strictly to racial explanations for the differences between savages and civilized men. Tylor, for example (1897:439; orig. 1881), cited the savage's lack of the "larger experience" of civilized cultures—a difference that is not clearly the result of "savage" genes. Yet still we must wonder whether this meant that savages lacked a larger experience because they were inherently stupid or that, as I believe Tylor meant in this passage, they did not have access to the scholarly knowledge accumulated and stored in the thousands of years of other humans' literacy.

Neither Tylor nor Morgan used biological analogies as extensively as Spencer did. Morgan reported that the emergence of what he called the "consanguine family" among savages afforded a "good illustration of the principle of natural selection" (1877:425), although he did not pursue the principle very actively. Tylor was moved to write, "History . . . and ethnography . . . combine to show that institutions which can best hold their own in the world gradually supersede the less fit ones, and that this incessant conflict determines the general resultant course of culture" (Tylor 1874, I:69; orig. 1871). However, when such pronouncements are separated from the meat of his analysis it becomes apparent that Tylor was not particularly interested in demonstrating the biological analogy, nor was he willing to acknowledge a great intellectual debt to Darwin (Tylor 1874, I:viii; orig. 1871; cf. Stocking 1968:97 and Opler 1964).

Yet both men shared to a degree in the "Social Darwinist" notions prevalent in their time. This was implicit in their assigning Victorian England and America to the highest known stages of cultural evolution (cf. Haller 1970). The bearers of civilization were "better and happier" than those at lower stages of evolution (Tylor 1874, I:31; orig. 1871).

This application of the "survival of the fittest" dogma imposed on much of their analysis a moralistic bias that was contrary to modern canons of objective social science, and the "racial" explanation for differences in evolutionary progress hindered scholarly inquiry into the roles of psychic unity and diffusion in change processes.

MATERIAL AND IDEAL FACTORS IN PROCESS

Morgan was unquestionably anxious to emphasize man's material relations as crucial factors in sociocultural evolution. Writing a year after the first volume of Spencer's *Principles of Sociology* was printed, Morgan observed, "It is accordingly probable that the great epochs of human progress have been identified, more or less directly, with the enlargement of the sources of subsistence" (1877:19). Technological inventions such as the bow and arrow and metallurgy were prerequisites for progress:

> The most advanced portion of the human race were [*sic*] halted, so to express it, at certain stages of progress, until some great invention or discovery, such as the domestication of animals or the smelting of iron ore, gave a new and powerful impulse forward [1877:39–40].

Engels' *Origin of the Family* (1972; orig. 1884) borrowed Morgan's discussion of the relationship between property ownership on the one hand and kinship systems, politics, and law on the other (Morgan 1877:218, 231, 531, e.g.). Engels also must have found congenial Morgan's observations about the tyranny of the propertied artistocracy (Morgan 1877:551) and the "unmanageable power" of property in the hands of privileged classes (Morgan 1877:552).[8]

[8]Morgan was a lawyer with considerable capitalistic investment interests. Thus Hobsbawm's comment (in Marx 1965:24; orig. 1857–1858) that Morgan "grew up in a utopian-socialist atmosphere" is false.

Yet in general there was a real ambiguity in Morgan's evolutionary scheme regarding the relative importance of material and mental factors (cf. Harris 1968:213 ff.). In his *Ancient Society* he sounded like a pitchman for the Enlightenment when he emphasized that "institutions of government [as other institutions] are a growth from primitive germs of thought" (1877:508) or when he singled out imagination as "that great faculty which has contributed so largely to the elevation of mankind" (1877:532). It would therefore be forcing the evidence to place Morgan in the same materialist camp as Marx, Engels, and Spencer.

Recently there has been some debate over whether Tylor could be classified as a materialist (White 1949a:364; Stocking 1963:795; Opler 1964). While Tylor mentioned the important effect of subsistence techniques on cultural development (e.g., 1897:168 ff.; orig. 1881), one of his primary concerns was the evolution of human mentality. This, together with the older Comtian notion of the analogy between individual and social development, is expressed in the final paragraph of his *Early Researches* (1964:241; orig. 1865):

[The belief that dreams have objective reality for primitives etc.] . . . belong[s] to that early condition of the human mind, from which . . . the ordinary ideas of Man and Nature held by educated men differ so widely. However far these ideas may in their turn be left behind, the growth which can be traced within the range of our own observation and inference, is one of no scant measure. It may bear comparison with one of the great changes in the mental life of the individual man, perhaps rather with the expansion and fixing of the mind which accompanies the passage from infancy into youth, than with the later steps from youth into manhood, or from manhood into old age.

The conclusion seems to be that both scholars were creatures of the post-Enlightenment and that they were not particularly concerned with an adherence to either of the two types of factors that their modern protagonists seem so eager to impose on them.

DETECTION AND DOCUMENTATION OF CHANGE PROCESSES

In striking contrast to Marx and Engels' specifically evolutionary work, that of Morgan and Tylor (and Spencer
as well) is crammed with ethnographic details from around
the world. But, of all the men, Morgan was the only one
to engage in protracted periods of ethnographic investigation
(e.g., Morgan 1851; 1870). However, Morgan and the others
obtained most of their evidence from classical scholars or
from missionaries, government administrators, and the handful of professional ethnographers who had lived among
primitive groups. Classical scholars, of course, could furnish
valuable insight into the customs of ancient Greece and
Rome. But determining the life-styles of extinct preliterate
groups at early evolutionary stages was obviously a more
difficult matter. Archeology, which was in its infancy, could
be of some help. But when used with discretion, two other
basic techniques were more useful.

One technique was to study culture traits that seemed
to be very old and that had somehow managed to survive
as anachronisms in present-day societies. Tylor in particular
wrote about the significance of such "survivals," as he called
them, for understanding earlier stages of evolution (and,
not incidentally, for use as proof of progress' triumph over
degeneration).

He wrote:

The ordeal of the Key and Bible, still in use, is a survival;
the Midsummer bonfire is a survival; the Breton peasants' All
Souls' supper for the spirits of the dead is a survival. . . .
[I]nsignificant, moreover, as multitudes of the facts of survival
are in themselves, their study is so effective for tracing the
course of the historical development through which alone it is
possible to understand their meaning, that it becomes a vital
point of ethnographic research to gain the clearest possible
insight into their nature [1874, I:16–17; orig. 1871].

The second technique was also in a sense a study of survivals, but one involving whole groups instead of isolated
traits. As Comte before them, Spencer, Morgan, and Tylor

felt that a study of contemporary "savages" could tell them a great deal about the savage stage of development thousands of years earlier. Yet Tylor, at least, explicitly recognized in this so-called "comparative method" the danger of going too far in assuming an identity between contemporary and prehistoric primitives (1964:239–240; orig. 1865). Morgan seemed much less wary when (for example) he attempted to use certain contemporary kinship terminologies as evidence for a past stage of group marriage (Morgan 1877:27).

Their ability to document change in a consistent fashion depended in part on the extent to which they were able to show the functional interrelationship of forms, as Spencer and Marx did, rather than simply to catalog or classify a series of diverse and exotic ideas and artifacts. Morgan was inconsistent in this, as usual. In his *Ancient Society*, he devoted five chapters to a discussion of the interrelationship of elements in ancient Greek and Roman societies; specifically, the linkages between descent, property, family form, and political forms. And he was able to show in masterful fashion how a change in one of these forms could be traced to changes in others. And yet he was also able to describe at length the features of Polynesian kinship systems without grasping the sophistication of the other aspects of Polynesian life, and the Polynesians ended up in his evolutionary scheme slightly above the Australian Aborigines and below most of the American Indian tribes (Morgan 1877:13–17; cf. Stern 1931:136).

Tylor was equally inconsistent in his devotion to functional interrelationships. In one important article, he used sophisticated functional analysis in tracing the relationship between changes in marriage and descent patterns; it was an exercise in method masterfully accomplished (Tylor 1888). Yet he warned in his *Primitive Culture* (1874, I:24; orig. 1871) that, in the reconstruction of man's past, "No kind of evidence need be left untouched on the score of remoteness or complexity, or minuteness or triviality." What then followed in this book was an amazing compilation of ethnographic tidbits on the development of language, systems of counting, myths, and so forth, with little attempt to convey any sense of functional interrelatedness. The evolution of culture was the theme in this and most of his other works, but the basic task, as he saw it, included a comparison of individual traits as the basic units, not of cultures as wholes (cf. Stocking 1968:81).

So, using their evidence and their assumptions about processes, could Morgan or Tylor cogently and scientifically account for the transition from savagery to barbarism, or from barbarism to civilization? Insofar as their conclusions about material factors involved in evolution could be scientifically verified, part of their general explanation seemed reasonable enough.

But what of the "germs of thought" or "imagination" mentioned as important factors? Morgan, for example, argued that the transition from matrilineal to patrilineal inheritance in Greek and Roman times was based on a "desire" to transfer property to one's own children (1877:343 ff., 470). How could this desire be verified? The logic was psychologistic: there was a change in inheritance; therefore, there must have been a desire for the change. He also made a number of references to a form of "natural development" of tribal confederacies, just as the transition from matrilineal to patrilineal descent was to him natural (1877:122 ff.). The natural development boiled down to a mentalist dead end: development took place because thinking men wanted it to happen. This may have been true, but to demonstrate this on the basis of Morgan's own evidence from the remote past is out of the question. Engels apparently saw the difficulty clearly, for in his adaptation of Morgan's ideas in the *Origin of the Family* (1972; orig. 1884), he ignored the "germ ideas" and concentrated on Morgan's materialism.

Diffusion and psychic unity were both *needed* to explain why the cultural evolution had taken similar paths in different groups and at different times. Yet neither of these dynamic factors could be scientifically verified merely by pointing to the widespread existence of similar social forms. And that observation, plus their own logic, was about all Morgan and Tylor had to go on. Also, without very careful explanation of the interrelationship of the two factors, they appeared contradictory.

Tylor seemed far more interested in showing that development took place than in showing the mechanisms by which it occurred. Perhaps his most extensive statement about developmental processes appeared in the final chapter of his *Anthropology* (1897; orig. 1881), where he cited the now familiar factors of warfare, property, kinship, and government. Spencer and Morgan, whom he mentions in his bibliography, covered this same group of factors earlier, and Marx and Engels before either of them.

I am arguing, then, that Morgan and Tylor were not primarily concerned with the mechanisms of change. Their evolutionary schemes were as much static categories for the classification of traits and institutions as they were dynamic models. And even as a classificatory scheme, Morgan's stage sequence was not very satisfactory. As his modern critics have pointed out, he could not successfully handle the problem of linking the level of complexity of *nonmaterial* social structures with the presence or absence of *material* culture traits: "In Africa, the bow and arrow was replaced by the more effective spear; and many other groups who have not the bow and arrow are high in other respects, but their status would, irrespective of this fact, be 'middle status of savagery'" (Stern 1931:136). His placing of the metallurgical but noncomplex ancient Britons in his scheme (see p. 52) is another case in point.

One of the reasons for this apparent lack of interest in process could have been a problem with evidence. To a degree, the evidence available to all the nineteenth-century evolutionists hindered their attempts to validate the mechanisms of change, particularly at lower stages of complexity. The validation was perhaps at its best when taken from accounts of classical civilizations or of late-feudal Europe—periods for which there were detailed descriptions with some time-depth. But in attempting to document mechanisms of change at the lower evolutionary levels, they could only turn to existing ethnographies, which usually said nothing about changes through time. The result was that some of the ways in which they used ethnographic evidence could neither prove nor disprove their conclusions about mechanisms. For example, in discussing the evolution of property concepts, Spencer noted that private ownership came about through warfare. For validation of this statement, he noted that the primitive Arawaks in South America had ill-defined private ownership, whereas more advanced Aztecs and Norsemen were warlike and had private property (Spencer in Carneiro 1967:195, 202; orig. 1882). Morgan and Tylor proceeded in much the same way with their evidence at times. In the absence of good data, then, examples were not of the transitional mechanism itself but of the "primitive" form in one society and the "evolved" form in another—and this amounted to classification.

Present Relevance of the Approaches

Marx, Engels, and Spencer have only recently emerged (or re-emerged, in Spencer's case) as "relevant" scholars in Western anthropology. Marx and Engels were ignored partly because of the scientific community's dogged refusal to separate Marxist social science from the Marxist political revolution of Lenin, Stalin, and Mao. In part, the creation of a somewhat inflexible and artificial boundary between the disciplines of anthropology and sociology was responsible as well. The reasons for Spencer's eclipse are not as clear. It certainly seems unwarranted in view of his competitive intellectual involvement with Morgan and Tylor and of his thousands of text pages about customs of the world's peoples.

Marx and Engels' materialism, their concept of class struggle, and their application of dialectics have all been influential in sociology for some time. Anthropologists are now using these analytical models in the study of political and economic problems of postcolonial economic development in the Third World nations, where class struggle and contradictions within social systems are rife (see, e.g., Magubane 1971). In such instances the analytical level is by no means the evolution of all human culture but, instead, the dynamics of specific sociocultural systems over relatively short periods of time—precisely the level at which Marx and Engels were at their best.

Morgan and Tylor's savagery-barbarism-civilization trilogy went out the window with the help of a dedicated group of early twentieth-century critics. But even under these circumstances, they and other nineteenth-century evolutionists made a contribution to the development of dynamic theory by providing a set of schemes to be reacted against. Then, later, the theme of general cultural evolution, the prospect of yet discovering the general laws governing cultural development, the concern with material factors (shorn of Morgan's "germ-idea" notion), and some concept of stagelike sequences of development—all were revived near the middle of this century, and the debt to the early masters was duly acknowledged (White 1959). In this revival the old evolutionary models themselves were not really the centers of attention that they had once been for Morgan. There were too many problems with the criteria of classification, and, besides, since the end of the nineteenth century most social scientists have assumed what Tylor and Morgan seemed so eager to prove: that general cultural evolution has prevailed over degeneration. I will describe the schemes of renascent evolution in Chapters Five and Six.

The discussion next centers on the attempt to discredit the general evolutionary approach in favor of a much more particularistic one. Yet, true to historical process, some of the contributions of the nineteenth-century scholars persisted in this and the other, newer schemes. The works of Marx, Engels, Spencer, Tylor, and Morgan, then, are decidedly not mere relics of interest only to historians. My task is to verify this assertion in the chapters to follow.

□□□□□□□□□□□□□□□□□□□□□□□□□□□□

CHAPTER THREE

THE HISTORICIST APPROACH

□□□□□□□□□□□□□□□□□□□□□□□□□□□□

The Setting

I N THE late 1800's Franz Boas left his native Germany and a career in physics to come to the United States and pursue a career in anthropology. He was a small but dogged man who had literally crossed swords with anti-Semitic colleagues as a student (proudly wearing the facial scars to prove it) and who, years later, endured starvation, freezing cold, and gnawing homesickness for the sake of compiling reams of painstakingly detailed ethnographic field notes. His life-style was characterized in a single word: *vorwärts!* (forward!) (Stocking 1968:147). These qualities alone might have earned him a place in the history of anthropology; but he was eminently more noteworthy for the dominant effect he had on American anthropology for almost half a century, and thus his personality, his work, and his ideas have been the subjects of almost as much copy as he produced himself during his long life.[1] To weave his contributions to the study of change into their historical context, however, I must return again to the development of evolutionist thought.

Lewis Henry Morgan, E. B. Tylor, Herbert Spencer, and Karl Marx suffered continually from a lack of carefully controlled data. But in the main, they paid attention to the demands of scientific responsibility (particularly Tylor and

[1]For example, Goldschmidt 1959b; Herskovits 1953; Rohner 1966 and 1969; Stocking 1968; Wax 1956; White 1963 and 1966.

Marx) as these had been formulated at their time. As so frequently happens in the history of the development of ideas, however, some of their basic arguments were treated as dogma by their followers, and some of their careful qualifications and hedgings on general statements were somehow ignored. In America the evolutionary ideas of Morgan, Tylor, and Spencer were dogmatized late in the nineteenth-century by men like Daniel Brinton and W. J. McGee. For example, Morgan and Tylor had been ambivalent about the relative importance of independent invention versus diffusion in accounting for widespread similarities of culture traits and customs. "Psychic unity," an important concept for them, was applied for two purposes: to account for widespread similarities when diffusion could not be demonstrated and, perhaps more important, to explain *why* the course of human history had proceeded through the steps of savagery, barbarism, and civilization. When treated by Brinton, however, psychic unity became *the* prevailing explanation for widespread similarity; diffusion, while not completely ignored, played at best a very minor role. And the progression from savagery to civilization continued as the grand pattern for deduction, a universal sequence that could be used uncritically for arranging sundry traits in their "proper" developmental relationship to each other without regard for the larger cultural contexts from which they had been ripped. Psychic unity and the savagery-barbarism-civilization trilogy were hailed as social scientific laws.

In 1895, Brinton presented a major address laced with evolutionist dogmatism before the American Academy for the Advancement of Science. By 1896 Boas had had enough. In a speech before the same group, Boas articulated his basic criticisms of that dogma and sketchily described his own approach (Boas 1940:270–280; orig. 1896). The ideas expressed in embryonic form at that early date guided him and his students for the next four decades.

Boas affirmed the evolutionists' conviction that an understanding of sociocultural change could only come through the reconstruction of the past. But he emphatically denied that the data then available proved the existence of any sort of universal laws. On the contrary, his own research had shown him that similarities of customs or traits among widely separated cultures could be explained by neither psychic unity nor diffusion but explained as the results of different historical developments leading by different paths to the same point. For example, clans could arise either through the amalgamation of small tribes or through the disintegration of large ones (Boas 1940:274; orig. 1896). If psychic unity were really a law, clans in every area would develop in precisely the same fashion. They did not, and this fact invalidated the strength of the psychic explanation. And, if traits that appeared to be similar were actually the result of quite different historical developments, would not the same conditions apply to whole cultures? Boas certainly thought so. Thus the savagery-barbarism-civilization sequence was also to be demoted from the status of a "law" on the basis of existing data. In his earliest writings, Boas was not willing to deny that such laws might ever be formulated (e.g., 1940:276; orig. 1896); he remained quite hopeful that they would be. But his optimism faded later in his career: "Cultural phenomena are of such complexity that it seems to me doubtful whether valid cultural laws can be found" (1940:257; orig. 1932). He came, then, to a repudiation of a search that had been a preoccupation of social science for over 150 years.

Boas also took the evolutionists to task for their application of the comparative method. A culture trait's relationship to its wider cultural context was crucial, he preached. It was hardly scientific, he continued, to rip traits out of their contexts, classify them according to their complexity, and then impose upon them some evolutionary sequence according to a predetermined scheme. This sort of pseudo-deductivism clashed sharply with his own cautiously inductive approach (Boas 1940:276, 282–283; orig. 1896 and 1920). Yet neither Morgan nor Tylor was consistently guilty of such excesses, any more than they were uncompromising advocates for psychic unity. Morgan, in particular, was often careful to trace the context and interrelationship of culture traits when he had enough data to do so. Boas' criticism could certainly have been more careful, then; due in part to its effects, the contributions of early evolutionists to the study of sociocultural dynamics were either overlooked or slighted among a generation of his students.

The Approach to Change[2]

It is not accurate to say that Boas' own scholarly goals and methods developed solely out of a reaction against evolutionary excesses, yet his own cautious approach in some ways appeared to be the antithesis of the earlier evolutionists'. But was there actually such a difference?

In drawing an apparent distinction between his own goals and those of the evolutionists, Boas noted early in his career that "the customs and beliefs themselves are not the ultimate objects of research. We desire to learn the reasons why such customs and beliefs exist—in other words, we wish to discover the history of their development" (1940:276; orig. 1896). In fact, this sounds much like the aims of Morgan, Tylor, Spencer, and Marx, even though Morgan and Tylor at times became preoccupied with the customs and beliefs themselves. History for Boas was where causation was lurking, waiting to be exposed by diligent ethnographic effort. But his historical interest was not in the great civilizations. He focused instead, as did most of his students, on

[2]Boas was a prolific, imaginative scholar whose interest ranged over a host of anthropological issues. My comments here are restricted largely to his contributions to the study of sociocultural change, and my conclusions about the work of him and his students are confined to this particular topic.

the task of reconstructing the pasts of nonliterate peoples. The real challenge was to determine past developments in the absence of written records and when archeology could be of little help.

Boas felt that historical sequences (and thus causation) could be exposed through a combination of two basic techniques: (1) intensive and thorough ethnography of cultures as wholes and (2) detailed comparisons of several cultures located in a limited geographical area. He preached that nothing should escape the ethnographer's notebook in the cultures he studied: kinship systems, subsistence techniques, ritual systems, language, folklore—all these and many more topics were to be carefully gleaned. But description, he cautioned, was not enough. An ethnography worthy of the name must include an analysis of the ways in which the customs and traits fitted together and of how they influenced each other. The influence of the local environment was also a key issue. And because there was usually very little written documentation of the cultures' pasts, the recollections of old, reliable informants served as the primary source of information on how patterns had changed through time. This information was supplemented by all other sorts of evidence available in a given situation. Once the ethnographies were completed, the careful comparison could begin. Customs and traits were compared to determine their similarities or differences within the geographical area and to chart their distribution among the several cultures.

Ideally, this combination of techniques could accomplish a number of tasks involved in reconstruction: the detailed comparison and informant's recollections could conceivably reveal the points of origin of traits and customs and could indicate the relative sequence in which those traits and customs spread to neighboring cultures. The study of the interrelationships within a culture allowed the investigator to understand better what influences were operating to modify a trait or custom once it had been introduced. And finally, the intensive ethnographic analysis could lead to an

understanding of the dynamics of interaction between the
local environment, the cultural patterns, and the individual
human being.

In its outlines it was not a very radical methodological
deviation from the work of some of the earlier evolutionists.
For example, Morgan had completed an exhaustive ethnographic description of the Iroquois in 1851. Morgan and
Spencer had been interested in the influence of the local
environment. All five evolutionists and many of their predecessors described in the last chapter concerned themselves
with tracing the interrelationships of traits and customs
within specified cultures. The origin and diffusion of elements of culture was a major preoccupation of some of
them. Only the task of discovering the nature of the relationship between an individual and the culture of his group
appeared to be one that had not been the concern of pre-
Boasian anthropologists.

Ideally, it was a comprehensive approach with a potential
for understanding dynamics. Actually, it was perhaps too
comprehensive a scheme, which Boas' own canons of empiricism and detail could never allow him to pursue in its
entirety. It was at the same time these qualities of Boas'
own work that constituted a major departure from the
work of the earlier evolutionists. In comparing the Boasian
and evolutionist approaches, then, I am suggesting that the
crucial differences lay not so much in the methodological
tasks themselves as in the way in which they were performed
and as in the level of abstraction at which the results were
applied. The evolutionists constructed general laws, whereas
Boas offered cautiously phrased descriptions of local developments. The evolutionists postulated world-wide diffusion,
whereas Boas described diffusion within a restricted geographical area, and only then if the transmission could be
proved. For the evolutionists, psychic unity was a causal
factor in change, and its universal influence would be demonstrated by historical reconstruction; for Boas, the causal
factors were unique to cultures located in a circumscribed

area and were so variable that they could not be safely predicted pior to intensive reconstruction within a limited geographical area.

So far, I have confined my remarks almost exclusively to Boas and his reactions to the evolutionist scheme. Now I want to broaden the discussion of issues in the historicist method and objectives and to sketch the contributions of some of Boas' famous students (not all of whom imitated their mentor's cautiously empirical style.)

Issues in the Detection and Documentation of Process

INDEPENDENT INVENTION VERSUS DIFFUSION

While Boas and his historicist students[3] flatly rejected what the evolutionists were doing with the psychic-unity concept,[4] still they were forced to leave open the possibility that similar traits in two different cultures might be a result of independent invention and development in each rather than of diffusion. Neither process was assigned a priority in the absence of proof, however; and proof was much more easily had in limited comparisons over small geographical areas, as Boas demonstrated repeatedly.

If the similarity was not because of diffusion, then there were two general ways in which the independent develop-

---

[3]I will be talking explicitly about A. L. Kroeber, Clark Wissler, Melville Herskovits, Robert Lowie, Alexander Goldenweiser, Edward Sapir, and Leslie Spier, although I expect some quibbling over whether all of them were, properly speaking, members of the "historicist" element in American anthropology. Some other students of Boas vehemently denied there was any such thing as a "Boas school," and most of them are known for their contributions to other than historicist-oriented research.

[4]Boas never denied, however, that universal psychic traits might exist among human populations.

ments could have occurred: by "parallelism" or by "convergence." Both are concepts frequently found in the literature of biological evolution. Parallelism in independent cultural development, the historicists believed, was relatively rare: it involved the independent progression of two similar culture elements through a series of similar alterations. An example (if we could ever know) might be that of the development of the game of *patolli* among the Aztecs and the game of pachisi among the Hindus (a famous issue broached by Tylor [1879] as evidence of widespread diffusion, discussed by A. L. Kroeber [1931] and re-examined by Charles Erasmus [1950]). It is possible that both began as simple games involving the use of lots (Erasmus 1950:382) and proceeded, independently and in parallel fashion, to develop into the fairly elaborate yet strikingly similar *patolli* and pachisi.

Convergence, on the other hand, was believed to be more common. Boas' example of the development of clans mentioned earlier in this chapter is one of convergence, in which, through time, and in different ways, two dissimilar elements come to resemble each other.

Parallelism, of course, was precisely what the concept of psychic unity was used to explain, and was in its most general application the old savagery-barbarism-civilization progression. Small wonder that A. L. Kroeber, one of Boas' first prominent students, was moved to observe:

Most culture parallels, even if indubitable, show . . . [a] quality of loose rooting in a more or less amateur psychology; and the similarities are themselves loose and vague—such as that most peoples can syllabify, or have some sort of chiefs or rulers, for instance.

By contrast, convergences are things that start out differently and subsequently assimilate. Here the phenomena may be quite sharply defined; and the factors that go to make them alike may also be definite [1948:540].

Here the typical historicist concern with the specifics of historical development is patent. But there was still a problem.

After psychic unity was destroyed as a cause for parallelism, it was necessary to offer a general explanation for those few indubitable instances in which parallelism *had* occurred, and, more important, for the more numerous examples of convergence. Boas and some of his students apparently wanted a general principle that could account for these occurrences but that at the same time would not contradict the crucial importance of understanding local historical development.

The principle of "the limitation of possibilities" filled the bill nicely. Alexander Goldenweiser, another of Boas' students, articulated it in 1913, although he claimed that Boas used it earlier (Erasmus 1950:384). It stated that convergence (and, by implication, parallelism) could be the result of similar logical, natural, or physical limitations operating on the development of traits and customs. The example most often used was that of a canoe paddle. If the purpose was to develop a hand-held instrument for propelling a craft through water where sails or long poles could not be used, there was a fairly narrow range of variation in the physical properties the instrument could have. It could not be too long or it would be unwieldy. It could not be too short or it would lose the propelling power of a man's two arms. It had to have a blade-like surface, although the shape of the blade could be leaflike, round, rectangular, or of some intermediate form. So, too, a group could trace its descent among kinsmen in only four ways: through the mother, through the father, through both the mother and the father, or through either parent to a combination of some maternal and some paternal relatives. In the case of the paddle, the limitation of possibilities was physical; in that of descent reckoning, biological. Of course, the wider cultural contexts of the traits in question exerted their own limitations. But the point is that the principle allowed a general explanation for similar culture traits resulting from unrelated historical developments in a way which was to the historicists infinitely more satisfying scientifically than the debunked psychic unity. How the principle operated in each specific case was, of course, still a matter for rigorous historical reconstruction, laced with down-to-earth logic.

But had the principle of psychic unity been debunked? I think Boas and his followers certainly believed it had. Seen from a different perspective, however, it could be argued that the difference between the Boasians' limited possibilities and the evolutionists' psychic unity was one of degree rather than of kind (Erasmus 1950:386). Limited possibilities was a more cautious and refined statement, but it was not by any means a contradiction of its predecessor. It did not challenge the presence of certain universal patterns of human psychology; rather, it viewed such patterns as one of a *series* of limitations on cultural variation that had been blown out of proportion by earlier evolutionists.

Diffusion versus independent invention was not the loaded issue for the historicists that it was for the evolutionists. The historicists remained open about which of the two was operative in a given situation and did not have to worry about diffusion contradicting some sort of general law (such as psychic unity). Unquestionably, diffusion occupied a more prominent place in the historicists' scheme of reconstruction primarily because the scheme itself called for comparisons of groups close to each other in time and space. Hence, independent invention was less likely.

DETECTION AND DOCUMENTATION OF DIFFUSION: THE CRITERIA OF PROOF

Still it was necessary to decide which, diffusion or independent invention, was the explanation for similarities in the development of certain culture traits and customs. If we pool a number of their statements on the subject, we find that historicists had four basic criteria for determining that diffusion had taken place.

1. *Space.* Were the similar traits distributed among cultures located close enough that information could have easily been disseminated from one to the other? If so, then the

possibility of diffusion was strengthened. However, absolute geographical distance alone could be a misleading criterion, because communication between peoples in close proximity could have been effectively blocked by natural or social obstacles between them: for example, mountain ranges, bodies of water, and perpetual states of enmity.

2. *Time*. The possibility of diffusion as an explanation for similarities was strengthened if the cultures involved were not only spatially close but coexisted at the same time. Obviously, the possibilities of communication between two nonliterate societies would have been extremely remote if one had become extinct well before the other emerged. (These two brief paragraphs by no means exhaust the ways in which temporal and spatial factors were handled by the historicists, as will soon be seen.)

3. *Complexity*. The case for diffusion as an explanation for trait similarities among cultures was strengthened if the traits were of such complexity that the chances of their independent development were remote. This assumption was actually a legacy from Tylor and Morgan. Morgan felt that the "gentile system" of kinship was too complex to have been reinvented and thus that it was diffused to the widespread areas in which it existed in his time (1877:377). And Tylor (1879) used an elaborate argument, including a calculation of mathematical probability, to demonstrate that *patolli* and pachisi were too complex to have been invented twice.

4. *Similarity of Form, Meaning, and Function*. The probability that similarity in two culture traits was due to diffusion was increased if the traits had a similar form, if they had a similar meaning, and if they were put to a similar use in the respective cultures in which they were found. One of the hoariest pedagogical examples of this requirement was the comparison of the pyramids of the valley of Mexico with those of ancient Egypt. Naive diffusionists pointed to the existence of the pyramids in both locations (knowing that the Egyptian structures were older) and used this ex-

ample along with others to posit a world-wide dissemination of civilization from the valley of the Nile (Smith 1928). However, a careful application of the criterion of similarity revealed that, although the pyramidal forms indeed looked alike, the meanings and uses of the pyramids in the Teotihuacán and Egyptian civilizations were quite different; thus, for all the insights gained from the intrepid voyages of the *Ra I* and *II*, a comparison of the pyramids in itself proves nothing about Egyptian-Mexican contacts, because not all the demands of the criteria of similarity can be met.

These four criteria were important in the limited comparisons and reconstructions Boas himself championed. But they were much more essential in grander schemes of reconstruction attempted by some of his students, such as Kroeber, who attempted to trace the patterns of diffusion over entire continents (Kroeber 1952:Chaps. 43, 47). If the criteria could not all be met in the larger studies, then the question remained open regarding diffusion versus independent invention of the traits and customs in question.

Obtaining proof that diffusion had occurred was one thing; but reconstructing the *order* in which a series of traits and customs had been disseminated, and thus reconstructing the sequence of their historical development, was quite another. This demanded more sophisticated methodological tools.

CULTURE AREA, AGE AREA, AND CULTURE CLIMAX

A culture area for the historicists was a classificatory device, not in itself a very useful historical concept but a necessary element in their reconstruction of the past. It referred to a group of "geographically contiguous tribes that exhibit so many culture traits in common as to contrast with other such groups" (Sapir 1949:425; orig. 1916). The similarity of cultures was in part presumably the result of their communication with each other, so that the boundaries enclosed a geographical area over which fairly intensive diffusion had taken place. It was thus a bounded system within which to study historical developments; usually the environment was relatively uniform throughout the area, which meant that one important variable accounting for intercultural differences was held more or less constant. And the areas were not so large as to prevent detailed studies of many individual cultures within their boundaries to get an idea of the range of cultural variation.

A method for determining the sequence in which traits spread across the area was suggested by Boas himself (1940:320; orig. 1916) and developed by Edward Sapir (1949; orig. 1916), Clark Wissler (1923; 1926) and A. L. Kroeber (1923:302). This, the so-called *age area* method, was based on a well-known assumption in biology (Kroeber 1952:58; orig. 1931). Its basic premise was that the relative age of an element of culture could be determined roughly by how far it had diffused from its point of origin within a given culture area. Thus, to borrow one of Kroeber's examples, the taboo on naming the dead and the girls' adolescence ceremony were universally found among the traditional Indian cultures of the California culture area, whereas property law and ground painting were confined to groups in the northwestern and southern portions of the area, respectively (1951a:107; orig. 1923). From this distributional evidence, Kroeber inferred that the taboos and adolescence ceremonies were much older than the property law of the Yurok or the ground painting of southern tribes.

The age area principle assumed a good deal about patterns of diffusion within and even between culture areas: that traits tended to spread outward in all directions from a point of origin in a pattern of concentric circles (Wissler 1926:183; he could not resist calling this the "law of diffusion"!); that the diffusion rate of traits tended to be uniform; and that as the traits diffused from their origin to the peripheries of the culture area they tended to lose some of their complexity. Wissler recognized that these assumptions had to be heavily qualified in almost every specific case. So he was continually making rather grand statements followed by exceptions and explanations of why specific cases did not conform to the basic age area assumptions (e.g., Wissler 1923:146).

But obviously traits do *not* spread at a uniform rate. Some (the horse and gun in North America are convenient examples) spread like wildfire; others, such as property law, remain confined to a limited area for generations. The movement of traits could retrograde and thus skew the assumptions about their relative age. And there was the whole question of the point or points of origin of specific traits: could not these be multiple, and could they not shift from one culture to another in an area?[5]

Kroeber's answer to this last question was "not necessarily." He used the term "culture climax" to refer to the portion of a culture area from which most of the material in that area had spread (1952:339; orig. 1939). A culture climax, Kroeber believed, tended to perpetuate itself: as it became more productive, it became more highly organized and thus better able to assimilate new ideas and techniques. With this greater input, the culture's production became even greater. The process was a slow one, however; so, barring "the introduction of a radically new subsistence mechanism, such as agriculture or the horse, [which] may occasionally cause a rapid growth . . . it may be taken for granted . . . that a climax in the historic period was also a climax, or at least a subclimax, in the later prehistoric period, and probably at least of [a] fairly high level of intensity before that" (1952:339; orig. 1939). But these climaxes of high intensity existed in only a few of the culture areas of North America. The question of the permanence of some sort of "culture center" in other, less developed areas remained a problem (Boas 1940:307; orig. 1936).

Both Wissler (1923:126) and R. B. Dixon suggested that

[5] R. B. Dixon (1928:69 ff.) was an early and articulate critic of the excesses of the age area scheme.

it was of little value to compare the distribution of two different traits in an area, because of the problem of relative rates of spread. Dixon shrewdly observed:

If we say that of two *different* traits the one having the wider distribution is necessarily or almost invariably the older, we are perhaps almost as likely to be wrong as right; if, on the other hand, we make the same assertion for two different forms or stages of development of the *same* trait, we are likely to be correct almost every time [1928:71].

Kroeber said practically the same thing three years later in comparing culture growth and organic evolution:

It is closely related groups of species or traits that must be compared, not distantly or unrelated ones: copper working with bronze, for instance, a simple with an elaborate complex of weaving techniques; not bronze with mudbrick-building, or a textile art with a religious cult. . . . In anthropology this limitation has generally not been recognized explicitly, has occasionally not been observed with due caution, and unnecessary attacks upon the principle have resulted [1952:58; orig. 1931].

Kroeber's criticism could easily be applied to his own earlier work (e.g., 1951a; orig. 1923).

CULTURE WHOLES AND CULTURE TRAITS

This is not a book about the definitions of culture; nonetheless, it is instructive to offer a few observations on the relationship between methodology in the study of culture change and "culture" definitions. Tylor's classic definition (1874, I:1; orig. 1871) described culture as a complex whole that consists of a series of subunits such as knowledge, morals, language, arts, and so on. The methodological inference drawn from this definition was that these subunits could be considered isolable areas of investigation. Tylor himself proceeded to do just that and ignored for the most part the introductory passage of his definition about culture as a whole. The historicists, too, paid a great deal of lip service to the holistic concept of culture.

In performing their research tasks, Boas and his students were best able to describe their versions of "cultures as wholes" as these existed at a single point in time. When reconstructing developments *through* time, however, they often found it impossible to work holistically and restricted their reconstructions to cultural subunits such as kinship, totemism, techniques of manufacture, or Boas' own favorite, folk tales. Folk tales, as George Stocking (1968:223 ff.) recently pointed out, were actually well suited to Boas' objectives. With some effort on the investigator's part, they could be reduced to a series of elements (plots, characters, style, vocabulary) whose distribution could be charted. At the same time, they were inevitably subjected to modification and reinterpretation by each culture, so as to make them fit into the prevailing context of local values and beliefs. Thus they offered evidence for the diffusion of culture traits through time and space and offered insights into how a diffused element was modified as it was integrated into recipient cultures.

The historicists' methodology for the study of change—as that of the evolutionists—focused on traits, and their definitions of culture itself lost much of the holistic orientation. For example, there was R. H. Lowie's famous observation (later amended) that civilization is a "thing of shreds and patches," a "planless hodgepodge" (1920:441). Wissler combined definition and methodology into a single summary passage: "In short, a tribal culture is a collection of trait complexes, developed and acquired in the course of tribal life; so the association of one with the other can be fully accounted for when we learn the events that brought them into these relations" (1923:71).

He apparently believed that a sense of the integration of elements would appear, almost magically, from a reconstruction of the origin and distribution of trait complexes.

My point is that *what* was being studied thus became in large part dependent upon *how* it was being studied.

ON PROCESSES: INVENTION, INTEGRATION, DIFFUSION

Early in his career, Boas wrote the words that were to be repeated again and again by students of sociocultural change: "The object of our investigation is to find the *processes* by which certain stages of culture have developed" (1940:276; orig. 1896). But Boas himself and some of his followers never seemed very clear about what they meant by "process" (cf. Rohner 1969:xvii)—or "history" for that matter (Boas 1940:305–310; orig. 1936). Kroeber certainly did not clarify the issue when he wrote, "History of course does not ignore process, but it does refuse to set it as its first objective" (1952:63; orig. 1935).

The historicist writings thus must be sifted to determine what they were referring to when they said they were discussing processes of change. And I think a distinction must be drawn between their theoretical, largely abstract statements about change process, and how they linked this theory with the data they collected.

Most historicists recognized in the abstract that invention, diffusion, and integration were all mechanisms of change. But invention was only lightly covered relative to other topics, perhaps in part because it evoked the specter of psychic unity. Occasionally it was ushered into discussions of the "clustering" of genius (Kroeber 1944), when the focus was more on the growth of inventions rather than on the process of invention. The point was in fact that when the culture patterns were "ready" for them, inventions tended to occur in clusters, such as the simultaneous discovery (which I here include with invention) of the biological principle of natural selection by both Charles Darwin and Alfred Russel Wallace. These were conclusions more about acceptance and integration than about invention.

Integration received a good deal of treatment in abstract, summarizing kinds of statements, in which readers were conscientiously advised that such factors as local values and patterns of organization operated to modify traits entering the cultural system from internal (invention-discovery) or external (diffusion) origins (Kroeber 1948:286–287; Wissler 1923:185). Boas himself was fairly successful in demonstrating how diffused traits of folklore were integrated (i.e., modified so as to mesh) with the pre-existing elements in various cultures of the northwest coast of North America (1940:422–423; orig. 1898). Yet, in spite of his programmatic statements, the integration of diffused elements did not rank as high in his list of research priorities as ethnographic descriptions of a single time period and as the tracing of element distributions (see Rohner 1969; Boas 1940). His followers seemed even more bent on tracing the diffusion of such elements as arrow-release techniques, items of clothing, the alphabet, and Kroeber's famous trilogy—salt, dogs, and tobacco (Kroeber 1952:263–282; orig. 1941)—than they were on demonstrating with the same painstaking care what happened to these traits and trait-complexes as they were accepted into a new cultural fold. One important exception was Leslie Spier's study of the Sun Dance (Spier 1921; see also Bennett 1944).

Distributional studies reached a climax in the work of Kroeber and his students between 1934 and 1938. Thirteen investigators obtained trait-distribution information on 254 tribes or bands in the American West, and turned out twenty-five monographs for the University of California's Culture Element Distribution Series (Kroeber 1952:263). The objectives were to more precisely classify cultures in the region and also to obtain "inferences as to their historic growth" (Kroeber 1952:263). The emphasis was clearly on diffusion and classification rather than on integration.

My point is not that classification and distribution charts were useless in the reconstruction of history; it is that historicists were not practicing all that they preached in the study of sociocultural change. One of the reasons why was noted by Boas himself:

It is intelligible why in our studies the problem of dissemination should take a prominent position. It is much easier to prove dissemination than to follow up developments due to inner forces, and the data for such a study are obtained with much greater difficulty. They may, however, be observed in every phenomenon of acculturation in which foreign elements are remodeled according to the patterns prevalent in their new environment, and they may be found in the peculiar local developments of widely spread ideas and activities. The reason why the study of inner development has not been taken up energetically, is not due to the fact that from a theoretical point of view it is unimportant, it is rather due to the inherent methodological difficulties. It may perhaps be recognized that in recent years attention has been drawn to this problem, as is manifested by the investigations on the processes of acculturation and of the interdependence of cultural activities which are attracting the attention of many investigators [1940:284–285; orig. 1920].

Fieldworkers seldom had the privilege of observing first-hand the process of invention or discovery, any more than they could be found waiting along with the natives as the next new trait arrived by diffusion. But at least the source of the diffused trait could be inferred by historicist techniques. The identity of the inventor, to say nothing of whatever processes may have been involved, was by and large forgotten by nonliterate peoples by the time the ethnographer arrived with his notebook.

As was so typical of much of his writing on general subjects, in the statement quoted above Boas offered seminal suggestions that were later proved prophetic in furthering the study of change. Yet in his works such statements appear almost as afterthoughts—mental meanderings that cut through what he apparently considered his more important ideas. For example, except for a few precocious efforts (see, e.g., Mead 1932), acculturation was not to become a primary interest for another fifteen years after the statement just quoted. As for the interdependence of cultural activities, if I interpret him correctly, the major emphasis on that aspect of ethnology was to be found at the time not in America but in Great Britain and France.

The historicists' substantive contributions to the understanding of the mechanisms of change were confined largely to the single mechanism of diffusion. However often they talked about "process," about "history," or about "process-history," the basic mechanism they focused on was the same. Kroeber justified this focus by statements such as, "The total part played by diffusion in human culture is almost incredibly great. This is a corollary of what has been said before, . . . to the effect that all cultures are largely hybrid composites of material that once entered them from the outside. Naively, human beings do not realize this to any great extent" (1948:412–413). Even Tylor's statement that "Civilization is a plant much oftener propagated than developed" (1874, I:53; orig. 1871) was cited to justify the intense interest in diffusion.

The historicists well understood the factors that could affect the rate of diffusion, or even interrupt its occurrence, fairly early in the period during which their techniques held sway. Sapir (1949:414 ff.; orig. 1916) cited a series of such factors succinctly: the trait would spread more rapidly if it was not surrounded by secrecy or taboo; if it could be quite easily separated from a larger context ("we expect a ceremonial dance as such to be much more readily transmitted than any notions there may be as to its function"); if it answered the "immediate needs or interests of the borrowers"; and if the groups involved in the transmission were all on "a friendly footing" and ideally spoke related languages. Unquestionably, after historicists had traced endless numbers of traits across the landscape, their awareness of the factors involved became increasingly sharp.

And the concept of diffusion was ramified and subdivided. Wissler (1923:159) distinguished between "organized" and "natural" diffusion, the distinction being the deliberate intent of the donor group to spread its culture traits. Dixon (1928:106) discussed "primary" and "secondary" diffusion, with primary diffusion being the diffusion of traits within a single culture area. Kroeber (1952:344–357; orig. 1940) wrote a famous description of "stimulus" diffusion, in which only the *idea* of a trait or custom reached the recipients, usually from donors quite far removed in space and time. Porcelain was one of his examples: Chinese porcelain found its way into Europe, where it was much desired; but the techniques of its manufacture did not diffuse along with the finished product, so the Europeans were stimulated to develop their own porcelain manufacturing processes.

For the historicists the documentation of the mechanisms of diffusion involved such considerations as what were the traits or customs involved, what was their geographical distribution, how might the distribution be explained, and when might the diffusion have taken place. Their methods of reconstruction led at best to inferential, probabilistic sketches of patterns of past development in nonliterate societies. This was a fact that critics of the entire approach, such as A. R. Radcliffe-Brown of England (1952:50–51), pointed out repeatedly and that Kroeber and others were forever defending as being questionable but crucial to the understanding of change. Kroeber evidently suspected at times that he was being "unscientific" in his methods and analyses, and in part for that reason he returned often to two somewhat contradictory arguments: the historicist method was essentially like that utilized by biologists in their tracing of past organic development—therefore, it was scientific (Kroeber 1952:70; orig. 1936); and yet, elsewhere, he stated that he was doing historical research, which was not like scientific research (Kroeber 1952:63–65; orig. 1935).

When applied as Boas himself thought it should be, the historicist methodology was unquestionably more scientific than much of that of the earlier evolutionists in the sense that much more data were demanded to make much more limited generalizations. But Boas himself stood accused of producing little in the way of scientific hypotheses or theories to be tested, and in this special sense, people such as Marx, Spencer, and Tylor—and even Morgan—were more-productive scientists. Even within his own camp, Boas locked horns with former students who had become restless with his plodding, cautious version of *"vorwärts!"* One famous clash took place between Boas and his student Kroeber in the 1930's. A brief account of the issues in that dispute serves to open another problem area in the determination of processes of change.

LEVELS OF ABSTRACTION

Boas was not patient with students who exceeded the limits of proof that he had so carefully instilled in them (Vidich 1966:xxv). The exchange between Kroeber and Boas in the pages of the *American Anthropologist* in 1935 and 1936 ranged along many issues, but the basic one seemed to be a disagreement about how broadly spatial and temporal diffusion should be traced and how generalized the resulting historical reconstructions should be. Boas reaffirmed his earlier tactical statements about making reconstructions within extremely circumscribed geographical areas and doing this only when the data offered incontrovertible proof for a given sequence. Kroeber, on the other hand, was arguing that reconstructions ought to be attempted even when exhaustive data did not exist to allow for certainty. He had, of course, done his share of the cautious Boasian sorts of distributions (e.g., Kroeber, 1951b:3–67; orig. 1922), but after the exchange with Boas he increasingly broadened his scope into continental and even hemispheric reconstructions (Kroeber 1944; 1952:379–395; orig. 1946).

His attempt is instructive for two reasons: it illustrated the absolute limits to which the historicist technique could be pushed; and it showed remarkable likenesses to what the evolutionists had been trying to do half a century earlier.

Kroeber's (1952:379–395; orig. 1946) objective in the

work was to trace the spread of civilization throughout the eastern hemisphere from its culture center in the Middle East and Egypt. After an introductory passage emphasizing the necessity of placing "items, complexes, or constellations of culture in relation to the totality of known culture," he proceeded to trace the diffusion of highly developed sculpture throughout the area and noted that "the same profile of events with its centrifugal trend recurs in other cultural productivities that are conveniently isolable—painting, for instance, and drama, and science, and probably technology" (Kroeber 1952:379, 380; orig. 1946). Thus for him the placing of traits in context meant in large part using them as markers for the spread of civilization—not determining the ways in which they were imbedded in the cultures growing and dying in space and time. And, in comparing the trends in Japan and Britain, he sounded very much like Morgan and Tylor:

Their developments were mutually relevant because both these advancedly individuated civilizations, even more different in outlook than remote in their spatial placement, *spring ultimately from the same root-stock of all higher civilization*—or, let us say, root-stock of heightening civilization [Kroeber 1952:380–381; orig. 1946; italics added].

He went on, however, to distinguish his own interpretation from one he imputed to the evolutionists:

The resemblances of the sacrifices of pagan tribes in Borneo and Luzon, of Lolos in Yünnan, of backward groups in British India, of West African Negroes, to the hecatombs of Homer and the burnt offerings of Aaron in Leviticus [fifty years ago] . . . seemed due rather to something emerging from men's makeup spontaneously, without reference to time and place and circumstances, and hence outside the concatenations of history. Now, in 1946, few if any would doubt the high probability of all these cases being interderived, at least through the whole breadth of the Eastern Hemisphere . . . [1952:386; orig. 1946].

Men like Brinton might have pushed the psychic unity

principle in similar analyses; but certainly neither Tylor nor
Morgan dogmatically dismissed diffusion as a process accounting for such similarities.

My point is not that Kroeber was necessarily wrong,
although archeological discoveries made in Southeast Asia
after his death (Gorman 1969; Solheim 1970) cast some
doubts over his diffusionist scheme. The point is that when
operating at the same level as that of the evolutionists,
Kroeber was forced into the same general explanations. He
may have been operating with the benefit of fifty years of
accumulated data, but in this study neither his technique
nor his conclusions were noticeably different from some of
his nineteenth-century predecessors. Again, then, I return to
one of my themes in this review: that in some cases crucial
differences between one approach and another, often described as being differences in both theory and methodology,
are in fact differences in levels of analytical approach—and
are not necessarily contradictory.

Boas and most of his followers focused on three analytical
levels: the trait, the individual culture, and the culture area.
But Boas made some penetrating statements about dynamics
at the level of individual personality, and several of his students later became leaders in the field of "culture and personality," although their inquiries in this early period were
often directed at the relationship between patterns of personality and patterns of culture in more or less synchronic
situations; time depth was of secondary importance. But
Boas insisted that the dynamic relationship between an individual and his culture was crucial and ought to be investigated—even though he himself did not regularly conduct
research on the subject. In another one of his prophetic,
programmatic statements, he managed to sketch what was
to become in the 1950's, 1960's, and 1970's a major focus
of research in sociocultural change:

The activities of the individual are determined to a great extent
by his social environment, but in turn his own activities influence the society in which he lives, and may bring about modifi-

cations in its form. Obviously, this problem is one of the most important ones to be taken up in a study of cultural changes. It is also beginning to attract the attention of students who are no longer satisfied with the systematic enumeration of standardized beliefs and customs of a tribe, but who begin to be interested in the question of the way in which the individual reacts to his whole social environment, and to the differences of opinion and of mode of action that occur in primitive society and which are the *causes* of far-reaching changes [Boas 1940:285; orig. 1920; italics added].

This last statement clearly suggested that the inquiry be carried into causation and process beyond the limitations imposed by diffusion of traits and suggested a different and potentially very fruitful level of analysis at which the historicists themselves did not usually operate.

ON "PRIME MOVERS"

It is evident in the historicists' search for processes of change that they assumed no preconceived causal or processual determinants—there were no prime movers as were in the materialism of Spencer, Marx, and Engels. For Boas and his followers, these were first, last, and always empirical issues, which meant for them that if there were any prime movers operating, such as the economic base, this would have to be determined by the data. Marx, Engels, and Spencer might have agreed on the requirement for data, but they would have nonetheless assigned first research priority to material factors. The historicists would not have gone this far. The investigator's attention was not necessarily drawn any more to economic traits than to other traits in the cultural inventory. In the lists of element distributions, economic traits did not preponderate over those of folklore, kinship, ritual, or linguistics. Their statements of intracultural dynamics, when they made them, did not include a primary causal element.

Boas was as hostile toward what he considered geographical or economic determinism as he was toward psychic unity and unilinear evolutionary schemes. Not that he ignored economic or geographical factors—his training in geography would not allow him to do that. But they were viewed as another part of the causal system, another variable in the multivariate approach to sociocultural dynamics. In part because of his influence, American anthropology waited until the 1940's to reexamine the possibilities of materialism as a research strategy.

Boas was justified in his skepticism about finding universal laws of cultural development, but the skepticism was in turn justified by his approach to the study of change. The problem was not so much a lack of data; it was, rather, that his view of intracultural integration, his criteria of proof, and his basic assumptions were in no way designed to lead to the formulation of general laws.

Present Relevance of the Approach

With only a few exceptions (e.g., Driver 1961), interest in tracing the distribution of culture elements was virtually dead among ethnologists by the 1940's. It has remained an important technique in archeology, however, in determining past developments from the distribution of traits such as pottery styles or dwelling designs. Reconstruction of the past is still not *passé* among ethnologists, as we shall see in the following chapters. But the more recent reconstruction approaches are only partially indebted to the energies of the historicist scholars of the 1920's and 1930's. In fact, many of the reconstruction techniques and assumptions used by modern cultural evolutionists are throwbacks to Morgan, Tylor, Spencer, and Marx—not to Wissler and Kroeber.

Anthropologists and other social scientists are still interested in diffusion as a process of sociocultural change, but this interest cannot be traced solely to the efforts of the historicists. The diffusion of traits from one culture to another is something that the more-recent acculturation approach considers to be only one of several major foci. Sociologists (e.g., Katz, Hamilton, and Levin 1963; Rogers 1962, 1969; Lerner 1958) are studying the transmission of new traits *within* a given culture. E. Katz, H. Hamilton, and M. L. Levin (1963:238) pointed out that this is actually a reawakening of an interest that was present in sociological writings about the same time that the concept was most popular among anthropologists. But in this reawakening, a great deal of emphasis is laid upon the importance of understanding the *acceptance* of diffused traits—something that the historical reconstructionists did not often consider in detail. Everett Rogers (1962), for example, divided the acceptance process into a number of stages and wished to know what characteristics are shared by those who are "early acceptors" of new ideas as compared to those whom he termed "laggards."

The historicists made a series of contributions that were considered enlightening but incomplete by representatives of subsequent approaches (such as that of acculturation): or that were continually and vociferously belittled (as by some representatives of modern evolutionary schemes); or, at worst perhaps, that were simply accepted with ultimate indifference (as was Kroeber's massive *Configurations of Culture Growth* [1944]). But please note that my account has ignored the value of their ethnographic contributions, gathered at a time when some informants could still remember the terrible impact of the expanding frontier. It makes no comment about their contributions to the understanding of kinship, to linguistic theory, or to the influence of culture upon personality. I have chosen to focus merely upon the contributions they made to the understanding of processes of change. So wide-ranging were the interests of some of them, particularly Franz Boas, that something is inevitably lost by generalizing even within this narrow avenue of inquiry.

CHAPTER FOUR

ACCULTURATION

I N THE United States the rise of enthusiasm for acculturation studies was sparked not so much by a reaction against the historical reconstruction of the Boas group as by a growing conviction that the distribution studies were simply not telling the whole story of sociocultural change, that they were incomplete. In England, meanwhile, the rising interest in what was termed "culture contact" was generated by a growing awareness of the forced changes of colonialism. Scholars on both sides of the Atlantic had been aware of both stimuli, however; it is not accurate to conclude that the Americans were motivated solely by theoretical sensitivity, or the British by practical considerations alone.

In this country the break between the historical and acculturation approaches was by no means an abrupt one. Acculturation was more a tendency that began increasingly to emerge in the works of students who had served their academic apprenticeships under Franz Boas or A. L. Kroeber. The first three acculturation studies all appeared in 1932 (Beals 1932; Mead 1932; Thurnwald 1932), although, as we know, Boas had suggested this approach in 1920. In England in 1929, Bronislaw Malinowski advocated a shift in emphasis to what he called "the anthropology of the changing native." He was clearly referring to acculturation, although his proposal was still couched in diffusion—and was blatantly imperialistic as well (Malinowski 1929).

After 1932, while Kroeber was still preoccupied with his distribution studies, acculturation studies grew in popularity. By 1936 the movement had become so important that a group of bright young anthropologists drew up a brief but concise memorandum designed to give general coherence to the approach (Redfield, Linton, and Herskovits 1936). And about the same time the American Anthropological Association launched formal discussions about whether the subject was "properly anthropological" (Beals 1953:622–623). These were interesting precedents in the development of American anthropology: an attempt to specify, in organized programmatic fashion, the ways in which a particular approach should be handled; and, at the same time, an attempt to legislate, in effect, what was anthropology and what was not. Kroeber, true to his own concerns, hinted that acculturation studies were merely a flash in the pan, a "whirl of vogue," and was critical of most of them (cf. Kroeber 1948:426–428). At any rate, the Association voted to table a motion to include acculturation studies in the realm of anthropological concern, and it was never reintroduced for a vote (Beals 1953:622–623). It really never had to be reintroduced: anthropologists' involvement in problems of American Indian administration, the contacts between cultures forced by World War II, and the postwar issues of decolonization added urgency to the growing prewar concerns, and acculturation was in solidly as a properly anthropological preoccupation.

Objectives and Methodology

The precedent for systematizing the approach to acculturation begun in 1936 was followed in 1954, when another memorandum on acculturation studies appeared (SSRC Seminar 1954). Although both memoranda proposed definitions for the concept, that of the 1954 group was broader yet simpler: "acculturation may be defined as culture change that is initiated by the conjunction of two or more autonomous cultural systems" (SSRC Seminar 1954:974).

The 1936 memorandum distinguished the concept from diffusion by noting that acculturation was more inclusive. In 1954, acculturation was clearly viewed as a *consequence* of diffusion, with the emphasis heavily on modifications resulting from diffusion rather than on the diffusion itself. Thus the focus in acculturation studies, as indicated by the two memoranda, was much more directly upon what in the last chapter was called the "integration" of traits and customs. The dynamics of change were to be sought in the *modifications within cultures resulting from contact with alien lifeways.*[1]

There were several parameters of the definition: first, acculturation referred to a *kind* of culture change—change taking place when two autonomous cultural systems meet. For the 1954 group, "autonomous" meant complete, structurally independent systems—that is, neither could be a part of some other, larger system, or dependent upon a larger system for its existence. Acculturation could take place between the Kickapoo and Potawatomi Indians in and around Horton, Kansas; but the result of what happens when Methodists and Catholics interact in Horton would not be acculturation—unless the Methodists happen to be Potawatomi, and the Catholics, Kickapoo. When pushed, this criterion of system autonomy becomes fuzzy. The 1954 memorandum attempted to make it as distinct as possible by stating that "An autonomous cultural system is what is usually called 'a culture' in the anthropological literature" (SSRC Seminar 1954:974), but writers before and since have tended to

---

[1] I will push this particular distinction between acculturation and diffusion because it is easier to conceptualize than other, slightly different ones (e.g., Herskovits 1966:170; orig. 1955; he viewed diffusion as "achieved cultural transmission" and acculturation as "cultural transmission in process").

interpret the criterion to suit their own specific objectives or methods (see pp. 19–20).

Second, "acculturation" refers to a *process* of change that has been distinguished from the processes of diffusion, innovation, invention, and discovery. Diffusion occurs in all cases of acculturation; obviously, traits or ideas have to be transmitted before they can have any sort of impact on the recipient cultures. But diffusion is one aspect, or one step, in the acculturation process. Innovation, or the origination of new ideas, is a process distinct from acculturation, except insofar as the innovation can be clearly traced to the conjunction of two or more cultural systems.

Finally, the concept may be used as an adjective, referring to a *condition:* "Group A is more acculturated than group B."

The objectives of acculturation studies included the now familiar one of understanding the processes of sociocultural change. Historical reconstruction was still an aim but was not as important as it had been for both the historicists and the earlier evolutionists. And, as I implied earlier, practical or "applied" objectives were emphasized in many studies of acculturation perhaps to a greater degree than in any previous approaches to change. The clash of Euro-American cultures with those of different traditions through global war or colonialism was producing problems that forced many anthropologists from their ivory towers in the hope that their studies of acculturation could somehow alleviate the problems in humanitarian ways. This last objective is not shared by all anthropologists today, however; and the practical efficacy of anthropological efforts is still a matter of considerable debate.

METHODOLOGICAL PERSPECTIVES

Both the 1936 and 1954 memoranda were primarily devoted to outlining the ways in which acculturation should be studied. I will present in abridged form the technique suggested by the 1954 memorandum, together with some methodological issues that emerged as the suggested program was put into actual practice.

The memorandum distinguished four distinct but inter-related facets which must be studied in any acculturation situation: the *cultural systems*; the nature of the *contact situation*; the *conjunctive relations* between cultures; and the *cultural processes* activated by the conjunction of the systems.

All *cultural systems* involved in the contact have certain properties that allow each system to persist as an independent unit. These properties are *boundary-maintaining mechanisms*, the *flexibility of the internal structure*, and *self-correcting mechanisms*. How each of these factors operates in any single system is variable; but how they operate in the systems in contact will have an effect on what happens during the course of the acculturation.

Boundary-maintaining mechanisms help limit participation in a given culture to a well-defined "in-group." The boundaries of a cultural system may be relatively "open," permitting active ingress and participation to aliens. The United States, insofar as an "American" culture exists, was for a time idealistically characterized as an "open" system. "Closed" systems, on the other hand, are those in which participation by "outsiders" is carefully and continuously limited. In some American Indian pueblos in the Southwest, the boundaries are closed physically as well as culturally: there is literally a wall around the village. Boundaries can be maintained by a number of devices, including deliberate isolation, perhaps behind real barriers. But there are more subtle and positive ways of maintaining cultural boundaries. Any ideology or activity that strengthens the group's conviction that its members are somehow better than members of other cultures—anything, in short, that tends to strengthen a group's *ethnocentrism*—can serve as a boundary-maintaining mechanism. Humor can serve this function nicely: a number of Potawatomi Indian raconteurs specialize in telling an endless series of "Indian-white man" stories around campfires at night. The theme is almost always the same. Superior-acting white men encounter an Indian, and, to ridicule him, ask him a series of inane questions. The Indian responds in Tonto-like language but finally puts the pesky white men in their places with a shrewd yet low-keyed punch-line. (Example: an Indian being ridiculed by white men for "stupidly" leaving his hips exposed above his leggings during a cold Kansas winter casually observed that his white brothers left their faces exposed without discomfort from the cold; therefore, he concluded, a white man's face must be about like an Indian's derrière.) Such stories are a source of great amusement among the Potawatomi but have the more subtle function of maintaining some boundaries between Potawatomi life-ways and those of white intruders.

Flexibility of internal structure refers to the culturally prescribed ranges of flexibility in such systemic aspects as the status structure, the arrangements of groups vis-à-vis each other, or in the variability in the ways of acquiring political power. It also refers to the "goodness of fit" among the various institutions in a system—how closely they are functionally tied to one another. Generally, autocratic systems under the exclusive control of elites tend to have inflexible internal structures. The memorandum of 1954 mentioned the social systems of the Pueblo Indians and Zulus as examples of rigid structures (SSRC Seminar 1954:976); then there are relatively inflexible patterns of interpersonal relationships, as among the Hutterites or Amish in this country. Flexible systems, on the other hand, characteristically lack these features.

Self-correcting mechanisms affect the ways in which the forces of conflict (e.g., factionalism and crime) are balanced by forces of cohesion or togetherness. In any system these two forces will be operative. But there is some considerable variation in the success with which they are balanced (see discussion of equilibrium, pp. 12–14). The effectiveness of the self-correcting mechanisms within any system, the memorandum suggested (SSRC Seminar 1954:978), may be indicated by such things as the frequency of rule-breaking by members of the system; the frequency of unsettled disputes; or the frequency of emigration from the system, assuming it is possible to do so (if emigration is not possible, the result could be a marked increase in the level of intrasystemic conflict).

So much for the three factors mentioned with regard to the facet of "cultural systems." The memorandum warned that these are not the only variables in the systems that could influence acculturation patterns but are merely what seem most often to be involved.

The question is *how* might they be involved? As an answer the memorandum suggested two alternative hypotheses, based on the important assumption that no one of the factors alone is usually crucial; their import comes from the combination of all three. First, it was suggested that what are called "soft shelled, invertebrate cultures" (with due apologies for the biological analogy)—that is, the systems that have permeable boundaries, flexible internal structures, and self-correcting mechanisms that are not very effective—are more likely to be susceptible to acculturative change than "hard-shelled, vertebrate" systems, with rigid boundaries, inflexible internal structures, and effective corrective mechanisms. But the memorandum allowed that the direct opposite of this hypothesis may also be applicable:

under certain conditions of extreme acculturation pressure the "hard-shelled vertebrates" may suddenly crack up completely; and . . . under other conditions it seems possible for the "soft-shelled, invertebrate" cultures to "ingest" great quantities of alien cultural material and still preserve many of their basic patterns and values [SSRC Seminar 1954:978–979].

In fact, examples of these latter conditions can be found in the acculturation literature.

There is one additional methodological task in determining the influence of the systemic factors in the culture change situation: it must be demonstrated that they operated in much the same way *prior* to acculturation. It is possible that a system becomes "hard-shelled and vertebrate" as a *result* of acculturation, thus nullifying the alternative hypotheses just stated. Obviously, the conditions cannot have the postulated influence if they emerge well after contact has taken place. Here, then, is one way in which historical reconstruction has been carried into acculturation methodology.

The second major facet of acculturation, the *contact situation*, deals with another set of potentially influential variables: the ecology and demography of the context in which acculturation occurs. In contrast to some of the other approaches reviewed in this volume, the memorandum conceived of ecological and demographic variables as being largely *limiting* rather than necessarily *deterministic* in sociocultural change. The distinction becomes difficult to maintain, however, if we reflect on the examples of ecological influence offered in the memorandum itself. For example, the fact that a culture had become dependent for survival on a single feature of the environment—say, bison—and that in acculturation this single feature was largely eradicated certainly set new *limits* for the "possible relationships between man and nature" (1954:979). The message is clear but perhaps understated in the memorandum, because a case for *determinism* could easily be made as well.

As for demography, one of the important considerations is the relative size of the populations in contact and the extent to which they are representative of all demographic categories in their respective cultures. A crucial fact in modern acculturation is that representatives of one of the cultures involved are predominantly mature males (SSRC Seminar 1954:980). A history of colonialism has shown repeatedly that acculturational conflict escalates when foreign soldiers, merchants, or administrators import their wives and children into the colonial areas. Other important demographic variables not explicitly mentioned by the memorandum could include the distribution of individuals and families in space (an obvious ecological consideration as well) and the relative morbidity figures of the cultures in contact.

The contact situation and the cultural systems, when properly analyzed, are important variables in accounting for what happens in a given situation of acculturation, but they do not get at the actual relations between cultures. They are stage settings or background features for the next major facet described by the 1954 memorandum.

Conjunctive relations refer to what goes on between cultures when they come into contact. The contact is not between "cultures" in fact, but between individuals and groups who establish communication links with each other. These links have two aspects, the first of which is *structural*—what the memorandum terms the "intercultural role network" (SSRC Seminar 1954:980 ff.). "Intercultural roles" refer to the types of links established between cultures (e.g., "religious," "mercantile," "military," and "administrative") and implies that each linkage is a paired, reciprocal relationship: for example, "missionary-convert," "buyer-seller," "conqueror-conquered," and "high commissioner–colonized subject." It is possible that the network could be diagrammed as a series of lines connecting the cultures in contact, each line being a "type" of intercultural role, with one of the pair of relationships at each terminal end.

But the diagram could only offer hints about the second aspect of the linkages, that is, *what is being communicated* between the elements of a paired relationship. Intercultural communication along the network may be restricted or specific, limited only to some members of the two systems—such as that between Jesuit priests and the Chinese emperor's children in the seventeenth century. Or the communication may be diffuse, affecting large numbers of people in various ways, as in colonial situations such as that existing between the United States government and the American Indians. The communication, of course, may consist of other, more subtle messages about attitudes such as ethnocentrism, racism, and other indications of domination-subordination. Often these subtle and perhaps even unintentional transmissions are more important in an acculturation situation than are the more obvious sorts of communication.

The memorandum emphasized that because it is actually people, rather than cultures, coming into contact with each other and because no one person or group can ever reveal *all* the patterns of their culture to members of another, *no complete cultural inventory or system is ever presented in an acculturation situation*; in the words of the memorandum, "no culture ever presents its full face to another" (SSRC Seminar 1954:983). What is transmitted about a given way of life is restricted, but there is another corollary of intercultural communication: what is transmitted is almost always reinterpreted by the recipients, either through their own prevailing values system or through some idiosyncratic variables arising in a specific context of communication.

In an informative and entertaining essay, R. H. Wax and R. K. Thomas (1961) described how this "filtering" of transmissions occurs in contact between American Indians and white people. Most American Indian groups place a high value on being silently reflective in interaction with others, each Indian being sure that when he speaks, he does so wisely. Whites, being unaware of prevailing Indian values, are apt to interpret this behavior as passivity and to make incisive remarks about "those dull, dumb Indians." They are viewing the Indians' interaction through their own value filters. Indians, on the other hand, are busily doing the same thing; that is, they are applying *their* values to patterns of white interaction. Whites, they observe, like to show friendliness, to put the other party at ease by making endless inquiries about family and weather, always smiling, shaking hands, touching, anxious to avoid prolonged pauses in the dialogue. It is precisely these patterns that put the Indian on his guard, because according to his value system such behavior is exhibited only by those who are trying to hide something. Earlier I portrayed ethnocentrism as a mechanism for maintaining cultural boundaries; here it becomes a source of static in intercultural transmissions.

In spite of the best efforts of the donor group, it is ultimately the perceptions and interpretations of the recipients rather than those of the donors that determine the areas of agreement or disagreement between cultures and the degree of acceptance of proffered ideas or traits. True, some acceptance of unpopular ideas is gained through coercion by the donors; but in almost every case the acceptance is token, superficial—and usually lasts only as long as the coercive pressure is applied.

The 1954 memorandum finally discussed acculturation *processes* as the fourth facet of acculturation. What follows is a hybridized version of processes drawing from the statements in the memorandum and also from a more recent summary (Spicer 1961).

Three more or less distinct steps are included in the acculturation process. The first, obviously, must be the transmission of ideas or traits: *diffusion*. The second is *evaluation* by the recipients, in which the diffused elements pass through the various sorts of perceptual and interpretative filters. The members of the receiving culture at this point exercise their selectivity in acceptance or rejection of new items, although the selectivity can be severely limited when the donor wields coercive power. If accepted on the basis of the evaluation, the new traits or ideas are *integrated* into the recipients' cultural system. It is this last step that has received much of the attention in the acculturation process, and I will say more about it in a moment. First, I should emphasize one obvious point: that these steps are *analytically abstracted* from the continuous flow of the process. They are usually not consciously applied, in checklist fashion, by the recipients of alien cultural material.

Now we turn to integration. Both the memorandum and

the Spicer volume offered a series of alternative patterns the integration might assume. It is useful to sketch them briefly here.

1. *Incorporation.* In incorporation, the donor's traits or ideas are integrated with the least possible disturbance to the recipient's pre-existing cultural system: the system remains largely unchanged. New traits which are radically different will be modified so as to fit more easily into the recipients' system. The net result is thus an increase in the *content* of items or ideas in that system rather than a change in its basic values or structure. There are logical limits, however, on how much new material—however heavily modified—can be incorporated without necessitating basic systemic changes. There are some cultures, such as that of the Navajos, that have been successfully incorporating alien traits for generations (Spicer 1961:529; Barnett 1953:56); but how much longer they can continue to do so is a real question.

2. *Replacement.* In some ways, the replacement process is the direct opposite of incorporation (Spicer 1961:531). Incorporation implies moderate to heavy modification of incoming elements; replacement involves little, if any, modification. In incorporation, new elements are added to the pre-existing content; in replacement, the new elements are *substituted* for pre-existing ones. Thus the net content of the receiving culture is not increased in replacement. The result is that the cultural system becomes a patchwork of elements that in some cases do not "fit" or mesh well with each other. Again there are limits to how much replacement can occur before the pre-existing system loses all coherence. There is some evidence that piecemeal replacement over several generations may in fact be more stressful to the recipient culture than a single, sweeping discarding of the old for the new. The Manus case briefly mentioned in the introduction to this book is a case in point (Mead 1956). Replacement as a process is also more likely to be found in

situations of directed contact, where the donor group is able to institute by force the changes it considers "best" for the recipients.

3. *Syncretism* or *Fusion.* Syncretism or fusion involves a combination or mixing of traits from two different cultural systems into a pattern that is different from either of them. Classic examples of this process include the "folk" Catholicism of Latin American peasants, a syncretism of pre-Hispanic and Spanish-Catholic ritual; and the peyote religion of modern North American Indian groups, whose participants commonly invoke "Our Father, the Sun" as well as Jesus Christ and the Virgin Mary (Bee 1965; 1966).

4. *Compartmentalization* or *Isolation.* Compartmentalization or isolation is really a pattern of nonintegration, in which traits of the donor culture, usually imposed by force upon the recipients, are deliberately held apart from the recipients' own pre-existing system. The acceptance is grudging and in name only. So long as coercive forces are present, the recipients act as if the new traits are part of their cultural inventory. When coercion is removed, the recipients in effect pack up the new traits until the negative stimulus returns. Examples of compartmentalization are numerous in colonial situations. One is that of the dual leadership system of the Pueblos in the eighteenth and nineteenth centuries (Spicer 1962:391 ff.). The Spanish conquerors introduced a system of hierarchical leadership ranks based on their own system of leadership. The Pueblos were forced to accept the new order, but they placed articulate and powerless "front-men" in the various ranks, meanwhile keeping their traditional system of theocratic oligarchy. When the Spanish were present, the front-men appeared to be the actual leaders of a Pueblo community. At other times, the front-men system was folded back into its compartment until it was needed once again.

A variant of the compartmentalization process is what the 1954 memorandum termed "reactive adaptation" (SSRC Seminar 1954:987). In this case the emphasis by the recipients is not so much upon keeping the alien traits at arm's length as in trying to bolster the sagging coherence of their pre-existing system. It may be manifest in surges of nationalistic feeling or, in its more extreme forms, in what have been called "nativistic" movements (Wallace 1956; Linton 1943). When acculturative pressure is felt to be uncomfortably heavy by the recipients, they may seize upon some aspect of their traditional culture for intensive focus—some ritual, perhaps, involving the participation of "true believers" that may or may not contain hopes for a miraculous reversal of the dismal acculturative trend. The Ghost Dance among the Plains Indians in the last decade of the nineteenth century was a nativistic movement in its extreme form (Mooney 1892–1893). Participation in this and less-bizarre movements seems to be its own reward insofar as it releases (temporarily) some of the pressure of directed contact.

This brief outline does not exhaust the possibilities of acculturation processes described either by the 1954 memorandum or by Edward Spicer (1961). These other alternatives have not been mentioned here either because a much different level of analysis is involved (as in *biculturalism*) or because they seem to refer more to *results* of acculturation than to integrative processes (as in *stabilized pluralism* or *cultural disintegration*).

It is important to note that none of these processes of integration is mutually exclusive; within a cultural system some traits may be incorporated, others replaced, and still others fused with incoming ones to form something new. Pueblo Indians who isolate the Spanish leadership structure may readily accept and incorporate the techniques of fruticulture. Yet, insofar as the data permit, it may be possible to determine that one of these processes dominates the others in a given cultural system for a given period of time. Thus, Navajo culture has been characterized as mainly an incorporative one, even though there are instances in which Navajo acculturation has included replacement, isolation, and fusion as well.

And there is one more fundamental point to be made: like diffusion, acculturation is never a one-way street. That is, any given cultural system is at once a donor *and* a receiver in the conjunctive relations. For analytical purposes, it is convenient to speak about "donor" and "recipient," even though to do so conveys the mistaken impression that a given system is *always* one or the other. Devices of convenience for analysis or explanation should not be allowed to mask the actual dynamics of the acculturation situation.

I have presented this lengthy abridgement of existing programmatic statements on acculturation in part because acculturation studies still comprise a large portion of the most recent work on sociocultural change. The several statements are also concise summaries of much of the existing knowledge about dynamics at the level of two or more interacting cultural systems. Thus, as the works cited, I have attempted to describe what acculturation studies ought to consist of as well as to convey some less specific knowledge. However, nothing very explicit has yet been said about the methodological techniques of the acculturation approach.

Methodological Issues

HISTORICAL RECONSTRUCTION: IS IT NECESSARY?

For most students of acculturation, as for the historicists, historical reconstruction is considered both necessary and risky. The risk becomes greater as one goes farther back in time and/or lacks good documentary or archeological evidence to support his statements. But it is considered necessary if one is to understand what changed and how that change took place. Ideally then, in acculturation studies historical reconstruction should be used to gain understanding of what the cultures in an acculturation relationship were like at some "base-line" or "zero-point" before contact between them took place (Herskovits 1941). But in some cases this is an impossible task, so the analyst must be satisfied to create his "base-line" only as far back in time as good evidence permits, and to carry his account forward from there. Even this somewhat limited methodological tactic is felt by some to be unacceptable or inapplicable. Robert Redfield, in his study of culture change in Yucatan, wrote:

Beginning with this culture as a point of departure, we find it unnecessary to commit ourselves to assertions as to the precise ways in which Spanish and Indian elements combined to make it up; our concern is with what has recently taken place in this culture and is currently taking place in it under influences exerted by increasing mobility and communication [1934:61–62].

He did, however, use aged informants to gain some insights into the past (1934:63). Bronislaw Malinowski voiced misgivings about reconstruction in more emphatic terms: while it may have been legitimate for what he termed "antiquarian anthropology" (1938:xxvi), it had no place in studies of culture contact.

if we were to survey the various aspects of culture . . . we would find everywhere that part at least of the "zero conditions" of the historical past, as it existed [in Africa] before the advent of the Europeans, is dead and buried, and as such is irrelevant. . . . Only forces of tradition actively influencing the sentiments of living men and women matter for them and those who have to deal with their destiny [1938:xxxi].

Malinowski's own version of acculturation methodology included "three orders of reality: the impact of the higher culture; the substance of native life on which it is directed; and the phenomenon of autonomous change resulting from the reaction between the two cultures" (1938:xxiv). Yet it was not clear from his statements how the "impact of the higher culture" could be adequately assessed without taking some pains to reconstruct precontact conditions.

In spite of Malinowski's preachings on the subject, British anthropologists, as those in America, continue to view historical reconstruction as an important portion of their methodology (e.g., Leach 1965; orig. 1954; Bailey 1960). Malinowski may have covertly been ignoring his own advice: one of his younger colleagues once observed, "Malinowski's theoretical denial of the value of historical reconstruction is . . . contradicted by his constant use of it, wherever he makes a good analysis" (Gluckman 1949:5).

So the question is no longer "Is reconstruction necessary?" but, rather "How far back in time should it extend?" This is ultimately up to the analyst. Again, few of those involved in acculturation studies seem as willing to push as far back as the historicists, but this is at least partly due to the fact that the acculturation analysts are trying to solve problems different than those posed by Boas and his followers.

THE "CULTURES-AS-WHOLES" ISSUE AGAIN

"The unit of analysis in acculturation studies is . . . taken to be any given culture as it is carried by its particular society" (SSRC Seminar 1954:975). But

Certainly it has hardly been demonstrated that the whole round of cultural behavior of any community or group of communities constitutes a coherent system. . . . [R]ecently there [has] been . . . a tendency to assume less comprehensive systems within the whole of a people's cultural behavior (Keesing 1958:410–412). It does not seem to us that if investigation moves more in this direction it would require abandonment of either our terminology or our concepts. They would apply in, for example, subsistence systems or security systems, as well as in whole cultural systems; they might in fact be more usable in that way than in connection with "cultures as wholes" [Spicer 1961:537].

The two statements reveal the methodological dilemma nicely. We saw earlier that in spite of the historicists' best intentions, there was really no way they could study cultures as wholes without breaking them down into traits or trait-complexes. Even when, in summarizing their analyses, they claimed to be presenting cultures as wholes, the result often was Lowie's "shreds and patches" sort of holism. The same thing could be said about acculturation methodology, as Ralph Beals (1953:634) pointed out a year before the SSRC memorandum: "In point of fact . . . no one has yet demonstrated a method by which cultures may be studied in their entirety." His comments were aimed at British "functionalists," but the Americans of the post-Boas period are fitting targets as well. While processes such as "incorporation" can be used to label an entire cultural system, this usage can come only after the integration patterns in a series of its subsystems or trait-complexes have been proven to be incorporative. This is implicit in the 1954 memorandum's statements about intercultural roles and is explicit in the contributions to Spicer's 1961 anthology. The candor of the Spicer statement on holistic approaches was thus very welcome even if a bit late.

The present impossibility of studying cultures as wholes does not mean that trait complexes or subsystems must be taken out of a wider cultural context in order to analyze what is happening to them. There is some methodological middle ground, which stops well short of tracing every single connection between every single trait-complex or subsystem in a culture yet which discerns the more important kinds of functional relationships between a particular complex or system and others within the culture as a whole. I believe the work of acculturation analysts has ranged more consistently within this middle ground than has the work of the historicists or Morgan or Tylor—none of whom seemed to be able to bring off a holistic methodology to match the doctrine that cultures should be treated as wholes.[2]

[2]One noble effort at a holistic analysis was Ruth Benedict's famous *Patterns of Culture* (1956; orig. 1934), more an attempt at holistic typology than dynamic, holistic analysis, although she did suggest that certain types of cultural configurations or *gestalten* influenced the sorts of new items that their bearers would most readily accept in contact with other cultures.

LEVELS OF ANALYSIS

The cultures-as-wholes problem is of course related to the larger one of the analytical levels at which acculturation can be studied. The analytical level for most acculturation studies is still often said to be whole cultures, but this must be understood in a way analogous to the anatomist who insists that his level of analysis is the human body. In both cases, what this entails is a dissection of included subunits.

Many acculturation analysts have followed Boas' advice in tracing the relationship between sociocultural change and various personality "types" (e.g., Hallowell 1948; G. Spindler 1955; Spindler and Goldschmidt 1952; L. Spindler 1962). In some cases it is difficult to say whether these are, properly speaking, acculturation studies or whether they belong more in the realm of psychological anthropology. The 1954 SSRC memorandum attempted to draw the line:

As far as acculturation is concerned, the psychological problem is to determine the depth of commitment to certain shared patterns and values and consequently to assess the difficulties of accepting changes. For what is important in this connection is not the structure or the orientation of personality itself but the extent to which certain basic values are internalized or rejected and the extent to which they function as selective mechanisms in acculturation [SSRC Seminar 1954:993].

In this sense, then, analyses at the level of individual personality comprise a fifth facet of acculturation studies, a set of extremely important variables that can affect the processes of acculturation at the higher, cultural system, level. The methodology is fairly complex and for the sake of continuity and consistency will be discussed in a later chapter of this book. To launch a discussion at this time would detract from the major focus of acculturation as here outlined, which is upon cultural systems rather than upon personality. I also think it is fair to say that when analysts have entered into an investigation of personality in acculturation, personality, not acculturation, has tended to dominate as the subject of inquiry.

At the opposite extreme, some analysts have gone beyond the level of a few cultural systems involved in a single contact situation and have attempted analyses of acculturation in entire ethnographic, national, or continental areas (e.g., Spicer 1961; Linton 1940). For the most part, however, statements at this very general level are summaries of findings at the cultural systems level in several different areas included in the survey, with some general statements about recurrent features in each of the specific cases. Spicer's 1961 anthology is a good example of how acculturation studies may be carried to a more general level of analysis, and it profits from the fact that all contributors used the same basic approach to their data.

THE BIAS PROBLEM

If acculturation is never a one-way process, then ideally an acculturation study should focus on *all* cultures involved in the contact situation. But what if one of the cultures is the analyst's or perhaps is another culture generally included within the "Western European Tradition?" Has his objective immersion in his own or any other related culture been sufficient to allow him to speak with certainty about it as well as about the non-Western cultures involved? Unfortunately, this problem has not been confronted squarely in many studies (Ray 1939:334). More often, the Western culture is almost taken for granted or, at best, given much less thorough treatment than other cultures in the contact situation (e.g., Linton 1940; Mead 1956).

There are several important reasons for this tendency. One is the conditions under which acculturation analyses have been made. Often their practical objectives are aimed at facilitating "modernization" or "development" of non-Western cultures. Modernization of Western cultures is not at issue, except insofar as development agencies or policy could be made more efficient or humane; therefore the Western culture does not receive as much attention. There is the related question of how effective the anthropologist can be to administrators of colonial or neocolonial regimes if he scrutinizes the administrators or their techniques too closely. He runs the risk of becoming a bother—or even a threat.

Another reason, particularly in acculturation studies without such overtly practical application, is the sheer amount of additional effort involved in attempting to treat American or European culture with the same degree of intensity as is devoted to others in the contact situation. It could be accomplished, of course. But the additional time and expense of this undertaking may not be balanced by radically new insights into acculturation processes in a given setting. So the trend continues to run in the direction of sketching the aspects of Western culture that immediately impinge on the acculturation setting—or seem most relevant to it— as a kind of expedient.

One notable exception is George Foster's *Culture and Conquest* (1960), in which the focus is upon the *conquistadores*—their cultural background, their native habitat, as well as their colonial objectives in the New World. The study has made a major contribution to modern understanding of Spanish-Indian acculturation by fleshing out the image of Spanish life, earlier portrayed in relatively superficial and even distorted terms.

DOCUMENTATION OF PROCESSES

Earlier I briefly discussed the problem of dissecting cultural systems for the analysis of processes. What the acculturation analysts have been cutting out for examination are not traits such as moccasin styles or arrow-release techniques or girl's puberty ceremonies but larger, more inclusive segments now called "systems" within a cultural system, or patterns: economic systems, kinship systems, residence patterns, religious systems, value systems, leadership patterns. And processes of change are no longer hunted down in studies of trait distribution in space or time by acculturation analysts but in studies of how some or all of these patterns or systems have been altered by contact with alien cultures. In the acculturation approach, *change mechanisms are the reactions of systems or patterns to external stimuli.* To be sure, diffusion is also a process or mechanism, but it is not change itself; it is the means by which new stimuli are introduced into pre-existing systems or patterns.

Tracing diffusion by acculturationists has become less speculative than it was in the 1920's, because the focus is on relatively recent or even on-going cultural transmissions that (theoretically at least) can be more readily documented. Both the diffusion and the integration processes are detected through the use of tactics outlined in the introduction to this book—that is to say through careful historical reconstruction, through the restudy technique, or (if financially possible) through the continuous monitoring of long-term exchanges of stimuli and their effects on receiving cultures. But, as noted in the last chapter, the historicist tradition for extensive ethnographic data-gathering has persisted as a basic task. Tape recorders and even videotape machines have supplemented the laborious note-taking, but the analyst's on-the-spot observation and occasional participation in the life-ways of acculturating groups have no substitutes.

In the detection of processes, the observation is of actors' behavior, of course, but a multitude of individual cases of behavior in a given context, say, "religion," are pulled together and the common elements are abstracted as "the religious system." The system includes the making and use of ritual objects such as altar materials, rattles, special costumes; beliefs such as in the omnipotence of God; and rituals such as *fiestas* to honor a particular saint. Alien elements can enter into any or all of these aspects of the religious system. It is the analyst's task to decide what those elements are and how they have affected the behavior and belief systems of the individual actors. To the extent that the effects have been common among a significant number of individuals, the analyst is justified in assuming that the "system" has been modified in a specified way. The methodological point here is simple: the analyst is observing *individuals* behaving or talking about their beliefs; but his end result will be phrased in terms of *systems* or *patterns*, not in terms of individual behavior. In the *description* of processes, it is the systems or patterns that are the focal points, not individual behavior.

And, in keeping with the historicist tradition, the majority of acculturation studies have adhered to neither a materialist nor an idealist line. They commonly take a multivariate approach, one which, as that of the historicists, assigns a priority to no single "prime mover" in theory, although in specific instances one system, such as the economic system or the system of values, may in fact be revealed as pivotal. There have been some attempts to seek general, cross-cultural principles about the relative speeds at which the various systems or patterns undergo change in acculturation. For example, it was once believed that technological systems, or systems of economic production, were among the first to change in contact, whereas values systems remained relatively impervious to early change (an example is Ogburn's famous "culture lag" theory [1957]). The 1954 memorandum (SSRC Seminar 1954:990) warned, however, that this condition "may be due in part to the emphasis placed upon technology in the Western world as well as to its evident superiority over most local forms." And others have detected an opposite trend in some of the newly developing nations: the values system has come to favor an enrichment of the technological system, but so far the technological system has received neither the knowledge nor the materials to enrich it. Values have thus changed before technology (Service 1960:118–119).

The 1954 memorandum further suggested (SSRC Seminar 1954:991) that components within a given system (such
as religion) may be differentially resistant to change, because

All culture segments [technology, social organization, religion,
etc.] have their concrete aspects, and these more explicit behaviors and apparatus are as a rule more readily mastered than
symbolic and valuational aspects. In religion, for example,
objects and rituals may be assimilated as readily as new tools.

And this view is essentially that stated by Sapir in 1916.

In this same, generalizing vein, some scholars have tried
to find regularities in the sequence of integration processes
as contact continues (Elkin 1951; Spicer 1961). In contact
between dominating Western and dominated American
Indian cultures, for example, there appears to be a sequence
of integration processes beginning with simple incorporation
of novel items, proceeding to incorporation of a more complex nature, and eventually leading to replacement as the
directed contact situation continues through time (Spicer
1961:539 ff.). But, although such regularities have been
detected in the Indian-white situation, Spicer believed that
"it is meaningless to posit such invariant sequences without
explicit statements of the conditions of contact as well as
the nature of the cultures in contact" (1961:541).

While there is no real reluctance to formulate general
principles or hint at cross-cultural regularities, there is the
familiar Boas-like caution about waiting until more data
are available. It only follows that the quest for "laws" of
acculturation process has never been a stated goal of this
approach.

One point needs to be repeated: an interest in culture
contact as a stimulus for sociocultural change is what dis-
tinguishes both the acculturation and the earlier historicist
approaches from their predecessors and contemporaries.
Both approaches tend to ignore innovation as a process, as
well as to ignore changes produced by a given culture's con-

tinuing adaptation to its natural environment. Internally generated changes—that is, those originating from within the cultural system—although recognized as important by the 1954 memorandum (as "cultural creativity"), are not usually dominant issues in acculturation studies. These internally generated processes are preoccupations in other approaches to dynamics, as we shall see.

Present Relevance of the Approach

There are numerous variations in the basic format of the acculturation approach as just described: some scholars have tended to emphasize one facet more than the others or to seek basic units other than systems or patterns for their analysis. Yet the variations have been relatively minor, and the approach suggested in the 1954 memorandum is still being applied today.

It is still being applied in most cases to practical issues of modernization or development involving the major powers of the East and West in contact with the so-called Third World countries. But although the format is much the same, the issues have become infinitely more complex. Some of them are methodological—for example, the difficulty of determining processes of integration when recipient cultures are being bombarded with a deluge of new ideas through the spread of literacy, use of such items as transistorized radios, and increased mobility between urban and rural areas. But also the issues of politics and scientific ethics are becoming ever more weighty for anthropologists and others interested in sociocultural dynamics as, in the name of "development," the bombardment becomes tragically literal. By comparison, a concern with what happens to a peyote ritual after the introduction of Christian elements (Bee 1966) seems ludicrously irrelevant. Anthropologists have become extremely sensitive to accusations that they are handservants of imperialism, offering advice on how "best" to foment developmental change while at the same time covertly pushing their own ideological-political predispositions and fattening their pocketbooks. For some, this has led to increasingly critical appraisal of the policies of major world powers with regard to "modernization" efforts among Third World cultures; others have refused to engage in acculturation studies whose results have clear potential for aiding domination of one group of people by another (although once the results of any acculturation study have been published, the investigator no longer has control over how they might be used by others). But again, the point: in spite of the increasing complexity of issues and methodological emphasis on analysis of cultural subunits, the acculturation approach remains viable in the study of dynamics of change through culture contact.

CHAPTER FIVE

OF EVOLUTIONISM, FUNCTIONALISM, AND HISTORICISM

ACCULTURATION studies did not contradict the historicism of the early twentieth century. They simply ignored some of the excesses (such as an occasional overenthusiastic use of the age area hypothesis) and elaborated considerably the whole problem of change initiated by culture contact. In fact, some of the leaders in the acculturation trend were Boas' own students, who had earlier participated in the historicist tradition.

We know from preceding chapters, however, that American historicism was not well received by British "functionalists" such as A. R. Radcliffe-Brown or Bronislaw Malinowski (who was in his own way also grappling with problems of change). And, beginning in the 1940's, the Boasian brand of historicism came under extended and bitter attack from another antagonist, Leslie White. His barbs were designed less to discredit the historical method than to reseat evolution as the dominant concept in sociocultural change, but his readers cannot fail to be impressed by the vigor with which he pursued both aims.

In this chapter I want to outline both the functionalist and Whitian evolutionist approaches to change by casting each in a role that is essentially antihistoricist (but not anti-*historical*). This is not to say that either approach was hammered out as a deliberate opposition to historicism, nor is it to suggest that whatever complementarity exists between them stems from their common antihistoricist position. Leading proponents of both evolutionist and functionalist schemes would vehemently deny these assertions. However, I intend to follow a theme suggested by others (e.g., Goldschmidt 1959a; Service 1962; Bock 1970; orig. 1963) and show that the two approaches can be complementary.

White's Evolutionism

Leslie White's major heroes were Lewis Henry Morgan and E. B. Tylor, although his writing incorporated a good deal from Herbert Spencer, Karl Marx, and Émile Durkheim as well. His own evolutionary theory, he insisted, was essentially that proposed by these men in the nineteenth century but benefitted from the additional anthropological data that accumulated since. Boas and his followers had been premature and scientifically suspect in their rejection of evolutionism, he wrote—premature because they never really gave evolutionary approaches a chance to accomplish their intended results and scientifically suspect because they distorted what Morgan and Tylor had said about such issues as universal stages and the importance of diffusion as a dynamic process (White 1945a:339).

He repeatedly attacked the cautious empiricism of the Boas group in passages like this:

In addition to being antimaterialist, they are anti-intellectualistic or antiphilosophic—regarding theorizing with contempt—and antievolutionist. In fact, they are opposed to so many things that someone has characterized their philosophy as "eclectic negativism." It has been their mission to demonstrate that there are no laws of significance in cultural phenomena, that civilization is—in the words of R. H. Lowie, the foremost exponent of this philosophy—merely a "planless hodge-podge," a "chaotic jumble" [White 1949a:368; footnotes deleted].

It has been pointed out that Lowie later recanted this characterization (Goldschmidt 1959a:40), but that does not make it any less effective as a demonstration of precisely what White was objecting to. Basically, what White said the historicists were against he himself was *for:* he pushed for materialism, for evolutionism, and for theorizing at the grandest levels of abstraction. His major quarrels with the historicists involved a now familiar set of interrelated issues: levels of abstraction, the role of history, and the nomothetic possibilities (i.e., the possibilities of determining *laws* of sociocultural dynamics). I will return to these issues later.

WHITE'S APPROACH

By *culture* we mean an extrasomatic, temporal continuum of things and events dependent upon symboling. Specifically and concretely, culture consists of tools, implements, utensils, clothing, ornaments, customs, institutions, beliefs, rituals, games, works of art, language, etc. . . .
We call the ability freely and arbitrarily to originate and bestow meaning upon a thing or event, and, correspondingly, the ability to grasp and appreciate such meaning, *the ability to symbol* [White 1959:3].

Much of the definition is like that one of Tylor's cited by anthropologists for decades. But the emphasis should be placed on "extrasomatic, temporal continuum"—for it is the key concept in White's scheme.[1] This is apparent in the following series of logical steps that White took in the explanation of his approach:
1. Culture depends on man for its existence, but *can* be analyzed as a *system in and of itself.* Man need not be considered a variable in the system, so long as it is clearly understood that *the level of analysis is the totality of culture throughout time*—not specific *cultures* at specific *times.*

[1]Culture considered as an "extrasomatic, temporal continuum" was not a conceptualization originated by White. Kroeber had much the same perspective years earlier in his article "The Superorganic" (1952:22–51; orig. 1917), as did still others before him.

2. All life can be understood as a process of capturing and utilizing free energy: trees convert solar energy into protoplasm; man converts food energy into new cells. Culture is fundamentally a *means* utilized by man for capturing and utilizing energy—that is its primary function. Thus (when considered as a system in and of itself) its dynamics are analogous to those operating at the organic level: the culture system captures and utilizes energy. And, as in organic evolution, as the energy captured and used by the system increases, the system itself becomes more complex and highly organized (White 1959:39; cf. Carneiro 1967:xxxv).

3. The cultural system can be divided into three subsystems. The most basic one is *technology*—tools, weapons, and the knowledge of their use—for here lie the means for capturing and utilizing energy as well as for meeting two other important requirements for cultural (and biological) survival: protection from the elements and defense against enemies. The two other subsystems are the *social structural* and the *ideological* or *philosophical* (White 1959:18 ff.; cf. Marx in Feuer 1959:43, orig. 1859). All three are in a mutually influencing interrelationship, but technology dominates by operating through social structure upon ideology: that is, both the social structure and the prevailing ideology are shaped mostly by the technology, even though they occasionally operate to stifle or limit the extent of technological development (White 1959:27–28). Thus White inserted a familiar (and probably necessary) hedge:

This theory states merely that of the various classes of forces within a cultural system, technology is the basis and the motive power of the system. It does not assert that it is omnipotent, independent of conditions and subject to no limitations [1959:28; cf. Engels in Feuer 1959:397; orig. 1890].

4. The technological subsystem controls the amount of energy captured and utilized by the cultural system; as the technology becomes more efficient, more energy is captured and utilized, which leads to development in the culture as

a whole. He stated this formally as the "law of cultural development":

"culture advances as the amount of energy harnessed per capita per year increases, or as the efficiency or economy of the means of controlling energy is increased, or both" (White 1959:56).

The law can be expressed as a formula: $E \times T \to C$, with E signifying energy, T technology, and C cultural development. Energy is more important than technology, however; technology can conceivably become extremely efficient without leading to development *if* the amount of captured energy is not thereby increased. Technology is "the vehicle, the means, the scaffolding, the skeleton; energy is the dynamic, living force that animates cultural systems and develops them to higher levels and forms" (White 1959:57).

The operation of this law is patent in the history of mankind: hunting-and-gathering subsistence produced a somewhat low level of usable energy (in the form of game and plants) in proportion to the amount expended by the hunters. Neither fire nor wind were significant as sources of energy in this earliest and longest stage of cultural evolution (White 1959:43–44). Energy capture was limited to what man's own muscle could provide as a means, and White estimated that in such hunting-and-gathering societies the amount of energy captured was limited to about 1/20 horsepower per capita per year (1959:45).

As soon as agriculture and, less important, animal husbandry were discovered, a whole new quantum jump in cultural evolution took place. Now man could *control* his sources of energy which meant greater yields in usable energy with less energy expenditure by man himself. This was the *agricultural revolution*, and following as a direct result of it came labor specialization, larger populations, ever more sophisticated technology (up to a certain point)—in short, *civilization* like that of ancient Mesopotamia, Egypt, Greece, and Rome.

Energy exploitation by culture then hit a plateau, forced

by monopolistic controls by elites, until the next major technological breakthrough, the *fuel revolution*. This corresponded to the growth of industrial production, which used coal as a major source of energy much greater than the potential of farming and herding. The amount of energy per capita per year underwent another quantum jump upward. But this time the development was more rapid and more spectacular than what occurred as a result of agriculture. White, as Kroeber before him (Kroeber 1952:339; orig. 1939), noted that as culture evolves the *rate* of development is *accelerated*. He continued:

The Agricultural Revolution required but a few thousand years to run its course. But the Fuel Revolution is only a century and a half or two centuries old at most, and already greater changes have been effected by it perhaps than by all earlier ages put together [White 1949b:385].

Goaded by war and the search for larger shares of the economic market, men developed their industrial technology to the point at which they could not profitably continue the full production in their factories. Thus there was another plateau, but a brief one, until the next and most recent breakthrough in the harnessing of energy, the *atomic revolution*. Man is still just past the threshold of applying atomic energy as a sophisticated tool of survival—or extinction—and White wished to offer no airtight predictions about where culture may go from here.

Like Morgan and Marx, White emphasized the basic importance of the shift from the primitive emphasis on kinship and on sharing of scarce resources to the emphasis on property accumulation and nonkinship connections of the state—Morgan's distinction between *societas* and *civitas*, respectively. And White's stages of evolution, rephrased in his more materialistic terms, are essentially those of savagery, barbarism, and civilization, although the atomic revolution was a wrinkle that Morgan or Tylor could not have added. White recognized that his approach represented nothing essentially new. All these notions—the focus on the highest levels of abstraction (i.e., "culture"); the search for "laws of development"; the materialism, with the pivotal role of energy; the tripartite segmentation of the cultural system into technology, social structure, and ideology—and others were to be found in the work of Morgan, Tylor, Marx, and Spencer. And White's vehemence in pushing his materialistic-deterministic scheme in his writing is also familiar. Marx's nemesis was modern capitalism; Tylor's was perhaps degeneration; Boas' was evolutionism; and, apparently, White's was the antievolutionism of Boas. For White, as for the others, the chosen path to wider acceptance of a conviction was through aggressive attack against its opponents as well as through repeated statement of the conviction whenever and wherever possible—even to the point of dogmatism. Of course, nothing draws critics like the scent of dogma, and White had his full share of detractors.

Issues in White's Scheme

THE INDIVIDUAL AS A FACTOR IN CULTURAL EVOLUTION

For White, man represents a biological constant in cultural evolution. Cultural evolution does not vary with racial variation; caucasoids do not have a monopoly on civilization—therefore, cultural dynamics are not to be discovered by delving into human anatomy and physiology. This, for White, would be fallacious reductionism. But man is more than flesh and blood; he thinks, feels, symbols, and so forth. He has a personality. Surely, White's critics declared, these attributes make a contribution to the dynamics of culture. White's response was a categorical statement of alternatives: either personality is *biological* or it is *culturally* determined. If the former, then it is irrelevant as a variable factor in culture change and can be disregarded along with other biological constants. If the latter, then all that is being said is "that culture causes or determines culture, but through the medium of human biological organisms, which is precisely what we are maintaining . . ." (White 1959:14).

With this orientation, his thinking about the role of "great men" in history was consistent with Kroeber's: that great men, geniuses, profound inventions, and so forth occur *when culture is ready for them.* "When certain cultural elements and conditions are present and in proper conjunction, an invention will take place; when they are not, the invention will not occur" (White 1959:16). Two of his articles were directly aimed at this issue: "Ikhnaton" (in White 1949b; orig. 1948) and "Man's Control over Civilization: An Anthropocentric Illusion" (in White 1949b; orig. 1948). Ikhnaton emerged as a man (or boy) dancing to the tune of Egyptian culture as a whole. Man, we are told in the second article, has no control over the course of culture, but he should keep trying to understand its workings.

THE NATURAL ENVIRONMENT AS AN EVOLUTIONARY FACTOR

The environment, White noted, is an important factor in the development of any given culture. But its influence must be carefully traced, because the relationship between a culture and its natural setting changes as the culture develops. Thus, he argued, a "mere inventory of environmental features" may shed no real light on environmental impact, because it does not take into consideration the fact that some of the features may be more relevant than others at different points in time. To use a contemporary example, the presence of coal on the Navajo reservation was not a relevant cultural consideration in the late nineteenth century. Now it is crucial in tribal politics and economics. The general accuracy of White's statement cannot be refuted. But he went on to insist that environment, like man the organism, is *irrelevant* to an understanding of "culture as a distinct class of phenomena," that is, as a total system through time (1959:51).

EVOLUTION VERSUS HISTORY AND FUNCTIONALISM

In most of his writings, White felt obliged to distinguish his evolutionary approach from those of the historicists and the functionalists (whose work will be described shortly). Much of the early heat of the resulting criticism of his distinctions has by now cooled, particularly because writers like Kenneth Bock (1970; orig. 1963) and Marshall Sahlins (1960) resolved the apparent contradictions. But the issue is important to an understanding of the kinds of data White used to support his general evolutionary theory.

He contrasted his "evolutionary process" with what he characterized as "historical process." Historical studies are particularizing; evolutionist studies are generalizing.

History is concerned with particular events, unique in time and place. Evolution is concerned with classes of things and events, regardless of particular time and place. To be sure, the evolutionist process always takes place somewhere and in a temporal continuum, but the particular time and the particular place are not significant. It is the temporal sequence of forms that counts. The battle of Waterloo or the assassination of Lincoln are defined and delimited by temporal and spatial coordinates. This is not the case with such developmental sequences as picture, rebus, and alphabetic writing, or stone, copper, bronze, and iron. Here it is the sequence of forms, the one growing out of another, irrespective of particular time and place, that is significant [White 1959:30; footnote deleted].

Perhaps the most cogent of White's critics on the role of history was A. L. Kroeber, who, as one of the Boas group, had his own ideas about what history should be. He detected in White's position an arbitrary categorization:

White . . . does "history" the signal but dubious honor of appropriating all that is most vital and significant in it and assigning it to evolutionism. . . . If he claimed the whole of the historical domain for "evolutionism," I should not particularly quarrel: the change would be nominal, like that of a color on a map. But it will not do to gut history and leave its empty shell standing around; there might be the embarrassment of no one's claiming it.

. . . I have maintained that much of what White calls "evolutionism" is history. . . . [Kroeber 1952:96–97; orig. 1946].

Kroeber's point is obvious: he and White were interested in some of the same sorts of dynamic relationships, although Kroeber lacked White's consistently materialist perspective. And surely Leslie Spier, working in the historicist tradition, was "doing evolution" in White's sense when he traced the development of the Sun Dance in a temporal sequence (Spier 1921). White himself was forced to "do history" when discussing the role of Ikhnaton in ancient Egypt, or when he attempted to account for the fact that Crow Indians deviated from the expected pattern of patrilineal descent: "But as it happens, we know something about the history of the Crow" (White 1959:152).

White also distinguished what he termed the "non-temporal, formal-functionalist" approach from that of evolution, singling out Radcliffe-Brown, Malinowski, Raymond Firth, Meyer Fortes, and C. Daryll Forde as exponents of functionalism (White 1959:31). Yet, as with "history," he used functional analysis in his own "evolutionary" studies—as indeed has practically every proponent of the several approaches to change that we have considered so far. His conception of the tripartite division of any cultural system into technological, social structural, and ideological components explicitly includes the assumption that the three are functionally interrelated (with the technological component being the most preponderant, of course).

Much of his major book, *The Evolution of Culture* (1959), consists of showing how elements of technology, social structure, and ideology were integrated in hunting and agricultural societies. His functionalism included both the sense of evolutionary development as well as the synchronic or atemporal emphasis found in much of Radcliffe-Brown's work.[2] In the several chapters on the function and evolution of social structure, he noted that the structure is linked to the prevailing technology and that it therefore functions generally to promote the most advantageous response to the biological needs of survival: subsistence and defense against enemies. The function of social structure, then, is to make life more secure for its component organisms. This is demonstrated in two ways: *synchronically*, by showing how a particular structure functions to promote the security of a group at a given point in time; and *diachronically*, by showing how a structure changes in response to technological developments and the resulting increase in a group's population (White 1959:144 ff.).[3]

My point is this: although White took considerable pains to distinguish the "evolutionary" approach from that of "history" on the one hand and "functionalism" on the other, he consistently resorted to *both* history *and* function in his analyses. His distinctions were aimed at particular *types* of history and functional analysis as he portrayed them, it is true—but his insistence on the distinctiveness of the evolutionary process tended to muddle the methodological issues, much as the insistent comments against evolution by Boas and his students obscured some real similarities in basic approach.

LEVELS OF ABSTRACTION

A source of confusion has been what sorts of evolutionary development White was talking about. First, there is the development of all culture through all time. His major book,

---

[2]But Radcliffe-Brown was not opposed to conducting studies of change through time, although he emphasized the evolution of *social structures*, not *cultural* evolution, as being worthy of study (1952:203; see also Mair 1957:240–241).

[3]A more recent study (Boserup 1965) reversed the causal relations from those given by White and argued that it is population increase that gives rise to technological development.

again, was about the evolution of *culture:* the development
of civilization to the fall of Rome. His theory of cultural
evolution applies, then, to culture—not to *cultures.* Well and
good. Environmental influence and the human organism
can be dismissed as constants at the level of general culture.
Specific *cultures* need not pass through all the stages of
cultural evolution; to require this as proof of the validity of
evolutionary theory, White felt, would be a confusion of
"the culture history of peoples with evolutionary sequences
of culture" (1959:18); "the cultural formulas have nothing
to do with peoples" (1945a:343).

But then:

The concept, or theory, of evolution is applicable to any
cultural system, whether it be our model of the culture of mankind as a whole, or the culture of any people, group of people,
or area *in so far as it can properly be regarded as a system*
[i.e., "only when and in so far as cultures can be considered
significantly apart from their relations and contacts with other
cultures"], or to those portions of the total cultural system that
can be treated as subsystems, such as technology, social organization, or philosophy, or to even finer subdivisions such as
writing, currency, the plow, Gothic architecture, geometry, or
the theory of reincarnation [White 1959:30, 18].

The cultural formula White proposed *does* have a great
deal to do with peoples, then—but only if the influence of
diffusion is disregarded. Tylor, upon whose scheme White
based his own, found no urgent need to exclude diffusion
from evolutionary consideration.

Unquestionably, White himself saw that it is possible to
use an evolutionary approach at several different levels of
abstraction. If he had consistently remained within a single
level, or made his shifts between levels more distinct, much
of the confusion would have disappeared. As it was, to those
who charged that technology might not be the prime mover
in all groups or that stagelike progression of culture does not
apply to cultures, his answers sounded evasive. He did not

meet all the objections squarely; he operated at several different levels of abstraction, then answered critics only from the most general level—one at which biological and environmental variables or other specific deviations are not relevant. Fortunately, his protagonists have cleared the issue by their useful distinction between *general* and *specific* evolution (Sahlins 1960:12–44).

DOCUMENTATION OF CHANGE PROCESSES

White's discussion of process was almost identical to that used by Herbert Spencer. Culture, White claimed, can be treated as if it is an organic system, which means that it operates in many ways analogously to biological evolution. Like Spencer, too, White usually led up to his points by a discussion of analogous biological principles—such as the tendency to proceed from simpler to more-complex forms; or the tendency to develop increasing specialization of component parts, coupled with the development of means to organize and integrate specialized units into working systems of survival.

But these general processes of segmentation, specialization, and integration can only be derived from an examination of *cultures* or subsystems of cultures; that is, to be able to discuss evolutionary processes in *culture*, it is necessary to detect them at the level of *cultures*. It is at this more specific level that White was able to offer some answers as to why and how $E \times T \rightarrow C$. It is here that he, as his evolutionist predecessors, made abundant use of functional and historical analysis. At the most general level, $E \times T \rightarrow C$ is a descriptive statement of what happens; it is not an explanation of how it happens. It is only when environment is *not* considered as a "given," or when culture contact is *not* ruled out of the "culture system" that explanations and mechanisms emerge. At the most general level, for example, it is not explained why technology tends to become more sophisticated; that is just the way it happens in culture. But such a statement smacks of psychic unity mysticism unless answers are provided from lower levels of abstraction. White implicitly recognized this when, for example, he noted that occasionally a shift from hunting-and-gathering to a horticultural technology need *not* lead to cultural development. The explanation is not found in $E \times T \rightarrow C$. It is traced to culture contact and to the fact that the group in question, the Kuikuru, felt no pressure to increase their energy output, because they were not being threatened by outside groups and because there was no economic incentive provided by trade with outsiders (White 1959:292, Carneiro 1957). And it is no coincidence that the steps into the agricultural stage of cultural development were taken first in the areas in which the local environment included a suitable climate for a fairly easy transition from intensive gathering of wild barley or rice to rudimentary domestication.

Some have tried to apply White's approach to single cultural systems (Meggers 1960; 1961) with results that have been challenged by others (Opler 1961). But this is the stuff of science, with a hypothesis offered at a single level of analysis being challenged and defended *at that level* by available evidence.

As Elman Service (1968:26; 1971:14) has stated, then, if the objective is to seek the evolutionary processes of sociocultural dynamics, the most general level is not exclusively the one at which to operate.

The Functionalist Approach

Again, all the scholars and approaches discussed so far were to a degree "functionalist," but some, such as Malinowski and Radcliffe-Brown and their students in America and Great Britain, were more functionalist than others. Much of their work was contemporary with that of the American historicists; and, as the anthropology of Franz Boas and his followers, it was in part a reaction against the perceived excesses of nineteenth-century evolutionism. Yet they owed a great intellectual debt to two of Leslie White's heroes: Herbert Spencer and Émile Durkheim.

There were significant differences between the approaches of Radcliffe-Brown and Malinowski, as in fact there were between them both and other functionalists. Here I want to ignore some of these differences in favor of a general distinction between "static" and "dynamic" functional approaches.

Functionalists have tended to focus more on social rather than cultural aspects of human life; that is, they have tended to emphasize the interconnections between various statuses and groups, as well as to emphasize the structure, the arrangements, these interconnections assume, more than the morality, the values, the meanings, or the artifacts that are cultural components of any human life-way. They assume that group life is a *social system,* in which the components are interrelated in such a way that a change in one of them may well lead to a change in some or all of the others. The scholarly objective is to analyze the ways in which the parts fit into the whole system—that is, to understand how the social system works. To see how a system works, the analyst must in effect hold it still long enough to get a good look at it. And in so doing, one of two alternative observations on the nature of the system can be made.

THE "STATIC" FUNCTIONALISM

The first observation is that the components of a system all play a part in its harmonious operation; otherwise, they would not be there. This perspective is basic to the "equilibrium" concept mentioned already in the first chapter; that is, that the system is regarded *as if* it is in a state of equilibrium in which the component parts are mutually adjusted into a working whole. To my knowledge no functionalist has ever insisted that this assumed equilibrium is *perfect*; still, critics in the past have called on some functionalists to make the denial more emphatically in their work.

This of course is not a perspective that leaves much room for a consideration of change. Time is not involved, except insofar as is necessary to allow the system to run through its periodic cycle—E. E. Evans-Pritchard's "structural time" (see Chapter One). This was the functional conceptualization of Radcliffe-Brown, and it is this sort of functionalism that was singled out by Leslie White as a basis for distinguishing his evolutionary approach from that of the "functionalists." As Wilbert Moore (1963) observed, such a perspective can only consider change as either trivial or tragic; trivial in the sense that the changes are so miniscule as to leave the system as a whole unaffected; or tragic insofar as a change in one of the system's components must inevitably lead to disharmony in the entire system. The perspective is nonetheless necessary in the preliminary steps of dynamic analysis—how otherwise could the analyst be able to determine what is changing and what is not?

THE "DYNAMIC" FUNCTIONALISM

Godfrey and Monica Wilson, students of Malinowski, conducted their functional analysis by using a second perspective on the operation of the social system, and this perspective has been used in the more recent works of anthropologists such as Evon Vogt (1960) and Clifford Geertz (1957) and of sociologists such as Wilbert Moore (1963). According to this alternative view, a social system *may* be in *relative* equilibrium, but there are always present certain sources of intrasystemic tensions or strains ("oppositions," as the Wilsons termed them [1945:125]). The attention of the analyst is thus directed not only to the ways in which the components fit harmoniously together but as well to the points at which they do *not* fit together—the sources of dysfunction. These dysfunctional elements, if radical enough, can lead to change in the social system. Thus it is assumed that the social system is not a harmonious meshing of elements *but a system for tension management.*[4] The Wilsons distinguished between what they termed "ordinary" and "radical" opposition within a system (1945:125). Ordinary opposition can be handled in any system by existing means of social control: criminals can be brought to justice, heretics burned, and so on, without producing any systemic change. Radical opposition is that which cannot be resolved except by changing the social system. The opposition may be sparked by two stimuli, one environmental, the other cultural.

disequilibrium . . . may arise either from social change resulting from pressure of the environment [e.g., floods, droughts, and earthquakes], or from change for . . . cultural reasons [e.g., new ideals, new uses for material resources, new knowledge, and new techniques]. Frequently an environmental change compels a social change in one institution, but all the other institutions of the society do not immediately change to match, and disequilibrium results. Or a new invention may be made and other institutions not be modified to match the change in technique. Thus disequilibrium may appear in a society previously in relative equilibrium [Wilson and Wilson 1945:133].

In applying their comments to Central Africa at the time, the Wilsons noted that the social system involving Africans and Europeans was becoming ever more racked with radical opposition or dysfunction: as the region underwent rapid industrialization, the other components of the social system could not keep pace. Life in rural villages was being upset by the emigration of labor into the cities. Racial tensions were exacerbated by the dependence of Africans on European wages and manufactured goods (Wilson and Wilson 1945:155) and by European demands for Africans' land. Again, none of these dysfunctional elements could be elimi-

---

[4]Although I portray this perspective as an alternative to that of "harmonious functioning," the two views are not necessarily mutually exclusive.

nated unless the social system as a whole was changed. It is interesting that the Wilsons regarded the Central African situation as a *single* system in which the parts did not mesh well rather than as a situation involving *contact* between two *separate systems,* African and European. This was more consistent with Radcliffe-Brown's pronouncements (1952:202) than with Malinowski's earlier methodology for the study of culture change in Africa (e.g., 1945:73 ff.);[5] but it was not consistent with the acculturation approach then being developed in the United States.

And, relevant to the complementarity of functionalism and evolutionism, the Wilsons sketched out a sequence for sociocultural development that, although they did not call it "evolution," could be viewed from an evolutionary perspective. They began by drawing the distinction between "primitive" and "civilized" societies, and then showed how movement from primitive to civilized could be characterized as an "increase in scale." Scale increases as the society's population increases and dependency relations become broader and more complex. The family or larger kinship group becomes ever less a self-sufficient subsistence unit, for example, and depends ever more on "outside" specialists and service institutions. Following an argument much like White's, Durkheim's, and Spencer's, the Wilsons noted that civilized social systems include a greater degree of specialization, which means *material* development:

It is only through specialization . . . that control of the material environment can be achieved, for it is physically impossible that one individual should master all knowledge, or be skilled in all the techniques of our society, or that we should produce what we do without division of labour. . . .

[5]Radcliffe-Brown (1952:202) charged Malinowski with "avoiding the reality" of social change by attempting to segregate European from African influences in colonial Africa, and concluded: "what is happening . . . in South Africa . . . [is] the interaction of individuals and groups within an established social structure which is itself in process of change."

Control of the material environment, in its turn, makes largeness of scale possible [Wilson and Wilson 1945:101].

Yet, in its most general statement, their scheme lacked the determinism of White's; the interrelationship between ideological and technological factors was not primarily unidirectional. In fact, the Wilsons' work was even somewhat atypical of the British focus on largely social factors at the time, in that they wrote a good deal about meanings and values—the stuff of culture (Mair 1957:232).

As I mentioned earlier, more recent functional approaches to change have also focused on dynamic processes originating in points of tension or dysfunction in the social system. A good example is that of Wilbert Moore (1963) that uses in part some ideas proposed earlier by sociologists Petrim Sorokin (1957; orig. 1937–1940) and Talcott Parsons (e.g., 1970; orig. 1960), among others.

According to Moore (1963:15), "fluctuations, variations, and uncertainties are characteristic of societies everywhere" and are an important source of flexibility in social systems: for example, "individual differences, complicated by differences in socialization, will prevent an exact and persistent duplication of role performances"; or different rates of fertility and mortality between generations could have effects on the existing social structure. These variations are usually trivial, on the order of the Wilsons' "ordinary opposition," perhaps, or Vogt's "recurrent processes " (see Chapter One). However, they are important insofar as they provide a *source of variability* in the social system from one generation to the next or even from one yearly cycle of "usual" activities to the next. Many of them can be brought back into line by imposing social controls or other sorts of checks. But, occasionally, "minor" variations occur at such a rapid rate that existing controls are only partially effective. Moore pondered the effects of "minor" variations in the socialization or enculturation of the young in a hypothetical case: in each individual family the variation is minor; but what if *most* of the families in a given group alter in a minor but distinctive way their socialization patterns in a single generation? The cumulative result could be a breakdown of socialization, as well as a major reassessment of existing values and standards of conduct (Moore 1963:17). Thus a minor change for the individuals could be a major change for the group. More commonly, however, the variations in one or a series of related conditions have a persistent direction from one cycle to the next, so as to appear trivial over a short term; but in a long-range, cumulative perspective, they can reveal a signficant change (cf. Maruyama 1965).

In addition to these usually routine sources of flexibility and potential change, Moore described a source of more-significant systemic changes that he labeled "the lack of close correspondence between the 'ideal' and the 'actual'" (1963:18). It lies in two different aspects of human existence. First, there is the discrepancy between man's actual ability to control his natural environment and the ideal of total control. Moore was not pushing environmental determinism but, rather, was noting that

Man has neither solved the problem of mortality nor a host of subsidiary but refractory problems of living in peaceful command of the universe. And anything less than total control of human biology and the non-human environment leaves ample opportunities for strain and innovation [Moore 1963:19].

The other general change-producing discrepancy exists between ideal and actual behavior:

Widespread recognition that human performance falls short of perfection may lead to the acceptance of more "realistic" standards, but this development is itself a significant change. Generally, however, ideals are somewhat more likely to be exalted than downgraded, and endure as a perennial challenge to imperfections (Moore 1963:20).

Both these general sources of change (i.e., the flexibilities and the inevitable discrepancy between ideal and real) have *evolutionary* as well as functional implications, Moore pointed out. The "trivial" meanderings provide a source of variations, as already mentioned, upon which change can build. The ideal-real discrepancy gives a *general direction* to the succession of changes through time—direction toward the perfect control of man's environment through enhanced technology or toward the development of institutions such as representative governments that close the gap between ideal and real behavior.

I have used these brief sketches of Moore's and the Wilsons' schemes as examples of how predominantly "functionalist" approaches, using the "tension-management" perspective, can deal with the phenomenon of change and in fact can dovetail nicely into "evolutionist" studies. But I have yet to discuss the critical issue of time depth.

FUNCTIONALISM AND THE ROLE OF HISTORY

Both Malinowski and Radcliffe-Brown were, along with White, persistent critics of the history practiced by American historicists. Malinowski was especially uncompromising in his attacks, as mentioned in the last chapter; and in his programmatic statements, he relegated history to a minor role in functional studies of change—even though he did not follow his own program in his substantive work. Radcliffe-Brown never went so far as to belittle the importance of history itself, even though he is best remembered for his synchronic, atemporal functional analyses. He was very concerned about the kind of historical reconstructions being made by the American historicists, however, much as he was with those of the nineteenth-century evolutionists: "My objection to conjectural history is not that it is historical, but that it is conjectural" (Radcliffe-Brown 1952:50). Proper history, in his view, gives documented evidence for the progression and interrelation of events through time; conjectural history lacks properly documented evidence: "To establish any probability for such conjectures we should need to have a knowledge of laws of social development which we certainly do not possess and to which I do not think we shall ever attain" (Radcliffe-Brown 1952:50; cf. Boas 1940:257; orig. 1932).

Part of the rationale behind these critiques involved, of course, an eagerness to disassociate their authors from the perceived shortcomings of other approaches. But more important is the fact that how "conjectural" a historical reconstruction may be is partly a matter of research objectives. If one wishes to go back to the origins of culture, obviously, conjecture must be involved; just as it must be when dealing with the past of nonliterates prior to their contact with Europeans. Functionalism—the diachronic functionalism discussed in this chapter—is less apt to use really conjectural reconstructions, because typically the approach is concerned with a fairly narrow time span. *But history is involved in all functional approaches dealing with change.* When the Wilsons described ideal-typical "primitive cultures," they used history. And when the sociologist Wilbert Moore discussed the dynamic effects of population increase, he used history. To ferret out the sources of tension within a system does nothing for the clarification of process unless the working of that system, the effects of tension, are observed as the system endures through time. It is as true with functionalism as with Leslie White's evolution: there can be no empirical documentation of change processes without considering events of the past.

EVOLUTION AND FUNCTIONALISM: A GENERAL SUMMARY

Two decades ago, both Leslie White and the leading proponents of functionalism in anthropology were essentially negative in their reaction to the historicism of Boas and his followers, while at the same time they emphasized the distinctions between their own respective approaches. In this chapter I have taken a different tack and have argued that laying emphasis on the distinctions between the approaches masks some important areas of complementarity (cf. Steward 1955:179; orig. 1949).

This is not to deny that real differences exist between them. Radcliffe-Brown's kind of atemporal functionalism was not evolutionist; nor, as mentioned, were most functionalists willing to go along with White's technological determinism. But with the injection of time depth and a discernment of developmental direction at a fairly general level of abstraction, such as that suggested by the Wilsons, functional approaches can become both evolutionary and deterministic (as Karl Marx once demonstrated). Another apparent difference is that White was primarily concerned with culture, whereas most functionalists have been more preoccupied with social structure. However, much of White's substantive description of evolutionary process involved social structural principles, just as the Wilsons' concept of social system dynamics involved cultural considerations.

The differences between these two approaches and that of the historicists were framed in part as objections to the latter's use of history. Yet both White and functionalists concerned with change used history liberally in their own substantive works. White, if anything, was even more "conjectural" than most of the historicists. If we leave aside the horrible mass of conflicting definitions, the quarrel over history actually seems to involve the issue of how best to use it rather than whether or not to use it at all.

In their discussion of dynamic processes, both White and the functionalists revealed a major departure from the work of the historicists in the very cursory treatment given to diffusion. In fact, White and the functionalists tended to focus on internal factors—factors within sociocultural systems —in describing dynamics rather than on external factors like culture contact. This is no more than a tendency, however, because neither White nor anthropological functionalists totally ignored the dynamics of intercultural transmission. I emphasize this because Bock (1970; orig. 1963) and Moore (1970; orig. 1960) in important articles discussed the functionalist preoccupation with immanent or intrasystemic causation. I feel their comments may be more apropos for American sociology than for anthropology, because anthropological functionalists like Malinowski and Firth and the Wilsons have been vitally concerned with intersystem dynamics.

White helped reawaken an interest in evolution as an approach to the study of sociocultural change, although he was aided considerably by the work of his near contemporary, the late V. Gordon Childe, in the 1930's and 1940's. He also reintroduced technological determinism as an integral part of the over-all evolutionary approach. Shorn of its dogmatic trappings and removed from its all-encompassing level of abstraction, White's perspective provided a stimulus for a broadening of anthropological interest in evolutionary studies. Functionalists, even the synchronic ones like Radcliffe-Brown, on the other hand, provided increasingly sophisticated insights into how elements of a social system are interrelated. And, as they have pointed out themselves (Parsons, 1970:97; orig. 1960; Gluckman 1968:227), such analysis is a necessary prelude to any attempt to understand how social systems change.

This chapter, then, has been in one sense an introduction to the next one. By sketching the complementarity among three apparently non-complementary approaches, I have tried to set the stage for the discussion of recent approaches that take this complementarity for granted.

CHAPTER SIX

VARIATIONS ON AN EVOLUTIONARY ECOLOGICAL THEME

W HILE Leslie White was at work on his updating of nineteenth-century evolution, Julian Steward had already published several articles dealing with another evolutionary approach to change—like White's, playing up materialistic factors but being much narrower in scope and much more involved with local environmental factors (Steward 1955; orig. 1936, 1937, 1938). To an extent, Steward's scheme was a reaction against the historicist explanations of dynamics that (he felt) slighted internal systemic and local environmental factors (cf. Steward 1955:208–209; orig. 1949). He had been one of Kroeber's students at the University of California and had contributed data to the Culture Element Distribution Study. But, in his own work, he chose to focus on "cultural ecology" and "multilinear evolution." He received early theoretical stimulation from K. A. Wittfogel and from V. Gordon Childe. Steward and White recognized each other's works to be important contributions but seemed always to be drawing distinctions between them rather than emphasizing their commonality (Steward 1955; 1960; White 1957).

Between the early 1940's and the late 1950's, Steward, White, and the writings of Childe and Wittfogel were virtually the sole representatives of evolutionary approaches, in part because of the tremendous impact of historicist and functionalist thinking on anthropological theory. By about

1960, however, it was apparent that evolution was no longer a social anthropological anathema. Steward (1955) and White (1959) had by then both published extended statements of their approaches, and their work had in part stimulated others: Sahlins (1958), Goldschmidt (1959a), Dole and Carneiro (1960), and Sahlins and Service (1960). In fact, the approach had become so popular that Sahlins and Service (1960:3) were moved to observe, "One may justly worry, even fear, that what may be called the 'band wagon effect' is about to take place with respect to evolutionism."

There is not space here to trace all the variations proposed in these and more recent treatments. I want to outline the significant areas of agreement and disagreement among them with special regard to the problem of process and continue to run the risk of overgeneralization for the sake of distinguishing a common coherent pattern to the approaches.

General and Specific Evolution

In 1960, Marshall Sahlins made explicit the simple but fundamental distinction between specific and general evolution that clarified Leslie White's approach considerably. Simply put, the evolution of *culture* is "general" evolution, a development of successive forms (hunting-and-gathering bands, agriculturalist, industrial revolution, Atomic Age) through long periods of time. "Specific" evolution, on the other hand, is the development of local *cultures* or groups of cultures through relatively short periods of time. The keynote of specific evolution is cultural diversity, brought about by a wide variety of localized factors: environment, diffusion, invention, and the like. In the general evolutionary perspective, all the diversity becomes merged into larger patterns that unfold in progressive fashion—"progress," as *objectively* measured, is the keynote of general evolution. Specific cultures arise, diffuse, proliferate, perhaps retrograde, or become extinct—leaving a very complex entanglement of specific evolutionary paths. But in the vinelike tangle can be detected a general course. This, Sahlins (1960:44) concluded, is what Leslie White's approach is designed to describe.

The same sort of general-specific distinction can be applied to the study of cultural subunits as well as cultures. One could, as the nineteenth-century evolutionists did, trace the *general* evolution of religion (Tylor) or kinship structure (Tylor and Morgan) or focus on *specific* diversity of kinship or religion as influenced by numerous local factors. Recently Morton Fried (1967) and Elman Service (1962), for example, have written general evolutionary studies of political systems and social organization, respectively. However, scholars have disagreed on the point at which specific evolutionary studies become general, and vice-versa, as the analyses shift through several different levels of abstraction (cf. Erasmus 1969:23–24).

The Adaptive Process: An Overview

A sociocultural system, as a species in the organic world (the biological analogy has been irresistible since Spencer's time), endures only as long as it can adapt to the features of its environment. The specific evolutionary approach has tended to regard any given sociocultural system as an *adaptive* system (Sahlins 1958:ix; 1960:23; Goldschmidt 1959a: 128; Steward 1955; 1968). The processes of adaptation give the system its dynamic character and thus its viability. In specific evolutionary approaches, the relationship between a sociocultural system and its natural environment—flora, fauna, climate, topography, soil fertility—is considered a dynamic one, generally tending in the direction of a more perfect exploitation of the environment. The means of exploitation (or adaptation) lie in part within the system's technology, which in turn may affect the other elements of the system in ways described by Morgan and White.

But in the specific evolutionist approach, the "natural" environment is broadened to include other nearby societies as well, which constitute another set of adaptive demands upon the system in question. The continuing adaptability of the system is also affected by the qualities it acquired during its past adaptation (Goldschmidt 1959a:133): "A culture is at the same time a product of its traditions, including diffusionary influences, and its adaptation to its natural habitat" (Sahlins 1958:x). This point is patent in the "law of evolutionary potential," which states in effect that the more specialized a system becomes in coping with a given set of adaptive pressures, the less able it is to adapt as successfully once these pressures change (Service 1960:93–122; see also Goldschmidt 1959a:137). For sociocultural systems, as for dinosaurs, *too* successful an adaptation to the environment can ultimately be fatal.

From this perspective, then, a sociocultural system is adapting not only to its natural habitat but also to alien sociocultural systems. Technology is regarded as an important adaptive mechanism, but it alone cannot create successful adaptation to other cultures; different elements of the system, such as social structure or politics, are in these cases also important adaptive mechanisms.

Such a perspective is in sum eclectic and approaches the problem of adaptive processes from a number of different directions. It therefore runs a certain risk of becoming overly particularistic, emphasizing the combination of *unique* environmental factors in the production of *unique* adaptations by each sociocultural system. This is precisely what the evolutionists led by White were attacking the historicists for. Rather than be caught in this bind, most modern evolutionist writers have attempted to limit their consideration of environmental variables to those that have *cross-cultural* significance and have attempted to trace developmental or evolutionary trends in not one but a series of systems through time. Their method is comparative, and their objective is to seek cross-cultural regularities in adaptive trends among sociocultural systems or among parts of systems such as politics or kinship. In fact, then, the strategy is to move from the specific to the general evolutionary levels of analysis without becoming bogged down with particulars but at the same time to include enough particulars to make the processes of evolution clearer. How successful this strategy can be depends in part on how each analyst handles his analysis of important factors in the adaptive process, including the *local habitat; impinging sociocultural systems*, past and present; and the *functional interrelationship of systemic elements*. I want now to examine some of the analytical alternatives for handling each of these potentially important factors.

Factors in Process of Specific Evolution

THE LOCAL HABITAT: CULTURAL ECOLOGY

Julian Steward (1955) helped to stimulate a major scholarly focus on the relations between man and his local habitat, or *cultural ecology*, although he was not the first to articulate the basic principles of this important relationship. He suggested a systematic way to study the dynamics of man-habitat interaction so as to get at processes and, at the same time, to provide cross-cultural generalizations. His method was based on a simple assumption: not *all* features of a given habitat are relevant to a given sociocultural system, nor are all systemic elements (e.g., religion, politics, technology, and kinship) equally affected by the man-habitat interaction. The analytical task is to determine what features of the habitat "bear upon the productive patterns" of the system by focusing on those systemic features "which empirical analysis shows to be most closely involved in the utilization of [habitat] in culturally prescribed ways" (Steward 1955:123; 37). The idea is to strip away all "irrelevant" aspects of both the environment and the sociocultural system so as to clarify the ecological relationship and its changes through time. This stripping away of all but those features most directly involved with exploiting the habitat leaves only the evolutionarily important portion of the sociocultural system, which Steward called the *culture core* (1955:37). The system's technology is the basic component of the core, but technology must always be analyzed in terms of the conditions of the local habitat.

The point needs an example. Conceivably, one could describe the aboriginal technology of the Shoshoni Indians of Nevada as "hunting and gathering" and could then shift to a discussion of the material traits involved (bows, clubs, nets, pits, corrals, and so on), in a manner somewhat like that of Kroeber's culture element distribution studies. Conceived as a series of material traits, the Shoshoni "technology" does not differ from that of a host of other cultures, nor does it reveal anything very significant about adaptive processes. But once this cluster of material *traits* is linked to hunting *procedures*, which in turn are linked to the *nature of the local fauna*, processual and cross-cultural statements are possible:

If the principal game exists in large herds, such as herds of bison or caribou, there is advantage in cooperative hunting, and considerable numbers of peoples may remain together throughout the year. . . . If, however, the game is non-migratory, occurring in small and scattered groups, it is better hunted by small groups of men who know their territory well. . . . In each case, *the cultural repertory of hunting devices may be about the same,* but in the first case the society will consist of multifamily or multilineage groups, as among the Athabaskans and Algonkians of Canada and probably the pre-horse Plains bison hunters, and in the second case it will probably consist of localized patrilineal lineages or bands, as among the Bush-men, Congo Negritoes, Australians, Tasmanians, Fuegians, and others. These latter groups consisting of patrilineal bands are similar, as a matter of fact, not because their total environments are similar—the Bushmen, Australians, and southern Califor-nians live in deserts, the Negritoes in rain forests, and the Fuegians in a cold, rainy area—but because the nature of the game and therefore of their subsistence problem is the same in each case [Steward 1955:38; italics added].

The example also provides a glimpse of Steward's "stripping away" approach in the final sentence, at least with respect to the local habitat. (The problem of stripping away secondary cultural features to get to the culture core is some-what more complex; I wish to postpone it for the time being.)

Again the major point: to be useful to studies of adapta-tion, technology in the cultural ecological approach must be placed in dynamic interrelation with significant features of the local habitat.

THE "CULTURAL" HABITAT: IMPINGING ALIEN INFLUENCES

Walter Goldschmidt wrote:

The brute fact of the matter is that the policing of evolutionary development ultimately rests in the external selective process: the fact that each society lives in a context of other societies which offer an immediate or potential threat to the society, against which the society must rally its forces [1959a:128].

Few contemporary evolutionists would argue with the impli-cation of this statement (which has a now familiar Spencerian ring), that the effect of this "external" factor must be inves-tigated, and many have stated as much in public. But the brute fact of the matter is that few evolutionists have practiced what they have been preaching. Even when the influence of alien systems is expanded to include not only military threat but the influence of diffusion of ideas and artifacts, as a class of factors it has played second fiddle to

man-habitat relations in many cases. For some, this treatment is justified by the data in particular situations (Sahlins
1958); for others, it is the result of a methodology carefully
designed to exclude precisely this set of factors (Steward
1955).

Sahlins (1958:200) pitted "historical" (diffusional) factors
against ecological factors in accounting for two different
forms of Polynesian social organization. The historical factors
fared badly, but then in this case so did the ecological ones,
because neither factor alone seemed completely to account
for the observed occurrence of the social structural forms.
The remainder of his study was devoted primarily to ecological sorts of explanations, in part because Sahlins believed
that the consistently high rate of diffusion in Polynesia, a
constant, could not account for the variety in forms of social
stratification (1958:x). One of the reasons he focused his
analysis on an area of shared tradition was to gauge the
relative roles of diffusion versus ecological adaptation as
causal factors in sociocultural systems.

Steward was more sweeping than Sahlins in pointing out
why diffusion processes were not relevant to his own studies
of multilinear evolution:

> If people borrow domesticated plants and agricultural pat-
> terns, it is evident that population will increase in favorable
> areas. How shall dense, stable populations organize their socio-
> political relations? Obviously, they will not remain inchoate
> mobs until diffused patterns have taught them how to live
> together. (And even diffused patterns had to originate some-
> where for good and sufficient reasons.) [Steward 1955:208].

The diffused traits in any sociocultural system give it its
distinct character, its "local color"; but these are "secondary
features," "which cannot per se produce the underlying condition of, or the need for, greater social and political organization" (Steward 1955:209). The major stimuli come from
the man-habitat relationship, in his view. Steward frequently
re-emphasized the secondary nature of diffusion as a causal

process and thus, as White, revealed a real disaffection with much of the "dynamic" approach forged by his historicist mentors.

But in 1956 Steward teamed up with Robert Murphy to write a brief comparison of adaptive patterns among rubber-tree tappers in South America and hunters of Canada. It was an ecological argument, fully developed. But in both Indian cultures a major dynamic factor had been contact between them and Europeans bent on economic exploitation, which the authors also emphasized. Perhaps the apparent contradiction in Steward's work is resolved by the fact that in his more extreme denials of the importance of diffusion, he was concentrating on comparisons of several different systems through extended periods of time; his level of analysis was much higher and his data relatively less accurate than in his and Murphy's tappers-trappers comparison. But my speculations should not divert attention from a basic methodological point: Steward's ignoring of the "local color" made it relatively simpler to trace the man-habitat relations, even at the cost of slighting the possibly crucial factor of culture contact.

Other proponents of the evolutionary perspective have recognized culture contact as an important causal factor in some cases. Elman Service (1962:136; 1971:157), for example, argued that in analyses of the evolution of social structure, authors (including himself) have biased their accounts by paying only passing attention to the effect of contact between "primitives" and alien, dominating sociocultural systems. The Basin Shoshonis of the American West, for example, were considered by Steward (1955) and others to be a classic example of a low level of sociocultural complexity, caused by a rudimentary technology in a forbidding desert environment. Service did not quibble with the evolutionary level, but he offered evidence to show that the condition was *not* traditional; that marauding groups of horse-mounted Piegans and Utes, and encroaching Europeans, were mainly responsible for the state of Shoshoni development. Furthermore, other groups at this same "com-

posite band" stage of evolution had all undergone decima-
tion, dislocation, or other sorts of disruption through contact
with more-powerful sociocultural systems (Service 1962:108).
Steward (1968:332), however, continued to favor his own
view of causal factors in aboriginal Shoshoni organization
over that of Service. In addition, evidence from other hunting and gathering societies favored Steward's conclusion that
the "composite band" was in all probability an aboriginal,
precontact, structure that was well suited to local habitat
and technology (Lee and DeVore 1968:7–8). Service report-
edly altered his own position concerning this view later, but
he nonetheless deserves credit for emphasizing the factor of
culture contact as one of important adaptive influence (Lee
and DeVore 1968:8).

Clifford Geertz (1963) combined culture ecology and
culture contact variables into a penetrating analysis of specific
evolution in Indonesia. Traditionally, the islanders practiced
two basic forms of cultivation. One form, swidden or slash
and burn, had a fairly narrow range of productivity, and
under situations of severe population pressure, new fields
had to be rapidly expanded—otherwise decreasing soil fertility drastically reduced the net crop yields. The other form,
sawah, or wet-rice paddy farming, was by comparison
infinitely more flexible. Simply by increasing the amount of
care lavished on the tending of the crop, the rice terraces
could support a significant population increase without
expanding the limits of the terraces themselves.

Beginning in 1619, the Dutch set themselves up as colonial
masters of the islands and turned parts of the *sawah* region
into sugar cane plantations. This caused a population pressure on the remaining *sawah* areas as wage-workers flowed
into the plantations. The adaptive result was a process
Geertz termed "involution," an "overdriving of an established form in such a way that it becomes rigid through an
inward over-elaboration of detail. . . ." (Geertz 1963:82).
The patterns of *sawah* agriculture were infused with this
involutive tendency: land tenure arrangements became more

complicated; ever more people were brought in to farm the same fields; ever more attention was devoted to the weeding, planting, and harvesting of the fields. As a result, the area was able to withstand the press of people because the *sawah* fields became more productive. The other components of the sociocultural system based on *sawah* cultivation, Geertz noted, also underwent involution—a minute elaboration of the basic forms of religion, politics, and kinship, without a change in the basic forms themselves.

In the swidden areas, on the other hand, small-scale private farming enterprises arose among the inhabitants, who were not used as the primary source of labor on plantations. The combination of ecological factors in the swidden area plus the different sorts of colonial pressure in the area revealed processes other than that of the monotonous routine of involutionary elaboration. The point is that the explanation of what happened in the Dutch colonization of Indonesia required both ecological and culture-contact variables.

IDEOLOGY AND INDIVIDUAL BEHAVIOR IN ADAPTIVE PROCESS

In no case is either ideology or individual behavior seriously examined as a causal variable in evolutionary process. Service began his evolutionary account by stressing the importance of ideology as a dynamic variable; but values, beliefs, and meanings—usually considered the essence of ideology—somehow became swiftly lumped into "rules," as in rules of residence or rules of descent or exogamy. Thus ideology apparently was a matter of social organization rather than a separate or separable sort of dynamic, in spite of the stated aims of Service's book (1962:28 ff.). In fact, most evolutionists, including White, have pointed out that ideology can act as a *limiting* factor in change in several different ways; and Service at least recognized it as a *dynamic* factor as well. But when the scholarly task is to reconstruct sociocultural evolution of the paleolithic, mesolithic, and neolithic—that is, at a general level before the advent of writing—it is impossible to assess the dynamic role of ideology. Again, the research aims, level of analysis, and data determine the variables considered.

For these same reasons, it is impossible for evolutionists to include exhaustive discussions of the dynamic role of individual behavior, White's analysis of Ikhnaton notwithstanding (this was, after all, a justification for *not* including individual behavior in evolutionary discourse). When individual factors are mentioned, they are characterized in terms of universal human needs (Goldschmidt 1959a) that together form a set of biopsychological limitations on the course of sociocultural evolution. Statements such as this by Fried are rare in most analyses:

> The genesis of the ranking society, in terms of individual psychology, may well lie in the demand for affect, so that some individuals seek reinforcement by giving more and more frequently than they should, thereby creating obligations among those that have received goods [Fried 1967:115; cf. Goldschmidt's concept of the "need for positive affect" (1959a:26–29)].

And Fried himself did not seriously pursue this line of causal inquiry. This observation is not for criticism (cf. Erasmus 1969) but for purposes of pointing out that dynamic processes can be pursued at several different analytical levels; it further implies that the methodology involved in rooting out process will depend on the analytical level involved.

FUNCTIONAL INTERRELATIONSHIPS: DETERMINISM AND PROCESS

According to some proponents of modern evolutionism, a deterministic perspective is not as readily applicable at the specific evolutionary level as it might be at the general level. In fact, the alternatives seem to be either to drop the notion of determinism entirely when dealing with adaptation or to construct a hyphenated label for a series of factors that, taken together, exert a "probabilistic-deterministic"[1] influence on sociocultural systems. Best known among the latter perspectives is that of Harris's "techno-environmental and techno-economic" determinism (1968:4). Elman Service favored abolishing determinism completely:

> *Down with prime-movers!* There is no single magical formula that will predict the evolution of every society. The actual evolution of the culture of particular societies is an adaptive process whereby the society solves problems with respect to the natural and to the social-cultural environment. These environments are so diverse, the problems so numerous, and the solutions potentially so various that no single determinant can be equally powerful for all cases [1971:25].

A good deal is apparently riding on which approach the analyst chooses to adopt. As Harris pointed out, without some attempt to isolate key variables that seem important in adaptation everywhere, we must rule out the formulation of scientific generalizations and, with them, the possibility of prediction of specific courses of adaptation (1969:203–205). When variables are isolated, however, the appearance often is one of deterministic cause-effect, regardless of the best intentions of the investigator. Service's statement raises the specter of bias through determinism. Without deciding the issue here, it is at least possible to discuss the perspectives on determinism in the more recent evolutionary approaches.

As mentioned earlier, almost all the evolutionist approaches are in fact materialistic, placing major or exclusive emphasis on man's productive relationship with the local habitat; and most of those approaches recognize White's and the nineteenth-century evolutionists' contributions in this context. Yet there have been attempts to reassess some of the early assumptions that have persisted along with materialistic determinism. Fried, for example, has explicitly

---

[1]That is, determinism is qualified "in probabalistic terms, *given a sufficient number of cases and in the long run*" (Harris 1968:245).

challenged the evolutionary significance of military organization in the less complex stages of development—stressed, we will remember, in Herbert Spencer's conceptualization of evolutionary process:

I think I will be able to show that the evolution of warfare and military statuses, at least during the earliest breakthroughs to more complex forms of society, *followed* and was *dependent upon* developments in technology, economic organization, and nonmilitary aspects of social organization [Fried 1967:105–106; italics added].

And later in the same book: "Rather than war and military roles being the source of stratification, it seems that stratification is a provoker of war and an enhancer of military status" (p. 216).

Another example: Malthusian materialism argued, as have most of the sociocultural evolutionists since, that increased agricultural production *leads to* increased population. Esther Boserup has proposed a provocative reversal of this notion:

It is . . . sensible to regard the process of agricultural change in primitive communities as an adaptation to gradually increasing population densities, brought about by changes in the rates of natural population growth or by immigration.

According to the explanation offered here, population increase leads to the adoption of more intensive systems of agriculture in primitive communities and an increase of total agricultural output [Boserup 1965:117–118].

Her argument is detailed and carefully qualified; I do it an injustice by mentioning it here almost in passing. The gist of it is, however, that a change to more "advanced" agricultural techniques from a "primitive" slash-and-burn (or swidden) technique actually results in *less* productivity per man-hour of labor. This is clearly recognized by the farmers themselves, who resort to more-advanced techniques of plow cultivation only when population pressure on the land makes it impossible to continue swidden techniques. More people must then work longer hours to maintain nutritional standards, but then more people are available for such work. When given a choice, farmers in noncomplex societies will not "develop" beyond the level of the swidden method. Increases in energy production per capita in the agricultural revolution, then, must logically have come from population pressure or, as Boserup suggested, from coercion of one society by another.

Here, then, are more "prime movers" of cultural evolution. Her hypothesis does not refute the scheme of general evolution proposed by White; nor does it usurp the important role of ecological-technological relations in adaptation. It does, however, suggest—tentatively—an explanation as to *why* technology has evolved and suggests that technology—at least agricultural technology, upon which all ancient civilization was based—may itself be a *dependent* variable. Yet it also replaces one of the ultimate questions of evolutionary causation with another: what accounts for population increases in specific cases?

Most evolutionary writers have shied away from the strident determinism of White yet stop well short of Service's "down with prime movers" mandate. Goldschmidt wrote that "our evolutionary hypothesis denies inevitability; it rather asserts central tendencies" (1959a:217). Thomas Harding (1960:57) warned that "No class or classes of cultural elements are inherently more suited for adaptive functions than others. It depends on the environmental factors present, as well as on the resources a particular culture has on hand or can borrow from outside." Yet, as Service suggested (1971:26), perhaps the time has come to treat the issue of determinism for what it really is—an *analytical perspective,* "a point of view which, like a telescope, should be used in a certain way for certain investigations simply because it works. It cannot be fruitfully argued as something that is empirically true or false." Strictly speaking, any attempt analytically to limit the variability of human life-ways to understand better the central tendencies or basic processes is determinism. But it is essential to the task of evolutionists, particularly to those who wish eventually to bridge the gap between specific and general evolution. General statements can only be built on the basis of specific regularities, and in order to determine the regularities of change processes among cultures A, B, C, D, . . ., some of the variations in each must be ignored, as Steward insisted. One need not, however, use Steward's methodology to get at the regularities.

STAGES AND EVOLUTIONARY PROCESS

One of the "survivals" of nineteenth-century evolution, as we have seen in the discussion of Leslie White's approach, is the concept of evolutionary stages. Steward (1955) and other evolutionists have proposed less-comprehensive evolutionary progressions than those of White. Fried described a sequence of political forms from "Egalitarian Societies" through "Rank Societies" and "Stratified Societies" to "The State" (1967). Service traced social organization from the level of "Bands" through "Tribes" to "Chiefdoms" and postponed discussion of higher levels (1962); but later (1971), in response to Fried's work, he suggested that only three "types" might represent aboriginal evolutionary stages: the "Egalitarian Society," the "Hierarchical Society," and the "Archaic Civilization or Classical Empire." I want briefly to discuss the way in which the mechanisms of transition from one stage to the next have been handled by the various authors.

In his "Cultural Causality and Law" (1955; orig. 1949), Steward described the evolution of civilizations based on irrigation agriculture. Without worrying about why village farming, the earliest stage in his sequence, might first have arisen, he described what social organization was functionally required to make the technological system work. Technology improved and productivity increased, leading to larger populations. The steadily improving technology and production involved the development of irrigation works of increasing sophistication and scale. Throughout this continuous process of improvement and increase, there were corresponding changes in the social organization (because the components of sociocultural systems are functionally interrelated). Finally, the productive limits of the irrigation technology were reached, and continuing expansion was possible only through warfare. Warfare had the effect of producing momentary expansion and florescence, then led to retrogression into a period of "Dark Ages" with declining population and lowered productivity forced by both the unmet demands of population pressure and the "abuse of the common people" by militaristic elites. The abuse of the people, reminiscent of Marx's class-warfare notion, was not a recurrent theme at each evolutionary level, however. In Steward's conception of process, the independent variables were environment, technology, and population growth; the functional relationship between the three variables and the rest of the "culture core" (basic religious, social, political, and scientific patterns) were clearly and plausibly traced.[2]

Service (1962), as we have seen, was much less willing to lean solely on technological-environmental factors in explanations of evolutionary stages; technology and environment alone, he argued, cannot account for the widespread similarity of bands. Needed as well are factors of competition, and social inventions such as the sodality to foster band cohesiveness (Service 1962:75). In the *transition* from the band stage to another, the impact of food production and population increase is major (Service 1962:110). Yet Service argued that these two factors alone make possible but do not

---

[2]Steward himself (1968:323) later recognized subsequent interpretations (Adams 1966) which held that irrigation was not so important in Mesoamerica and Mesopotamia, two of the areas of civilization in his earlier comparison. My intention here, however, is to play up his description of process and largely to ignore the implications of more recent data for his original scheme. The method, in other words, is still viable even though the conclusions may be challenged. Steward was always open to changes in his approach and conclusions—a key characteristic of a true scholar (Manners 1973).

cause a new level of evolution, the tribe. Again, a crucial causal factor is competition with other groups—just as it was with Spencer and White—with tribal organization being one effective way of organizing a mass of people into an efficiently competitive group. Tribal organization arises, then, in favorable productive areas, from a need to compete effectively. The social structural mechanism is the formation of pan-tribal sodalities, groupings that in effect link groups of bands together; clans serve such a purpose, as do age-grades or military societies (Service 1962:115–116). In the transition from the tribal to the next higher level, the chiefdom, increasing food productivity again plays an important role; but a necessary causal variable is *specialization,* either by *locality* (as where local groups each produce a different sort of goods, which are then redistributed within a given region so that each group receives a full range of products) or by *individual* specialization (as in the case of leatherworkers, farmers, fishers, and potters each contributing their special products to the commonweal) (Service 1962:145).

Morton Fried also included both technological and other sorts of variables when he accounted for the transition from one stage to another, as, for example, in the emergence of stratified societies:

population pressure; shifts in customary postmarital residence patterns; contraction or sharp natural alteration of basic resources; shifts in subsistence patterns arising from such factors as technological change or the impingement of a market system; development of managerial roles as an aspect of maturation of a social and ceremonial system. I explicitly reject warfare and slavery as initiating conditions . . . [Fried 1967:196].

All the schemes described here have in common the argument that technological productivity and population density must increase if successive stages of evolution are to emerge, and none of the schemes seems particularly concerned with explanations for the increases themselves. That is, in the discussion of the processes of sociocultural evolution, certain basic factors receive relatively little analytical attention. This has not changed since the nineteenth century; but how much more complex the processual statements are, even since the time of White's early writings and even with the limiting of certain variables! And yet they remain speculative, as they must because of the nature of the data that support them.

Detection and Documentation of Processes

THE TASK OF RECONSTRUCTION

A common feature of virtually every evolutionary study, general or specific, is the task of reconstructing past developments, either in single sociocultural systems, in clusters of systems, or in components of systems such as social stratification, politics, or social organization in general. This is an apparent similarity to the scholarly task of the American historicists; but, to repeat, the evolutionary approaches lack the particularism of the historicists, which is to say that their emphasis is upon more general similarities and trends through more extended periods of time. And there is the relative de-emphasis of the diffusion process.

The two approaches share some other common features. Evolutionists, probably even more so than the historicists, are consciously applying conjecture, inference, or logical deduction, milking the last drop of suggestion from the sketchiest of evidence. Given the task they have set themselves, this is what they *must* do, because time has erased much of the really good data they require. This was precisely the kind of problem facing the evolutionists of the nineteenth century, and it is not surprising that the contemporary evolutionists have adopted some of the earlier methodology.

One of these techniques is the comparative method, shorn of the excesses of context-ignoring Victorians yet still being one of the few means of "help[ing] the imagination to flesh

out the outlines of ancestral cultures" (Service 1971:151).
The typical documentation of evolutionist assumptions now
begins with a statement of the hypothesis, a survey of whatever ancient evidence may remain to support it, and liberal
use of evidence from more-recent groups existing in what is
assumed to be a similar context (e.g., Fried 1967; Service
1962; Sahlins 1958; White 1959). There are still problems
with the method, as the evolutionists themselves have
recognized since Tylor's time. One is the fact that more
recent "survivals" of presumed earlier, more widely spread
levels of evolution—such as the Bushmen of the Kalihari or
the Arunta of Australia—have themselves been changing
through time. The crucial question is how rapidly and how
drastically this change has been going on. As a rough and
ready, rule-of-thumb sort of approximation, it can be
assumed that the change in such marginal groups had been
neither drastic nor rapid—particularly in ecological relations
—prior to recent intensive contact with dominating cultures.
The assumption is implicit in Thomas Harding's "principle
of stabilization" (Harding 1960:53 ff.), which stated that a
sociocultural system tends to adapt (change) only as much
as is necessary to keep its basic form intact: "cultures at rest
tend to remain at rest"—although both the principle and
assumption must be used with extreme caution.

Steward insisted that the key features of both the habitat
and the culture core were to be *empirically determined* by
the analyst in each case. His approach was largely inductive
within an ecological framework and avoided the particularistic pitfalls of the historicists. The problem is how to
document the change process so as to allow evolutionary
conclusions rather than local cultural histories. Steward did
it by limiting possible variables still further. He compared
the sequence of changes in *similar* culture cores, all of which
were set in essentially *similar* local habitats—for example,
small horticultural villages set in semiarid climates, where
irrigation was required if agriculture were to develop to its
fullest potential (Steward 1955:178–209). He was able to

demonstrate that cultures in the several areas of comparison did progress from small farming villages through a succession of almost identical sociocultural stages. He concluded that the similarity was caused by the similarity of the local habitats and the application of similar adaptive techniques (such as irrigation). His conclusion was, again, nothing startling, and even premature (cf. Adams 1966); but his explanation of *how* the similar stages evolved was much more detailed and rigorous than had been attempted previously. Had the local habitats and productive techniques not been similar, the sequence would not have been similar in the different regions; and had it not been possible to understand the interrelations of techniques and habitat, it would not have been possible to understand the evolutionary processes involved.

Sahlins later (1958) attempted to approach the dynamics of the technology-habitat relationship in a different way. Instead of comparing adaptations to similar environments by different sociocultural systems, he traced the effects of different environments and technologies among representatives of the *same* cultural tradition. He assumed that the systems involved in his comparison, those usually grouped into the culture area of Polynesia, had at one time stemmed from a common source. The ensuing changes in features such as social stratification, he felt, could be traced to the development of different technologies, which in turn were adaptive responses to different environments encountered as Polynesian mariners sailed outward from their original homeland. The stratification systems on coral atolls were, for example, different from those on the high volcanic islands in the area, in large part because different technologies were required to exploit effectively the two different sorts of environment (Sahlins 1958:250–253).

Again the basic assumption is that technology influences the other components of a sociocultural system (social stratification in this case); but for a rigorous explanation of specific adaptive mechanisms, technology must be placed in the context of the local natural habitat. Steward's and Sahlins' studies made complementary general evolutionary points: similar ecological adaptations give rise to a sequence of parallel developments in unrelated sociocultural systems; and different ecological adaptations can lead to divergent development, even among systems once sharing a common heritage. Their more substantial contribution, however, is the description of processes by which this occurs.

The reconstructive bent of most evolutionist writing means also that the documentation of change processes is difficult—for all the attempts to specify the relationship between environment, technology, and other systems and for all the stripping away. The farther back in time the evolutionary sequences are pushed, the more difficult it becomes. For this reason it makes sense to take a deterministic approach to system-habitat interaction, because the causal properties of other factors may be impossible to assess. "Guesstimates" based on material factors are much less wildly speculative than those that posit ideological factors as a cause, given a near total lack of specific data. To be sure, the comparative method reveals that ideology *tends* to be a dependent variable, yet its role remains conjectural in some cases largely because it cannot be precisely documented. What I am saying is simply that the nature of the research objective *plus* the quality of the data have a determining effect on methodological assumptions.

MEASURING EVOLUTIONARY PROGRESS

White proposed a potentially quantifiable measure of energy utilization in 1949.[3] A number of other measures of

---

[3]He established a "base line" for calculations by estimating that in preagricultural societies, where "human energy" was the sole energy source, the average adult male could generate about 1/10 horsepower and that 1/20 horsepower was about the per-capita average once children and other nonproductive members were included (White 1949b:369).

the extent of objective "progress" have appeared both before and since. Scholars universally agree that this is a difficult task, particularly when one wishes to reconstruct past pre-literate evolutionary stages, yet all are apparently agreed that such a universal yardstick could make comparative analysis of several different adaptive mechanisms much more rigorous. So far there seem to be few measures that can be universally applied, again because the data in some cases simply do not allow any but the roughest calculations.

Sahlins (1958) used surplus production of food commodities and the extent of their redistribution as a measure of technological efficiency in his Polynesian study. He showed that the amount of stratification was directly correlated with the size of the group involved in the redistribution of the surplus and with how frequently the food was redistributed. In another work (Sahlins 1960:21), he suggested some other criteria for measurement of general evolutionary progress but did not suggest how these might be quantified.

More recently, Harris (1971:203 ff.) proposed a formula designed to calculate "food energy"—the number of calories annually produced by a group. The formula is $E = m \times t \times r \times e$, in which E is food energy in calories, m the number of food producers, t the hours of work per producer, r the number of calories expended each hour by each producer, and e the "average number of calories produced for each calorie expended in food production." Using data supplied by R. B. Lee (1969; orig. 1966), he reckoned that a band of Bushmen hunters and gatherers has an average food energy output of about 23 million calories— about 2100 calories per day per person in a band of 30 people. Swidden agriculturalists have significantly higher E's, and irrigation agriculturalists higher yet: more than three billion, for example, in a single Chinese village of about 700 people.

In the United States, the agricultural labor force of about five million in 1964 produced some 260 trillion calories. Clearly, such a formula could be used in quantifying the degree of sociocultural development when good data are available and when the comparative figures are adjusted to compensate for different group sizes. It would also be necessary to show what proportion of each group's total population is engaged in food energy production. Food energy is, however, just one type of energy produced in modern industrialized societies.

Population growth and distribution have been the basis of several measures of development (e.g., Naroll 1956), but Fried (1967:112) warned that figures comparing the density of population at two different evolutionary stages do not always take into consideration the different patterns of land use. Hence, a large hunting band and a small tribal society may have the same density figures, but actually the tribal group may be located in one dense cluster in a restricted portion of the total land area while the band may be dispersed in small groups throughout a land area of the same size.

Coon (1948) constructed a multivariate quantification system, measuring the level of evolutionary development according to four factors: degree of individual specialization, extent of trade, number of different institutions to which an individual belongs, and the complexity of institutions (cited in Steward 1955:90). Carneiro (1962; 1968) proposed a Guttman scale analysis of development, ordering societies from "lower" to "higher" in complexity on the basis of the presence or absence of a series of traits (e.g., "trade between communities," "taxation in kind," "code of laws," and "monumental stone architecture"). This approach allows a given society to be ranked according to degree of evolutionary development but, perhaps more important for the analysis of process, gives some inkling of the approximate sequence in which a set of traits appears in that development.

In criticizing Coon's efforts, Steward (1955:90) pointed out an important consideration that is applicable to many efforts at quantification of progress: when used cross-culturally, they frequently ignore the important *qualitative* differences between systems, specifically "the qualities of [their] . . . institutions, and . . . the specific developmental and ecological processes which produced them." It is fair to conclude, however, that because a given methodological approach may be more suitable to answering one set of questions than another, it is not therefore wrong. Quantitative measures may ignore qualitative differences, but should not be abandoned for that reason alone.

RECONSTRUCTION AND THE PROBLEM OF DOMINANCE

The problem of dominance in reconstruction has been neatly stated by Service:

> It seems obvious that what has been missing in cultural evolutionary schemes is a way of talking in evolutionary terms plainly about what are its salient dynamics: the evolutionary dominance of modern advanced societies in the forms of colonialism and imperialism, and the reactions of some societies to this dominance in various forms of revolution. . . . [C]lassic evolutionary schemes failed to take into account the obvious facts of the interaction of cultures in terms of dominance, reactions to it, and the variable degrees of succcess on either side of the encounter. *There is no inner dynamic of inevitable orthogenetic change, particularly when any change can be thwarted by another society's dominance powers* [1971:10–11; italics added].

He then suggested that the concept of adaptation, implying adaptation to the natural habitat as well as to other sociocultural systems, allows for dominance relations to be considered. We have seen how Geertz, for example, accomplished the necessary balancing of cultural and habitat factors, as Service himself attempted to do in his reassessment of the "deviant" features of band-level organization.

But, in my opinion, these two examples are exceptions to the general tendency of recent evolutionary work, even when that work is recast as a study of "specific evolution" or "adaptation." The major focus, as mentioned earlier in this chapter, is still upon system-natural habitat relations and the dynamics of the interrelationship between the internal components of a given system or "type" of system. In short, I think (with Service) that it is not only the "classic evolutionists" who have failed to take intercultural dominance into account, and I think that the explanation lies in what it is most modern evolutionists are trying to do.

This raises the related issue of whether evolutionary approaches are equipped to deal with contemporary problems of directed change and international development (cf. Erasmus 1969). I would argue that they are, or can be, if they can successfully incorporate the variable of dominance into their schemes without losing a sense of the other factors involved in the adaptive process. Such general principles as Service's law of evolutionary potential have some applicability to the present: the most dramatic evolutionary advances can be expected among less specialized sociocultural systems. Because of this relative lack of specialization, they are better able to borrow and capitalize upon technological advances discovered after considerable trial and error in more specialized systems. Service applied the law to a comparison of the rise of industrialism in Communist China with the industrialization process in the West and concluded that Western industrial dominance is forcing a confrontation with China and other developing nations (Service 1960:120 ff.).

As mentioned before, Geertz (1963) provided a method for combining ecological and dominance factors in an understanding of recent issues. Morton Fried (1952) and the Murphy and Steward study of tappers and trappers (1956) also contained important methodological leads, although the application was primarily to events of the past. Given a change of focus to more contemporary issues, the question becomes one of distinguishing between "evolution," "acculturation," and "cultural ecology." In studies such as these, the distinction is most difficult to make.

Summary

Service stated (1962:26) that a general evolutionary perspective, like that of Leslie White, is useful provided

(a) that the environment is held constant, which is to say that culture as a totality is regarded as a closed system in order that only its own internal integration is under consideration; and (b) that the actual mechanics of evolutionary change are not being described.

This chapter has been more concerned with specific evolution, the approach that does *not* hold environment constant and that *does* attempt to describe the actual mechanics of evolutionary change. With the concept of specific evolution has emerged the notion of sociocultural systems as *adaptive* systems. This in turn has tended to dilute the strictly technological determinism of White's scheme by assigning causal priority to local habitat and intersystem contact. Yet most evolutionary approaches still emphasize material factors, particularly the basic nature of technology-habitat interaction.

The primary aim of both specific and general evolutionary studies has thus far been a reconstruction of the patterns of past sociocultural development. Specific evolution, however, is more involved with a study of mechanisms or processes. Reconstruction, particularly with accompanying problems of sketchy data, makes a materialist-based approach a most reasonable one, even if it is inevitably speculative. To be sure, a modern application of the nineteenth-century comparative method allows for some guesses about ideological factors in prehistoric systems, but these must always be sketched in after the material conditions are reconstructed. And there is no way that individual motivation can be determined. Whatever the methodology employed, then, the documentation of the mechanisms of transition from band to tribe, or from tribe to chiefdom, cannot be made with the same accuracy as more contemporary dynamics. This does not mean evolutionary reconstruction should be abandoned.

The evolutionary writers of the 1960's and early 1970's have all acknowledged a debt to the earlier work of Leslie White and Julian Steward and, ultimately, through White, to the nineteenth-century evolutionists (even though the Marxian dialectical approach has not been used extensively, if at all, and class conflict has not yet become the popular focus in studies of evolutionary process by anthropologists). Yet it should be clear that some debt is due to the early functionalist scholars, as well as to proponents of the acculturation approach.

CHAPTER SEVEN

PSYCHOCULTURAL PROCESSES: INDIVIDUAL BEHAVIOR AS A LEVEL OF ANALYSIS

S O FAR in this narrative, dynamic processes have been described as features of sociocultural *systems:* systems adapt; systems are integrated but may be subdivided into subsystems or components for closer analysis; all culture is a vast system that has a reality of its own and that follows a certain detectable course of development; and so forth. I have argued that as analytical approaches, ones that hold a series of other variables constant or "given," these perspectives are legitimate and even necessary. But one of the constants keeps lurking on the periphery, just out of focus, in spite of several attempts to discount or ignore it: individual human behavior. Common sense tells us it is by no means a constant once it is removed from the periphery and incorporated into an analysis of dynamic factors.

My task in this chapter is to introduce two somewhat different approaches to sociocultural change that incorporate psychological variables. My aim in doing so is not to demonstrate that the other approaches we have considered are necessarily wrong or even incomplete. It is, rather, to illustrate one of the themes of this book: that what factors are considered and how they are treated depends on the sorts of questions the analyst wishes to answer.

Innovation

In anthropology, the scholar who has unquestionably contributed the most systematic and comprehensive discussion
of innovation processes is Homer Barnett. In analyzing his
field data from the Northwest Coast in the late 1930's,
Barnett concerned himself with the question of how alien
traits were incorporated into an on-going sociocultural system
—something that Boas had suggested years earlier but that
had not been consistently practiced by his students. Barnett
arrived at two fundamental conclusions: (1) that culture
traits, whether material or nonmaterial, are not "discrete inflexible wholes" but can be subdivided into qualities of form,
meaning, function, and operating principle, any of which
can be modified by recipient peoples, and (2) that the
processes of modification and incorporation are basically
mental processes, occurring in the minds of individuals
(Barnett 1942). Neither of the observations was particularly
startling, but both were important assumptions in the innovation approach that emerged a decade later.

In 1953, the year his book on innovation was published,
Barnett participated in the SSRC Seminar on Acculturation
(see Chapter Four). By then he was so firmly committed to
his own approach that he chose not to co-author the
seminar's memorandum, and he added a "mildly heretical"
postscript instead (SSRC Seminar 1954:1000–1002). His
argument was an old one, but again most germane to his
innovation approach: that culture and social structure have
no reality; they are abstractions, convenient scientific short-
hand. But, he charged, in the minds of many social scientists
they had been transformed from mere conceptualizations to
reality, with inevitably distorting and misleading results. He
stated succinctly his own views on the nature of culture:

In dealing with culture we are inevitably dealing with multi-individual *ideas*, that is, with ideas shared by more than one person. But this sharing does not make them . . . supraindividual with an autonomy of their own. They are no different from any other ideas. They have the same place of residence, and they are subject to the same principles of thinking as idiosyncratic ideas. They do not act with forces and features of their own, and assuredly they do not behave like wind or stone.

. . . No matter how [the] . . . problem [of change] is viewed, it takes on an ultimate *mental* reference [Barnett 1953:15; italics added].

It is not productive here to pursue the obvious areas of contention between Leslie White and Barnett. The important point is that by describing the nature of culture, Barnett was describing what he intended to study as the primary elements in culture change: changes in ideas. And, because multi-individual ideas are subject to the same principles as idiosyncratic ones, the analyst could justifiably concern himself with *how* "new" or "different" ideas emerge in individuals. This, for Barnett, was the key to processes of sociocultural change, although the emergence of new ideas simply makes change possible—it does not cause it to take place. Change results from the *acceptance* of the novelties by the group.

THE PROCESS OF INNOVATION

Innovation is the recombination of previously existing ideas into a new idea (or *mental configuration*, in Barnett's terms). The process is rapid, complex, and often subconscious on the part of the individual. *It is essential to keep in mind that the process goes on within the individual's brain, and that its basic units are ideas* (mental configurations), *not material items.*

To illustrate a simple kind of innovation, pretend for a moment that you are a young child, and you want to build a toy car "just like a real one." The problem is the headlights. You know they are round, shiny, metallic devices mounted on the front of Dad's car; this is a pre-existing configuration.

You know that tin cans are also round, shiny, metallic objects but are used to hold food, an entirely different function from that of the headlights. This is another pre-existing configuration. By *analyzing* the two configurations, that is, by breaking them down into separable qualities (roundness, shinyness, metallic, used to hold food, used to light the roadway, etc.) and then *matching* or *identifying* similarities in these configurations, you are able to *substitute* two empty tin cans for "real" headlights on your toy. The three steps—analysis, identification, and substitution—together comprise the innovation process. Again, few people are conscious of such innovative sequences, and many innovations are much more complex than this example. Incidentally, *differences*, rather than similarities, among pre-existing configurations may be the important consideration for the innovator, when an innovation represents the opposite of the pre-existing configurations. Avant-garde innovations in recent Western clothing and cosmetic fashions seem to be a result of this latter process. Just at the time when both women and men are wearing their hair "unusually" long, the Sunday newspaper supplements carry pictures of the latest "bald" look, in which members of both sexes shave their heads completely.

Why do people innovate? Finding the answer to that question, said Barnett, "is admittedly a formidable task, the more baffling and confusing the deeper the probing goes" (1953:97). He then deliberately did not probe more deeply, but instead referred to "wants" as "incentives to innovation." He did proceed to outline the various sorts of wants or needs that can be inferred from innovative behavior, such as the need for personal credit from one's peers, the need for self-identity, and the like; but he was content to keep such wants as givens in his scheme for the sake of focusing on the process of innovation itself.

Innovation is *not* a process limited only to geniuses or inventors. Everyone innovates, and most are unaware that they are doing so because the innovative combinations of configurations are so fleeting and at times so trivial that they never force themselves fully into the individual's consciousness. Countless other combinations are stifled as soon as they are born because they are whimsical or outrageous or at least improbable. The rates at which individuals innovate do apparently vary, as does the relative emphasis placed on innovations in one or another components of a group's life-way. For example, innovation among lower ranks of enlisted men while in their line of duty is discouraged by the American military, whereas it is a vital process in modern American art. Both the rate and nature of the innovations, in short, are influenced by their cultural setting. I will return to this point in a moment.

ACCEPTANCE OF INNOVATIONS

Earlier I mentioned that Barnett was concerned with how alien traits are integrated into a receiving group once diffusion has occurred. He noted that this integration, or *acceptance* of alien traits, also entails innovation. In other words, whether the "new" trait is introduced by some creative person within the group or comes to the group from the outside, the recipients will innovate during their acceptance. We know already from the discussions of acculturation and diffusion that incoming traits will inevitably be modified by recipients. Barnett described what factors are important in the modification process, from the perspective of the individual acceptor-innovator (1953:Chaps. XII–XIV; 1964). Generally, the individual must assign some sort of *meaning* to the innovation—it must have significance *for him*; and from his perspective, acceptance must bring with it some *advantage* he would not otherwise enjoy. If both conditions are not present, then the innovation will probably be rejected. Exactly how does innovation play a part in acceptance? The potential acceptor first *analyzes* the proffered novelty in terms of his pre-existing configurations that he believes are relevant. He then matches or *identifies* components of the new with those of the old and, according to his criteria of evaluation, decides whether or not to *substitute* the new configuration for the pre-existing one. The apparent difference between *innovation*-innovation and *acceptance*-innovation is that the "new" configuration originates in the former and not in the latter. But, in fact, Barnett (1953:330) argued that the novelty for the innovator is not quite the same as the novelty for the acceptor. The reason is the philosophical-psychological one that the mental configurations of two or more people are never identical. Even though the acceptor may *think* his "new" configuration is exactly that offered by the innovator, it is not; inevitably the acceptor adds to the novelty of the innovator's "new" idea.

DETECTION AND DOCUMENTATION OF
THE INNOVATION PROCESS

One major problem exists in detecting the analysis, identification, and substitution steps of the innovative process: they must be inferred from an actor's behavior. Substitution, it is true, may be directly observed in behavior—as with the "bald look" mentioned earlier. But who is to say, aside from the actor himself (if he is aware of it), when one configuration is substituted for another if apparent changes in behavior are *not* involved? In fact, Barnett's description of the innovation process is an exercise in logic, liberally laced with the psychology of learning and perception. That is, knowing what we do about human mental activity, there are actually only a limited number of ways in which new mental configurations can emerge—if in fact all configurations stem from previous ones. Barnett succeeded in describing the sequence that seems to fit best with present knowledge. Logically, some sort of analysis *must* take place before units of combination can be identified. And, logically, substitution of the new for the old *must* occur if there is ever to be any change in mental configurations. Barnett's scheme is much more complex than I have attempted to portray here, but the three steps are the basic ones.

Barnett believed that with the proper sorts of data, the three steps (together with their ramifications) can be empirically demonstrated. That is, the pre-existing configurations used in the innovation can be identified, as well as can what happens to them in the innovator's mind. This example comes from a recent religious movement among Indians of the Pacific Northwest:

> The development of Shaker ritual and doctrine reveals many instances of behavioral innovations. . . . John Slocum, the founder of the cult, equated himself with a Catholic priest and so initiated the practices of listening to confessions, using a hand bell to mark intervals in the ritual that he introduced, and wearing a white vestment [Barnett 1953:234; letter references to Barnett's paradigm of innovation omitted].

In this case the configurations are relatively easy to sort out. Other analysts using the same data would probably come to the same conclusions. But what of more complex innovations? Or of situations in which the pre-existing configurations are not so clear-cut? In such instances, Barnett's scheme must be applicable—but this can never be more than an assumption, because it can never be determined one way or the other.

In other words, it must be assumed that if Barnett's scheme is applicable to all cases that he documented, it is applicable as well to cases that he did not, and could not, document. This is scientifically a risky, if necessary, condition. More pressing, though, is the whole issue of getting inside the mind of the individual to account for *specific* manifestations of the innovative process. It is one thing to know the principles of the innovation process; it is another to assert a knowledge of how these principles operate in the mind of a specific individual at a specific point in (past) time, particularly if the innovator in question is not the analyst himself.[1]

Yet this places demands on the model that it is not equipped to handle. Perhaps it is enough to know the range of basic innovative processes without bothering much with an application to specific cases. After all, innovation is not sociocultural change; it is a *source* of change whose inner workings, in the absence of data of unusual detail, can only be assumed. It is, in fact, rather difficult for the analyst to get his teeth into the innovation process itself, except, when data permit, to be able to reconstruct what pre-existing configurations were combined to produce innovation "X". Barnett told us how new ideas originate, and did it in a convincing manner, I think. But the crucial consideration for sociocultural change seems less the process of innovation than factors affecting its nature, rate, and eventual acceptance of its products by the group. To understand these factors, described by Barnett in some detail (1953), it is necessary to consider the *sociocultural context* within which innovations take place; and it is also important to consider the biographical and psychological backgrounds of *advocates* (those who urge acceptance of the innovation by the group) and of *acceptors*.

CONTEXTS, ADVOCATES, ACCEPTORS

Generally, innovation potential will be greater among individuals in sociocultural systems (1) that have a relatively large inventory of culture traits (both material and non-material) and that are relatively "open" in the sense that communication of ideas among various groups is fostered;

[1]This situation is analogous to the state of our knowledge about general evolutionary processes in biology (mutation, selection, drift, and hybridization) as opposed to what little we know about the whys of specific adaptations in the remote past.

(2) in which there is a generally good possibility for immigration into the system;[2] and (3) in which competition between individuals or organizations is not squelched (Barnett 1953:Chap. II). On the negative side, innovative potential is usually quite high in situations of disaster or among groups who feel themselves to be rejected, devalued, or humiliated by other groups in the same sociocultural system. In the latter cases, to say that the innovative potential is greater is not to say that the innovations themselves necessarily will alleviate the disaster or end the humiliation; under such conditions the rate of innovation is likely to be speeded up, and with more innovations, the chances are greater that one of them will be a solution to the problems.

Here it is possible to see some connection between the likelihood of innovation and the potential for sociocultural evolution, for rate of innovation becomes an adaptive factor in situations of ecological stress. And, the wider the range of the cultural inventory, the greater the number of configurations that can be brought to bear in coping with ecological stress—so that, from an innovation perspective, a sociocultural system becomes better able to adapt to changing demands as it becomes more complex (i.e., increases its cultural inventory). So, too, could the "plateaus" of Leslie White's evolutionary scheme (periods of relative stagnation following the major revolutions in energy usage) be described in innovation terms as deliberate attempts on the part of elite power-holders to stifle the communication of ideas and innovative competition. There are qualifications to these generalizations, of course. One of the primary ones is that *rate* of innovations says nothing particular about the *acceptance* of innovations. To borrow from the theme of Elman Service's law of evolutionary potential, a sociocultural system might become so elaborate, so complex, that even though solutions are offered, they cannot be accepted be-

[2]Barnett (1953) cited the impressive contribution of novel ideas made by those who immigrated to the United States. See also McClelland 1964:175; orig. 1962.

cause the system cannot be reorganized along innovative lines. The converse of this generalization is also applicable of course—extremely complex innovations may be *too* complex to be accepted by some groups.

Again, innovation is going on all the time, among all individuals. Only when considered within a sociocultural context, however, can it be understood why groups vary in their rate of innovations or why some types of innovations are more readily accepted than others. Acceptance also usually depends in part upon how, and by whom, the novelty is "sold" to the group, and at this juncture the role of the advocate becomes extremely important.

Barnett pointed out that often the advocates or "salesmen" of the novelty are not those who originally innovated it. Christ had his Paul of Tarsus, and Mohammed his Abu Bekr (Barnett 1953:300–301). True, the great American inventors of the nineteenth century were frequently their own salesmen, holding money-making demonstrations at large public gatherings; but nowadays the cost of necessary equipment and materials, coupled with the economic power of large corporations, has eliminated backyard shop or basement putterers as potentially important contributors. They have all gone to work for the large corporations.

A moment's reflection on the subject will provide the reader with a series of qualities that make a "good" advocate almost anywhere: pleasant personality, probably; expertise in a field relevant to the novelty he advocates (or perhaps merely the *suggestion* of expertise—witness the television commercials for patent medicines that featured actor-advocates dressed in the working garb of physicians); some widespread popularity; and so on. Members of elites, incidentally, do *not* always make good advocates. They may be the objects of hatred rather than of emulation by potential acceptors; or, they may fear a loss of their elite status if they endorse important changes in the sociocultural system (Barnett 1953:404).

It is difficult to generalize briefly or coherently beyond

this about what "types" make good advocates or about what features are shared by those others who accept innovations more readily than their peers. This is because the types partially hinge upon a given sociocultural context. A "good" advocate to Euro-Americans might sound like a braying huckster to an American Indian. A typical "early" acceptor type in one context may be that of the insecure deviant, constantly seeking personal security or identity by eagerly experimenting with a succession of novelties (Barnett 1953:378 ff.). Or, in another context, early acceptors might be found primarily among the secure, "pillar of the community" types who can afford to take the calculated risks involved in trying out something new (Rogers 1962:169–170). However tied they may be to specific contexts, these are issues of great practical as well as theoretical significance, and Barnett and others have offered a series of suggestive hypotheses for further testing.

For Barnett, then, innovation is the basis of all sociocultural change. Diffusion, evolution, stresses and strains within systems—all are ultimately products of the human propensity to create new ideas out of old ones. But, again, there can be no sociocultural change without acceptance of the innovation; and, immediately when we broach the issue of acceptance (or even when attempting to understand a specific innovation), the larger sociocultural context becomes a crucial variable. All this is to say that even though the analytical level focuses upon the individual mental process, no specific example of change is intelligible without invoking variables from the more inclusive sociocultural level of abstraction.

VARIATIONS ON AN INNOVATION THEME: MAZEWAY REFORMULATION

A *mazeway*, according to A. F. C. Wallace (1956:266), is an individual's unique mental image that includes

perceptions of both the maze of physical objects of the environment (internal and external, human and nonhuman) and also of the ways in which this maze can be manipulated by the self and others in order to minimize stress. The mazeway is nature, society, culture, personality, and body image, as seen by one person.

No two mazeways are ever identical among members of the same sociocultural system. What makes the system itself work is a measure of predictability to individual public behavior; for example, whatever the contents of an individual's mazeway, we in this country may be reasonably sure that he will stop his car at a red traffic light.

The mazeway is an individual collection of strategies for reducing stress. It is, like Talcott Parsons' and Wilbert Moore's concept of the social system, a stress-reduction or stress-management mechanism for the individual. And, again analogous to the functionalist conception of the social system, the mazeway of the mature individual tends to change only as much as is necessary to reduce new or different sources of stress. The mazeway can be altered, and behavior changed accordingly by means of the innovation process as outlined by Barnett. To the extent that the new behavior is duplicated (i.e., "accepted" by the group, presumably because others experience stress from the same source), sociocultural change occurs.

For present purposes, it is important to note the linkage between the mazeway concept, functional models, and the process of innovation. But also, the mazeway concept having been introduced it is important to discuss briefly what I regard as one of Wallace's major contributions to the understanding of sociocultural change: the revitalization process.

Occasionally, particularly in imperialistic situations or those otherwise including a somewhat impermeable division between groups of dominating haves and dominated have-nots, but also in natural disasters, war, or other sorts of severe environmental alterations, the stress upon some or all members of the society becomes intolerably great. The list of stress-reducing strategies in members' individual maze-ways has been exhausted without any notable reduction in the stress from the blockage of access to desired goals. At this time, an individual within the group undergoes a sudden and very radical mazeway resynthesis (Wallace 1961:148; 1956:270). Typically this occurs as the result of a dream or trance or some other sort of hallucinatory experience.

The individual "reborn" through his experience and now a "prophet," then reveals essential features of his new mazeway (a "code" including an innovative strategy for dealing with the persistent source of stress) to others who become followers. But they become followers only after they themselves innovate additions to their pre-existing mazeways by means of what Wallace calls *hysterical conversion* (1961:152 ff.). The phenomenon is familiar enough. It occurs in large crowds of people, most of whom are already prepared to seek some sort of solution to their plight; it is induced by suggestive stimuli such as repetitious musical rhythms, repetitious harangues by the prophet, endless dancing, hunger, fatigue, and other factors. The individual may faint, begin convusive twitching, "speak in tongues" (glossolalia), or undergo nothing so physically spectacular; but he is converted to the belief of the prophet and thus believes that a solution to his mental stress is imminent.[3]

A prophet or leader and his followers thus create a social movement of a kind Wallace called a *revitalization movement*, one designed by its adherents to create a more satisfying culture (1961:144). How successful the movement is to this end depends on how effectively it has been organized by the "prophet" or leader and his cadre, how rational its program for change is in face of the realities of the wider sociocultural context (cf. Linton 1943:233), and how successfully the movement adapts to resistance against it. A successful movement eventually becomes "routinized" into the existing sociocultural system, and a new "steady state" or relative equilibrium is established.

[3]R. Firth (1963:242; orig. 1951) might have argued that the act of spectacular conversion is itself a partial alleviation of the mental stress. See also Gerlach and Hine (1970) for the role of conversion in Black Power and Pentecostal movements.

Many revitalization movements in history have been unrealistic by Western standards: often pathetic and bizarre attempts by primitives engaged in a final battle for cultural coherence against the forces of civilization. The Ghost Dances of 1870 and 1890 among American Indians (Mooney 1892–1893) and the series of so-called Cargo Cults among Melanesians (Worsley 1957) are among the best-known examples. But use of terms such as "hysterical" and "bizarre" should not mask the applicability of the revitalization model to contemporary processes among modern nations. As Wallace (1956:277) pointed out, the Russian Communist revolution provides an excellent example of a revitalization movement, as does the more recent revolution in the Peoples' Republic of China. Yippies and Black Muslims and Young Americans for Freedom in this country are examples. Some of these cases suggest that not all leaders of revitalization movements undergo mazeway resynthesis during trances or hallucinations and that not all conversions are necessarily "hysterical." Such terms tend to undermine the eminent shrewdness and realism of some revitalization movements (cf. Gerlach and Hine 1970).

A tendency to focus on the overtly *religious* elements of revitalization efforts (implicit in the use of the term "prophet") may also divert attention from the *political* effectiveness of such movements. I am thinking here specifically of the numerous separatist religious sects in colonial Africa, which in some cases represented the sole means by which politically active Blacks could become influential without risking immediate suppression by the authoritarian colonial regimes. Certainly Wallace himself was cognizant of the often hazy distinction between "religious" and "political" revitalization movements (cf. Gerlach and Hine 1970).

Wallace made the interesting observation that in revitalization movements only the leader (and perhaps a few of his hard-core followers, I would think) undergo a nearly complete mazeway resynthesis. The rank and file converts simply add a new repertoire of public behavior (and presumably an alternative mazeway structure) and are thus capable of reverting to the pre-existing mazeway in the absence of continuing stimuli from the movement. This is explicitly recognized by many revolutionary leaders in their efforts to maintain some measure of revolutionary or revitalization emotion among their followers once the immediate obstacles have been overcome. Hence the phenomenon of periodic purges of members who do not display the proper enthusiasm, and the almost constant attempts to convince the rank and file that their sources of stress have by no means been eliminated. The leader himself never reverts to a pre-existing mazeway. He remains a resynthesized "prophet" with "almost paranoid intensity and stability" (Wallace 1961:154).

In Wallace's words,

It is impossible to exaggerate the importance of these two psychological processes [mazeway resynthesis and hysterical conversion] for culture change, for they make possible the rapid substitution of a new cultural *Gestalt* for an old, and thus the rapid cultural transformation of whole populations. Without this mechanism, the cultural transformation of the 600,000,000 people of China by the Communists could not have occurred; nor the Communist-led revitalization and expansion of the USSR; nor the American Revolution; nor the Protestant Reformation; nor the rise and spread of Christianity, Mohammedanism, and Buddhism [1961:154–55].

With all due acknowledgement of the importance of innovation and mazeway reformulation as general processes, let me restate the problems with them as useful analytical tools. As general processes analogous to reproductive fitness in evolutionary biology, they are logical and helpful in understanding in the abstract what happens within individual minds in situations of sociocultural change. But, like reproductive fitness, without extraordinarily detailed data they are unable to account for the specific changes in a specific sociocultural system at a specific time in any but a superficial and even circular way: In what ways does the mazeway change in situation "X"? In ways designed to reduce the amount of stress on the individual. How much stress is necessary to produce such change? Enough to change the mazeway configuration. In other words, the concepts describe what *must* take place, but they often cannot reveal how in fact the processes do (or did) take place in a specific instance. They depend on sociocultural, biological, and natural environmental factors for their specific qualities. This larger context is so important that, without extraordinarily detailed data, a general knowledge of how innovation and mazeway resynthesis operate is helpful but virtually incidental to processual analysis of a given sociocultural change.

Achievement Motivation

So now we come to a fundamental processual issue in the understanding of sociocultural change: what is the relationship between the dynamics of individual motivation and the dynamics of the sociocultural system? A psychologist, David McClelland, and his associates have provided some interesting, suggestive insights as a result of over twenty years of research on achievement motivation in human groups (McClelland 1961; 1964; orig. 1962; McClelland and Winter 1969).

There are several assumptions basic to the achievement motivation theory: one is that human beings everywhere have basic motivations toward achievement (i.e., the attainment of excellence or mastery), toward power (the manipulation of others), and toward affiliation (harmonious personal relations with others). Individuals vary in the extent to which one or another of these motivations is dominant in their interaction with their external environment (including other individuals). The relative strength of these motivations might be measured empirically through such instruments as Thematic Apperception Tests (in which the subject is shown a series of pictures of individuals in various settings and is asked to compose a story explaining each picture) or other tests that can be devised by researchers.

McClelland and others concentrated on achievement motivation as being most crucial to economic development of the individual and (theoretically) of the sociocultural system. They assumed that economic development was in turn crucial for development in other aspects of the sociocultural system in the modern world. They were, in short, interested in seeking answers to pressing practical problems of modernization and were less concerned with reconstructing the past. They were also anxious to add to existing theory on the psychology of motivation.

In their research they repeatedly found a high correlation between a strong individual need or motivation for achievement and success in business (McClelland 1964:168 ff.; orig. 1962), as well as a tendency for those with high achievement motivation (abbreviated n Ach) to gravitate to business rather than to other professions.

Now, if the individual n Ach could vary, what about the n Ach of entire groups or nations? The hypothesis was that such intergroup differences could be documented, but not, for obvious reasons, by administering thousands of Thematic Apperception Tests (TATs). Instead, the researchers chose what they considered the equivalent of the TAT at the group level: popular stories transmitted to children in preadolescent years, either orally or in the form of schoolbooks. Based on the number of themes in this literature that were clearly transmitting achievement orientation rather than power or affiliation, the analysts were able to construct a ranking of nations as to the dominance of the achievement motive in national culture.

Next, they attempted to link the national achievement motivation with national economic development. By using "kilowatt hours of electricity produced" as a rough but best available measure of contemporary total development, they found that there was a significant correlation between the achievement theme and subsequent national economic development (McClelland 1964:171 ff.; orig. 1962). Furthermore, when data were available, they were able to demonstrate that this correlation had existed historically—in England, for example.

There were two waves of economic growth [in a three hundred year period] . . ., one smaller one around 1600 and a much larger one around 1800 at the beginning of the Industrial Revolution. Each wave was preceded by a wave of concern for achievement reflected in popular literature, a smaller one prior to the growth spurt around 1600 and a larger one prior to the Industrial Revolution [McClelland 1964: 170–171; orig. 1962].

The fact that economic development occurred *following* the rise in achievement motivation suggests that the *n* Ach was one (but not *the*) causal factor in the development. McClelland's own comment was less qualified: "What clearer evidence could one ask for? What people are concerned about determines what they do, and what they do determines the outcome of history!" (1964:171; orig. 1962).

There is the problem of determining the causes of achievement motivation in a given sociocultural system, and on this subject McClelland and associates have not been clear. The need is instilled in children through child-rearing techniques and education, and it has followed sweeping revolutions such as those of the Communists in China and Russia, for example. But these findings simply pass the question on to other, pre-exisiting factors. Whatever its ultimate causes, however, early in the research it was assumed to be a very basic motivation, presumably learned early in life. As such, according to prevailing psychological theory, it could not be easily instilled in adults.

The implication of this assumption was gloomy for those interested in fomenting developmental change (see Kunkel 1970:98 ff.). In a sense, it offered no alternatives to the *status quo* of some "underdeveloped" areas whose populations lacked a strong n Ach. Regardless of the amount of material aid poured into these areas, without n Ach in at least a portion of the population there could be no lasting developmental change. McClelland and his team finally decided to challenge the basic assumption: to try to instill an achievement motivation in adults through an intensive but brief (5–10 days) educational experience. If it worked, the program could provide a valuable tool for developmental change at a very low cost (leaving aside here the moral issues involved, which McClelland and Winter [1969] described in some detail).

The series of experimental seminars held in various countries produced evidence that the achievement motive could be instilled in some but not all of the participants.[4] That it could be instilled at all was of real significance, but the crucial issue for sociocultural change was *how such educational programs affected the community*. Unfortunately, a research design to determine this had to be abandoned for lack of funds. The best that can be done to date is to project the significance of the seminar results into a wider context and to estimate the implications for significant change (McClelland and Winter 1969).

One of the implications is that, as with innovation, achievement motivation is partially dependent on sociocultural variables—not merely for its presence or absence, perhaps, but also for its net impact on the sociocultural system. Stated formally, it appears to be a necessary but not sufficient factor in economic development. Of determining importance is the *opportunity structure*, that is, the possibilities in the system that achievement motivation can be rewarded in some way.

It cannot be stressed too often that all the evidence showing the importance of n Ach for business or entrepreneurial success

[4]The procedures used in the seminars were described by McClelland and Winter (1969). Basically they amounted to familiarizing the students with the achievement motivation research, sensitizing them to achievement motivation cues in personal behavior patterns, and having them practice "achieving" behavior in a series of role-taking exercises.

applies largely to situations in which opportunity is held more or less constant across individuals or firms, and where success is at least moderately probable [McClelland and Winter 1969:16].

For example, as a group, businessmen who took the seminar in India showed a significantly higher level of entrepreneurial activity two years later than a control group who had not taken the course. But those who were more active had an important feature in common: they were in a position either to direct or heavily influence procedures in their business firms. Those taking the course who were not in such a structural position did not increase their entrepreneurial activity. For achievement motivation in a population to lead to sociocultural change, there must be some perceived chance of success for "new" techniques. Conversely, when there are few or no perceived opportunities for success, the achievement motivation of the group may decrease. But both—achievement motivation *and* opportunity—are necessary for change. Providing opportunities alone, without n Ach, is often not enough to produce significant alterations in the pre-existing sociocultural system (McClelland 1964:174; orig. 1962), as experts in directed cultural change know very well (cf. Bee 1970).

Now, "opportunity" is ultimately what the achiever himself perceives about his chances for success in a proposed undertaking. And, by definition, a sociocultural system is composed of interrelated components. This means that for the individual the opportunities in the economic component of his existence may be offset by barriers in the religious realm, or in the more inclusive value system. Often these cultural barriers are conceived in terms such as "traditionalism" or "fatalism" or "image of limited good" (Foster 1965). While McClelland's data are not conclusive, they suggest that where the potent combination of n Ach and opportunities exists, the traditionalistic or fatalistic factors are *not necessarily* hindrances so long as the individual is left to decide for himself how best to achieve. In their study of Indian businessmen, for example, McClelland and Winter found that the seminar participants judged to be "traditional" were just as active after the course as the "modern" ones.

> How is it that people who were cautiously fatalistic, who avoided conflict, who did not believe in planning, and who strictly followed traditional caste rules were just as likely to expand their businesses after achievement motivation training as those who claimed to be modern on all these issues? The conclusion seems compelling that much of what has been written about the changes in attitudes that are necessary for business improvement is misleading. . . . What does seem to be essential is that the man develop a strong faith in himself as an origin or agent of change, as someone who can solve problems efficaciously on his own. . . . The most effective strategy, in other words, appears to be to change the man's self-image by direct instruction on this key point, and then to leave the rest to him [McClelland and Winter 1969:349].

But there must be a limit to the extent that traditional values can be compatible with individual achievement. For example, it is a rich Sioux cattleman indeed who can conscientiously adhere to the traditional practices of sharing his abundance with less well-to-do relatives and still show signs of continuing economic achievement (cf. Eicher 1961–1962:193). Unless his resources are great, he in time would be forced either to fly in the faces of tradition and needy relatives for the sake of his own enterprise or to allow tradition to rule and let his cattle herds dwindle. In the complex, modern society, tradition may be much less of a barrier than it is in the closed, corporate folk community (Wolf 1957).

A related issue is what effect the competition resulting from achievement motivation has in situations where economic resources are limited. The achievers' gains in such situations may be others' losses, resulting in a net lowering of the total productive output of the group (McClelland and Winter 1969:94). McClelland and Winter's response to this argument was not very satisfactory: n Ach, they asserted, is not inherently a need to compete with others but is, instead, a drive for excellence. Competition exclusively for scarce resources is a motivation for power, not achievement, in their terms. Yet clearly when achievement is expressed in terms of gaining greater profits and when the total profit possibilities are limited, it is difficult to see how n Ach does not involve competition. Again, the potential effects of this situation in communities with limited resources deserve careful consideration by development agencies.

Recast in terms of the theme of process or mechanisms of change, achievement motivation is an important psychological factor that can have an effect on the sociocultural system. It is one kind of motivation to innovate, translated into a useful analytical concept because its strength can be inferred quantitatively. Obviously, it cannot predict what innovations will be made; but it can predict what group is most likely to produce economic innovations, and it can even say something about a group's potential for economic development (i.e., it can say something about whether certain sorts of innovations are likely to be accepted). It can do so, however, only when other crucial variables in the sociocultural system—such as opportunity structure and resource limitations—are taken into consideration. As is true of innovation, then, the influence of achievement motivation on sociocultural change is most usefully observed in the context of a given sociocultural system. Yet crucial information is lacking, because the impact of a group of individuals with high n Ach has still not been studied by the McClelland team.

Psychological Factors in Sociocultural Processes

A combination of two analytical levels is needed to assess psychological influences in a specific case of sociocultural change: that of individual behavior and that of the sociocultural system. In a sense, we are confronted at the individual psychological level of analysis with a problem similar to that at the level of general sociocultural evolution: abstract processes described at either the most general or the individual level are not in themselves sufficient to account for changes in specific sociocultural systems over given periods of time. This is not to detract from their significance. To perpetuate the overused analogy, it would be almost as unthinkable to abandon innovation or mazeway reformulation or achievement need as to abandon mutation and natural selection as general processual concepts in biology.

Speaking of sociocultural evolution, the reader may by now be asking, "Which approach is the *right* one, evolution or innovation?" The answer quite obviously depends on what sorts of analytical questions the researcher is asking. The two approaches are applicable to different sorts of problems. If, for example, the objective is a reconstruction of changes induced by ecological stimuli in sociocultural systems, then innovation is not very helpful, particularly if the changes occurred in the remote past. Or, if one wishes to trace the relationship between plant domestication and sociocultural development, innovation is not a crucial issue. In both cases it is assumed to be operative, but it is not and cannot be the focus of the research. If, on the other hand, the analysis seeks answers to the question, "What effect did John Slocum and Mud Bay Lewis have on the Indian Shaker religion of northwestern America?" (Barnett 1953) then obviously innovation is a crucial consideration. Or, if a medical organization wishes to know the impact of the introduction of new techniques such as acupuncture on the practices of its members, innovation-acceptance is a valuable analytical approach.

There are clearly some "middle range" issues that are amenable to either type of approach—evolutionary or innovational. Skillful analysts can isolate both necessary and sufficient determinants in the specific sociocultural system alone without invoking psychological variables (functional-ists as well as evolutionists take this perspective). Others insist that in such cases psychological variables are necessary (if not sufficient). It seems unproductive to argue about which approach is "best" without also including a consider-ation of the types of problems the approaches are designed to cope with and the availability of relevant data.

In the next chapter I want to continue the theme of the interrelationship of individual and sociocultural factors in change. I have intended the discussion here in part as an introduction to what follows, by isolating concepts like innovation and achievement motivation and discussing the problems of studying individual psychological variables in sociocultural change. But I must add that I have not touched at all upon a significant body of research into the *effects* of sociocultural change upon individual psychology. Such important questions about the extent to which differ-ences in sociocultural adaptation are reflected in psychologi-cal adaptation to change have been studied by scholars such as A. I. Hallowell, George and Louise Spindler, and A. F. C. Wallace. They have been ignored here for the sake of focusing on the causal interrelationships between psycho-logical and sociocultural factors. I have been asking what psychological processes are involved in processes of change, and I have been ignoring what effect sociocultural change has on the mental processes of individuals.

CHAPTER EIGHT

ENTREPRENEURS, BROKERS, AND DECISION-MAKING

A GAIN the question must be asked: *what* is it that is changing in sociocultural change? For Homer Barnett (1953), the changing elements were ideas or individual mental configurations. For A. F. C. Wallace (1961), they were mazeways. For others, including some functionalists and evolutionists whose works have already been described, the *forms* of sociocultural subsystems were what changed: kinship (Murdock 1949); politics (Fried 1967; Sahlins 1958); ritual (Geertz 1957); economics (Dalton 1971). Yet in most cases the raw data came from a single source: individual human behavior. Innovation, strictly speaking, is not behavior; it is a mental process that may or may not lead to behavior. Economic change, to be sure, involves behavior, but often at such an abstract level that the individual's contribution to the pattern is difficult to handle analytically.

The several approaches synthesized in this chapter have in common a focus on the behavior of individuals as a locus of sociocultural change processes. None of them represents a rejection of the innovation theory. They have simply been less preoccupied with the precise individual mental processes involved. They also have assumed a good deal about motivation and have not bothered to prove or disprove the presence of certain motivational universals. And they have recognized explicitly that it is interaction between indi-

196

viduals in a specific context that is the stuff of sociocultural forms—that to understand what gives rise to forms and how they change, the analyst must focus on individual interactions in specific settings (e.g., Barth 1967).

Basic Assumptions of the Approaches

Individual behavior involves individual decision-making. "What will work?" "What is considered proper?" and "How is this behavior going to help me?" are questions that most of us have asked ourselves at some time during our lives before deciding how to act in a given situation. By no means all behavior involves this deliberate calculation; it may be irrelevant in some actions, such as spontaneous expressions of happiness. Or it may be subconscious or "automatic," ingrained through years of enculturation— such as stopping at a red traffic light. Yet few actions of consequence from the individual's perspective are taken without first thinking about alternatives, and it is these actions that generally have the greatest significance for sociocultural change.

The decisions are not made in a vacuum. Depending on the nature of the action, other individuals' behavior is a factor to be considered; the prevailing system of values in the group is another; the natural environmental setting may be another; the amount of anticipated benefit from various action alternatives is yet another. In short, decisions about which behavior is "best" in a given situation always involve considerations of *incentives* and *constraints* surrounding alternatives available—the perceived advantages and the limitations or drawbacks.

Social scientists are able to describe patterns or forms of a group's social structure or culture to the extent that there is general consistency to the decisions of its individual mem-

bers—to the extent, that is, that individual members tend
to opt for the same sorts of behavior in a given context
labeled "economic" or "political" or "ritual." This implies,
then, that in any sociocultural system, there will be a general
agreement among members about the nature and effectiveness of various incentives and constraints, even though the
precise individual perceptions of these may vary (cf. A. F. C.
Wallace's "organization of diversity" concept [1961:27 ff.]).
Obviously, the general *agreement* makes for stability of the
system; the *variations* in individual perceptions are a potential source of change, as suggested in Barnett's innovation
model.

Another basic assumption is derived from what is known
in economics as the "maximization" model (e.g., McClelland and Winter 1969): *that human beings everywhere tend
to choose the personal action that they feel will gain them
the greatest benefit* (or avoid the greatest loss) *with the
smallest expenditure of resources* (Barth 1963; 1966; 1967;
Erasmus 1961; Bailey 1960; Kunkel 1970). Whether the
assumption is justified has been hotly debated (Hempel
1965:463 ff.; as cited in Kunkel 1970:32); but if we grant
that it is, if it is to be of use in the study of sociocultural
change it must be carefully qualified: for one thing, not
all behavior has such a "maximizing" motivation behind it.
And "benefit" is not always calculated in the same way,
either within a given cultural system or among different
cultures. Benefit could be monetary increase, but it could
also be social recognition of one's expertise; it could be the
avoidance of unpleasant situations; or it could be a nebulous
mental state such as a "sense of accomplishment." This
wide range of variation presents certain methodological
problems that I will describe later on. "Expenditure of
resources" is also a calculation involving different elements
in different situations. Money and other forms of material
wealth are, of course, resources; but so is time, and so is
physical energy or effort; so is prestige, or political power to
influence the decisions of others. It would thus be very

misleading to conceive of "maximization" in narrowly economic terms, although among its most obvious examples are those involving economic transactions. This assumption about maximization in decision-making is not meant to imply the more general assumption that all human beings are always conniving seekers of self-gratification. Again, not all behavior is maximizing, and that which is may be constrained by the existing values system in the group as well as by a number of important physical or social limitations. And behavior aimed at maximization is not always successful, either—successful from the actor's perspective, that is.

Next, it is necessary to assume a condition that McClelland's research has documented in part: that although all individuals make decisions from among behavioral alternatives, there are some who tend to push the constraints harder than others or to circumvent some of them, so as to create new alternatives. Typically, such individuals are at the same time more concerned with maximization than are others in their group. Remember, however, that McClelland carefully limited his focus to *achievement* motivation, or to the urge to maximize one's potential for excellence. According to the assumption being discussed here, this is but one sort of maximization; others are involved as well.

Such individuals, who exist to a greater or lesser extent in all cultures, have been called "entrepreneurs" by economists, a term picked up by other social scientists and applied to individuals whose maximization is not necessarily economic in nature (Barth 1963; Kunkle 1970; Bailey 1960, esp. 256–257). Eric Wolf has suggested "cultural broker" as a term that refers to individuals engaging in a more restricted type of entrepreneurship, one particularly common in acculturation situations (Wolf 1965; orig. 1956).

Entrepreneurs tend to be more willing to take risks than others in their group; they tend to be the first to try out new techniques of business, politics, or other social inter-

action. They tend to take quick advantage of new opportunities for maximization whether these new opportunities are
the result of changes elsewhere in the sociocultural system
or its physical setting, or are simply old conditions perceived
in new ways by the entrepreneurs themselves—again, the
innovation described by Barnett (1953). Like all decisions,
some of those made by entrepreneurs are bound to be
wrong, and they may lose everything. But sometimes their
decisions lead to greater maximization, and herein lies the
importance of the entrepreneur for sociocultural change.

If the entrepreneur's new ways of allocating resources
(whatever these may be) have been successful in increasing
his benefit with less expenditure, then his actions are apt
to be imitated by others in his group—to the extent that
his techniques become known, to the extent that others
share his ideas of what constitutes "benefit," and to the
extent that they have similar resources to marshall and
expend in similar ways. If the new behavior is spread
through the group and recurs consistently enough to become
institutionalized as "the way to do things," sociocultural
change has taken place.

With all these assumptions and qualifications, then, it is
argued that one of the approaches to the genesis of sociocultural change in a group is to focus upon the activities of
entrepreneurs. But it is important to remember that entrepreneurial activities are significant in sociocultural change
*only to the extent that they have an effect on the behavior
of others in the group.* If this is not kept in mind by the
analyst, what results is a series of microstudies focused on
entrepreneurial behavior without any sense of the impact
of this behavior on others. Again, this has methodological
implications that will be discussed later.

These several assumptions add up to a view of the sociocultural system and its dynamics which is as follows: every
system is the abstracted pattern of individual behavior, much
of which is the result of individual choices from a number
of perceived alternatives. The choices are made after con-

sidering the perceived incentives and limitations or constraints of each alternative. Individuals tend to choose the alternatives that offer the highest personal benefit at the least cost (in terms of resources). A change in an individual's behavior is the result of a perceived change in the incentives and/or constraints surrounding a set of alternatives. Some individuals more readily than others tend to perceive these changes and alter their behavior in an attempt to exploit their opportunities. Under certain conditions, these new behavior patterns become institutionalized in the group, and sociocultural change has taken place.

Constraints: A Pivotal Consideration

Much of the literature has described at length the relative importance of several types of constraints as variables in sociocultural change. I want to review the major factors here, but I must remind the reader that the precise nature and effectiveness of each varies from case to case.

Values—the conceptions of what is good, desirable, or proper shared among group members—operate in two ways. On the one hand, they include the goals that an individual ought to strive toward and the basis for calculating the relative pay-offs of the various alternatives. On the other hand, they set limitations on the range of alternatives and on the nature of the pay-offs. For example, in our society, it is considered "good" to have a great deal of money (a goal), and how much money can be received from each of a series of alternatives for economic behavior is a factor in deciding which alternative to accept. Yet values also limit the alternatives by specifying which are "acceptable" and which are not. One can inherit money, which is all right with the prevailing value system. One can also work his fingers to the bone to become a "self-made man," which is even more in accord with the value system. But one should not work his fingers to the bone in staging a robbery, because robbery is not a valued means in mass society. Thus, robbery, for many persons at least, would be quickly eliminated as a behavioral alternative for getting money. Values, from this perspective, are forces of persistence, operating as selective factors on the range of behavioral alternatives.

Yet, values themselves obviously change through time (cf. Rokeach 1973). Some persons in our society have opted for behavior that explicitly rejects "more money" as an economic goal in favor of "just making enough to get by." For these persons, the valued goals have changed perhaps because the means of reaching the goals have been cut off. In other words, the persistence of valued goals in a group may be based in part upon the existence of the group's behavioral means of attaining them. It is also possible to conceive of situations in which the goals themselves remain unchanged but the range of "acceptable" behavior to reach them becomes broader or narrower. In "ends justify means" fashion, robbery or violence may become valued behavior for a group desperately needing money or seeking an end to other sorts of deprivation. It is in such situations (such as the violent revolution engendered by class conflict) that the innovative behavior of entrepreneurs can have an important impact. The more general point is that values and behavior can be viewed as influencing each other in a circular fashion.[1] Values tend to limit behavioral alternatives, but new behavioral alternatives carry with them the potential for changing pre-existing values.

As we know from earlier chapters, *material* factors as constraints on behavior were recognized even before the advent of Marxist materialism. They impinge most evidently in problems of economics or ecological adaptation, although they are by no means limited to these contexts:

[1]The role of values in a group's life-way has been discussed by Ayoub (1968), Barth (1966), and Rokeach (1973).

for example, the relationship between political power and control of material resources, or that between social structure and exploitation of material resources. I have already described in some detail the ramifications of material factors in sociocultural change, and it would be needlessly redundant to go over them again in the approach now being considered. It is necessary, however, to point out that an important consideration is the perspective of the *actors* regarding material constraints. An "objective" analysis of the potential of a given natural environment cannot necessarily give an insight into the ways in which the people are using it, for example. The people may recognize clearly that they are not making the most efficient use of their habitat's potential but may be prohibited from doing so or may not wish to do so because of other sorts of constraints, material or nonmaterial. Further, changes in the nature and effectiveness of material constraints may be a result of objectively documented changes in material conditions, but they need not be; changes in actors' *perceptions* of the conditions can be equally significant as a source of alternative behavior patterns even though the conditions themselves remain objectively unchanged.

No battle lines have been drawn among proponents of the decision-making approach to change regarding which—values or material factors—are the most important constraints. In fact, as implied in the discussion so far, both are considered operative, and they can affect each other in given situations. A masterful analysis of the mutual influence of values and material constraints was provided by Bennett (1969) in his study of adaptive strategies among plainsmen of Canada.[2] He noted, for example, that a rancher's job makes it practically impossible for him to take a vacation; he must stay close to his ranch and stock to ensure that

[2]Bennett's study actually lies in the realm of cultural ecology, but has been included as an example of the decision-making approach for reasons I will make clear later on.

all goes well. This material constraint is reflected in a prevailing set of values in which an individual derives pride from his "stability and localism" (Bennett 1969:185). Elsewhere in the study Bennett noted that the nature of the local environment makes raising sheep a much more productive enterprise than cattle ranching. But among the ranchers there is a stigma against sheep and sheepherders, and the ranchers place a positive value on the less productive enterprise (Bennett 1969:182). This latter example serves also to show how maximization must always be understood within a particular set of constraints perceived by the actors themselves.

In addition to values and material conditions as variable factors, certain *social structural* conditions can affect the impact of entrepreneurial behavior. Mead (1964), as Barnett (1953), has described the crucial importance of *communication* of information between entrepreneurs and the population at large, for example. New patterns of maximization will never catch on if they cannot become known to others. (I should add that in certain contexts, the entrepreneur may deliberately suppress information about new techniques until he is able to get the jump on his competitors). The easier it is to communicate ideas among members of a group (i.e., the fewer the social structural barriers to communication), the greater the chances of acceptance of new behavior judged to be favorable or advantageous. Here, too, it is possible to see how the social structural factors can be influenced by both material and valuational ones. Communication may be difficult in areas of dispersed settlement and rugged terrain without systems of roads or electricity. Communication may also be inhibited between members of different socioeconomic strata, in part because it is not considered "proper" for the rich or powerful to associate with the poor.

Typically, too, the acceptance of new ideas by the group at large depends to an extent on the group of close associates surrounding entrepreneurs. Individuals in this group may play the role of advocates (Barnett 1953) in bringing new behavioral alternatives from the entrepreneurs to the larger population. They may also play the role of advisors to the entrepreneurs, feeding them needed information or suggesting modifications of entrepreneurial techniques. Successful businessmen or politicians usually have formal or informal staffs that serve both functions. Mead (1964:xviii) used the concept of *evolutionary cluster* to refer to such groups:

> among the conditions which make it possible for a man of exceptional ability—that type of exceptional ability which we call genius—to make a contribution to cultural change is the special composition of the cluster of individuals with whom he interacts and through whom he interacts also with others.

One of the implicit points here is that communication of information is crucial in two directions: *from* the entrepreneur to the larger population, and *to* the entrepreneur from a variety of sources. Social structural features may facilitate and/or inhibit this communication.

Another social structural feature of potential importance is the extent to which membership in a group is "fixed" instead of "flexible." Examples of "fixed membership groups" include modern Indian tribes (Clifton 1965) or other organizations in which membership is acquired instead of achieved. Fixed membership groups, Plotnicov (1962) suggested, may tend on the whole to be better able to cope with pressures to change than other groups whose membership is flexible (i.e., based on achieved criteria or bound together only by common interest). Members' responses have a wider potential range, because loss of their fixed membership is not a major threat to their innovativeness. In theory, then, the Kickapoo tribe of Indians should be potentially more innovative than the Republican Party or the Congregational Church when confronted by stimuli for change.

Detection and Documentation of Change

So much for the abstract summary. But how can it be applied to real-life situations? For example, as accurate as it may be to say that sociocultural systems are patterns originated or generated by individual behavior, it is obvious that no one observer, or even a small team armed with videotape equipment, is capable of documenting all examples of individual behavior in all contexts. The task has to be focused on the behavior of *some* individuals in *some* contexts, and the formidable methodological decision involves which individuals in which contexts should receive major attention as potential harbingers of change. It is in choosing a context that the analyst may invoke his own preconceptions about prime movers or pivotal factors in sociocultural change. For many, economics, politics, and ecological adaptation are crucial contexts for any group's existence and for the study of dynamics. Even these contexts must usually be narrowed to consider the economics of the marketplace, the politics of local-national level interaction, or the ecology of herdsmen in a single sociocultural system. The assumption usually is that a study of new alternatives and decisions in any one of these settings has important implications for change in the entire system, even if the implications themselves are not fully traced out.

As for individuals within the selected context, most analysts have tended to focus on entrepreneurs or brokers, because it is by these individuals that the initial steps in the change process are usually taken. Ideally, however, the focus must shift at some point to those who either accept or reject the entrepreneur's innovations, if the aim is to understand how new ideas can lead to change in group behavior patterns.

To understand an existing sociocultural system (or a portion of it) and to detect the emergence of new behavior patterns, the analyst must determine the major constraints that limit the range of behavioral alternatives. This is a very ticklish operation, because no matter how exhaustive the investigation or how intimately familiar the analyst is with the subjects of his study, it is still difficult to know for certain how a given entrepreneur perceives the constraints limiting his alternatives in a given context. This takes us back to the emic-etic issue raised in the first chapter.

From whose perspective are the constraints best portrayed, the analyst's or the actor's? Some (e.g., Barth 1967; Bailey 1960) argue that it is the actor's perceptions that are important and ought to be the point of reference, and this has been assumed in the discussion so far. Yet it is practically impossible to climb inside another man's mind, particularly when he belongs to an alien cultural tradition. So, without really confronting this methodological issue head on, the analysts seem content to focus on the more obvious constraints and incentives inferred from their observations of behavior and its settings. And, they limit themselves to the settings in which the major constraints and incentives are relatively more clear-cut for both observer and actor—such as economics or ecological adaptation—rather than settings in which the major constraints may be more covert—such as the composition of love poems or shamanistic practices. Therefore, *the description of "relevant" constraints will always contain an element of approximation, and no analyst can legitimately insist that he has accounted for all the constraints operating upon actors' behavior in a given situation.*

The identity of the entrepreneurs and the nature of the constraints on their behavior must be determined by the timeworn ethnographic technique of intensive observer involvement in the system being studied. He must participate as much as possible in the life of the group, constantly noting the behavior of its members. He conducts extensive interviews with key informants and collects responses to survey-type questionnaires. And the involvement must usually be a lengthy one, because values and other sorts of constraints are not readily detected by one who is not intimately familiar with the behavior patterns and environment of the group.

The Events of Change

But, according to this approach, what does the analyst look for, even if we assume he has narrowed his context to economic or political behavior and has singled out the individuals he believes to be entrepreneurs? Obviously, he must concern himself with the situations that have potential for producing change in the pre-existing system, situations that Mead (1964) called the "points of divergence" in the flow of systemic processes, points at which an individual is presented with a chance to change his pattern of resource allocation in the hope of greater benefit.

Where to look for these points of divergence depends on the kind of context the analyst chooses to observe. For Bailey (1960), whose focus was upon political change among hill tribes in India, the focal points were conflicts between political rivals. He described in detail the principal individuals involved in the conflict, the behavioral alternatives that they had to choose from, and the tactics they employed. In essence, and translated into the jargon used in this chapter, he found that there were three different sets of alternatives for behavior in political conflict among the Konds of India. One set included the traditional alternatives of *tribal* politics; another included patterns of conflict in *caste* interaction. And, more recently, the influence of the *national government* on the local villages revealed a third set to local political entrepreneurs. Whereas several generations ago, a given local political or legal issue sparked conflict waged according to the limits of tribe or caste alternatives, modern entrepreneurs are increasingly choosing their tactics from alternatives in the national set during conflicts over local issues. Bailey offered an example of an entrepreneur's unsuccessful attempt to use a new set of alternatives to his advantage:

[A] man from Rupamendi attempted to use his role as a citizen of India and as a tax-payer, whose name appeared on the Record of Rights, to own and cultivate land in Baderi. His [choice of action] . . . was an appeal to a system of land-holding which was in conflict with the traditional land-holding system of the Konds. The latter lays it down that no-one who is not a member of the village community ought to hold land in the village. The [national] Government system implicitly says that community-membership is irrelevant to the holding of land. But the [action] . . . failed. . . . This case shows that [choices of new alternatives] . . . lead to structural change *only when they are usually successful, and when the actor by directing his allegiance elsewhere gains his end* [Bailey 1960:252–253; italics added]

Bailey (1960:253) further argued that disputes in the political arena can have two outcomes: they can reaffirm the existing set of alternatives by squelching the effectiveness of new ones; or they can demonstrate that the pre-existing alternatives are no longer perceived to be the most efficient for personal maximization and that they must give way to new ones. The latter outcome "is, so to speak, a proclamation of social change."

Bailey's research tactic was to focus on events of political conflict concerning a single or related set of issues: power and landholding in a village and its environs. He then analyzed the disputes as cases of individual decision-making from among different sets of alternatives. By interviews and intensive dissecting of the tactics in the dispute he was able to determine the major constraints operating for the principal actors and could determine not only why one set of behaviors was chosen by an actor but also why others were not. And within broad limits he was able to detect trends of change, such as a weakening of traditional clan alliances as constraints in political behavior.

Margaret Mead (1964) traced the impact of an entrepreneur in the South Pacific during a revitalization movement in 1946. The man, Paliau, and a group of followers capitalized on the effects of a preceding Cargo Cult movement in the area of the Admiralty Islands (the one briefly described in Chapter One, in which people destroyed most materials of their pre-existing way of life in hopes of the miraculous arrival of new material goods from across the sea). When the cargo did not appear, the peoples of the region were at a point of divergence, ready for new alternatives. Paliau, aptly dubbed "the man who met the hour" (Mead 1956:165), appeared and with the help of his evolutionary cluster presented a new program for action that the people accepted. Mead's tactic in this case was to attempt to document carefully the key decisions made by Paliau himself, the role of his cluster of lieutenants, and the sociocultural context in which the events of change occurred. In this way she felt she could assess the impact of this particular entrepreneur on the larger population and thus gain some insight into the role of entrepreneurs and evolutionary clusters in sociocultural change.

Fredrik Barth (1963) and his colleagues have compiled an anthology of essays that focus on the role of the economic and political entrepreneur in sociocultural change in northern Norway. By knowing some of the sociocultural background and by observing in detail entrepreneurs' public behavior in economic or political contexts, they have succeeded in spelling out the important constraints that operate in the selection of behavioral alternatives. Specific events have been carefully dissected to wring out all possible information about the relative effectiveness of the several important constraints and incentives. In one of the essays, Harald Eidheim (1963) analysed a politician's behavior in a manner quite similar to the approach employed by Bailey (1960).

So the analyst zeros in on particular events: political meetings, religious revivals, fishing for herring, buying and selling commodities, or whatever, according to the objectives of his research. As the events unfold he is careful to note the behavior of key individuals in the events and to note the factors that seem to impinge on their behavior. He is alert for changes in either behavior or constraints in a series of similar events through time; and he tries to determine the impact of the changes on the group as a whole. This is a large order for a single analyst operating alone. It is perhaps best conducted by a team, whose individual members share a common perspective on the research problem. Even under these circumstances, however, *it may well be fruitless in the detection of dynamic mechanisms* unless the research setting has been carefully selected.

Methodological Problems in the Event-Analysis Approach

However much insight he may gain into the persisting systemic structure by such an approach, there is no assurance that the analyst will be able to witness the sorts of decisions that lead to eventual change. There are several ways in which this risk can be reduced. One is to select a group for whom major *material* constraints have been recently (or are about to be) changed. Many efforts at international development, for example, include hydroelectric projects, massive technological assistance, or resettlement schemes. Such programs are obvious alterations of existing material constraints for target groups, and the chances are good that their maximization behavior will be altered as a result. An analyst can gain information about such projects before he commits a great deal of time and effort to finding a site for his research.

But the contexts need not be restricted to "development." Occasionally, nature intervenes to produce radical changes in existing constraints—such as a typhoon on Ulithi (Lessa 1964) or volcanic eruptions on Tristan da Cunha. Less often, but perhaps more happily, a group may benefit from windfalls such as being "discovered" by jet-set tourists eager to immerse themselves in exotica or from learning that they are living on top of rich deposits of some valuable mineral. (I should add hastily that these may be mixed blessings, however.) Any of these circumstances may lead to significant sociocultural change, and the analyst may be able to time his arrival in the local setting so as to witness the effects of the new constraints on the behavior of members of the group.

Or, the analyst may choose to study the mechanisms involved in a series of sociocultural changes that have already occurred, much as Mead (1964) did in her reconstruction of the events leading to acceptance of the Paliau movement in the South Pacific. The task involves reconstruction of fairly minute details, so as to provide the clearest documentation of change mechanisms and the role of individual decisions; therefore, the analyst must not allow too much time to elapse between the series of changes and his visit to the group involved.

A third, and much less satisfactory alternative is to rely heavily on documentary evidence in tracing the genesis and impact of individual decisions. Such sources as minutes of public meetings, newspaper accounts, agents' reports to superiors, and the like may give clues as to who decided what and when and may even offer a glimpse of the incentives and constraints impinging on those decisions. But if the principals themselves are dead or cannot remember the event clearly, the best that can be hoped for is a very rough approximation of change processes through the event-analysis approach (cf. Bailey 1960:254; Bee 1967).

The effectiveness of the approach is therefore extremely dependent upon the availability of good data about decision-making, which is to say that it is usually limited to changes over brief periods of time.

Another prerequisite is that the analyst be able to gather information about a *series* of decisions regarding closely related issues through time; the more cases the better. If he is able to observe only a few events in which the decisions seem important and novel, he is in no position to know whether the cases indicate a trend toward change or are simply random variations. Using a medical metaphor, Bailey likened new decisions to "malignant symptoms" in parts of the pre-existing sociocultural system ("the body-politic"):

But we have no means of telling from . . . [a single] action alone whether the body-politic will survive and cure itself, or whether it will die. After the event we can be wise. . . . In other words, we need to have seen a large number of patients die of the disease, before we can say, on diagnosing the first symptom, that the disease is likely to prove fatal [1960:255].

Declared Bailey: "We can only identify change retrospectively" (1960:255). What this means is that however carefully the analyst has selected his field location, however accurately he has identified the entrepreneurs, and however able he is to witness important events, he still cannot be sure he is witnessing events of change until he determines the *impact* of the events (specifically the frequency with which the "new" choices are repeated in subsequent events). In some cases, the only way to determine the impact is to monitor the behavior of individuals over extended periods of time—perhaps several years. This can be accomplished by the continuous presence of observers (a most desirable but financially unfeasible method [Vogt 1960]) or by a series of carefully planned restudies at periodic intervals. Another alternative is to train members of the group itself to conduct the necessary observations, so long as they can be properly reimbursed for their efforts and provided that their observer role does not jeopardize their pre-existing status in the group.

As I have implied already, I believe that some of the anthropological literature that focuses on the role of entrepreneurs has tended to become more involved with the entrepreneurs' decisions than with the impact that they have upon the larger group (e.g., Barth 1963). This is not necessarily a fault; these sorts of studies have followed a research strategy that places priority on the genesis of change rather than on the acceptance or institutionalization of change. But it is difficult to create a potent combination of the event-analysis level with a more inclusive analysis of the general impact of new behavior (see Bailey 1960:254–255).

Other studies have focused less on specific decisions made by specific individuals and have concentrated on changing patterns of *group* decisions about resource allocation (e.g., Bennett 1969; Barth 1967; and [more programatically] Erasmus 1961). This approach adds latitude to the requirements for "good" data, because the behavior of one or two individuals at particular points in time need not be documented so exhaustively. The objectives are still to determine the nature of the incentives and constraints operating upon behavioral change, but the general trends in that change itself usually have become apparent already. The task is to understand why the trends occurred as they did, and, more important, whether they might continue into the future. A brief but enlightening example of such an approach is provided by Barth's (1967) study of the Fur.

The Fur of Darfur: Group Decisions About Resource Allocation

The Fur of the Darfur province of Sudan usually make their living from farming. The husband and wife of the typical household each cultivate their separate millet fields and keep their separate cash accounts. The woman is obligated to cook and brew beer for the man; the man is obligated to provide the woman with some cash for consumer goods such as clothing. But otherwise, the household is not

a single unit of consumption. This typical behavior constitutes a general set of decisions about the allocation of
resources (time, food, cash) in a general context (the household).

Some Fur families have become nomadic herders, with a
corresponding change in resource allocation. Under these
conditions, the husband and wife pool their cash resources;
she farms and cooks while he herds, and they form a joint
unit of consumption rather than the usual two units of the
farming household. The explanation, Barth (1967:666)
allowed, could be acculturation: the Fur herders have been
in contact with Baggara Arabs—who are also herders—and
have simply copied the latters' life ways. But the acculturation explanation is weakened by the fact that still another
group of Fur have much the same pattern of pooling of
resources and joint consumption, even though this third
group's subsistence is based upon neither farming nor herding but on the cultivation of irrigated fruit orchards. Furthermore, there is no evidence that the orchard cultivators
have borrowed these consumption patterns from other
groups.

Instead of viewing these changes as acculturation, Barth
argued that they are the result of rational decision-making
from among new alternatives:

The advantages of . . . jointness in [millet] cultivation are
rather limited, only slightly reducing the labor input required
for the same result, and few spouses choose to work jointly.
But in a situation where one of the spouses can specialize in
herding, the other in cultivation and dairying, cooperation offers
great advantages. Similarly, where a pooling of labor in specialized arboriculture and fruit-picking gives far greater returns
than millet cultivation, it is also clearly to the advantage of
both spouses to go together over production and share the
product jointly [1967:667].

The key variable thus is not contact with other cultures but
"the advantage of joint production over separate production." As Barth himself noted, this is hardly a surprising

conclusion. But it is based on an approach that leads to an understanding of process rather than to a classificatory or descriptive account that offers no such understanding. It explains *how* household form A (separate consumption) changed to household form B (joint consumption) by concentrating not on the forms themselves but upon the behavioral alternatives upon which the forms were based. Barth argued that if analysts continue to be preoccupied with sociocultural systemic forms themselves rather than with how such forms came into being, the understanding of sociocultural processes will continue to suffer (1967:661).

Barth's conclusion about the key variables involved in this case was not a categorical rejection of the importance of culture contact as a dynamic factor in other cases. Rather, the decision-making approach puts the influence of contact into perspective as just another possible variable to be considered.

In describing how these several changes have taken place, Barth made no special reference to the behavior of entrepreneurs, nor did he attempt to zero in on particular events of change. He focused on the collective pattern of decision-making of a group of individuals and attempted to explain the different patterns he observed, patterns that had already become established (institutionalized). What mattered was that the patterns were present; who initiated them was analytically irrelevant. The focus was largely retrospective, concerned with explanation after the fact, just as Bailey (1960:255) declared it must be.

Is the Study of the Entrepreneur Really Necessary?

Of course it is helpful to understand the role of the entrepreneur and his advocates in the processes of sociocultural change, because such individuals usually break the ice of tradition (however thin it may be). But it is not always possible to specify that role very clearly in all situations in which the decision-making approach is useful, so its influence must in some cases be considered a given. My point is that it is possible to study the influence of constraints and incentives on decision-making among alternatives without being able to study the precise effect of the behavior of a handful of key individuals.

I am arguing that there are two variations on the single decision-making theme: one is the detailed study of the behavior of entrepreneurs in a series of similar contexts, which is aimed at understanding how culture changes originate and what their future course might be. The other is a more general focus on changes that have already occurred, in which the objective is to determine why the group selected one particular set of behavioral alternatives over another. The two variations ought to fit together nicely; theoretically they do just that. Actually, however, the extensive requirements for data and the circumscribed time period for analysis of the first makes it difficult to fit with the second.

Limitations of the Approach

Two obvious limitations on the decision-making approach involve level of abstraction and time depth. The effectiveness of the approach, it seems to me, lies principally in its ability to specify the factors involved in the selection of new kinds of behavioral alternatives. The rigor is diminished as the level of abstraction becomes higher and as the time depth becomes greater, for there are analytical and temporal points beyond which decision-making data are either irrelevant or impossible to obtain. When operating at the level of general sociocultural evolution, to take an extreme example, we need not know, nor can we find out, the decision-making process or the identity of the entrepreneur or evolutionary cluster who first developed the idea of domesticating wild seeds. At the general level, the relevant information is that agriculture was added to man's store of techniques for harnessing energy. We cannot know if the new technique was the result of acculturation, or was independently developed again and again within a specific region like the foothills of Asia Minor. In a more specific case, if the transition in Fur subsistence from millet horticulture to herding had occurred in the more remote past, we would be unsure about the influence of the neighboring Baggara Arabs.

Another sort of limitation lies in the ability of this approach to generate testable generalizations. I have carefully avoided calling the decision-making approach a "theory," because it postulates no particular relationship among a series of variables. Rather, it makes certain theoretical assumptions that it does not attempt to prove. An example is the maximizing tendency among human actors and its relationship to the acceptance of new behavioral alternatives. The approach is just that—a scheme for determining how sociocultural change takes place. The conclusions it produces are usually specific to a given situation, such as the factors involved in the household behavior of the three Fur groups, or the role of Paliau and his advocates in the new order among the Manus. As an approach, however, it can be applied to all situations for which necessary data are available. It is a statement about what conditions to investigate, not a statement of laws, corollaries, or principles.

A related observation, also seen as a limitation by some (e.g., Harris 1969:203), is that it is an *eclectic* empirical approach. That is, it is inherently neither materialistic nor idealistic—but potentially both. It can be made into a material approach if the particular analyst wishes to use it in that fashion. The analyst can consider only the material constraints impinging on a particular behavioral change, and, to the extent that his data allow him to do so, can conclude that these material factors alone are both necessary and sufficient explanations for the observed change. The same holds true for the ideological constraints. But the major applications thus far have included both sorts of factors as influential in the changes that they have documented (e.g., Bennett 1969; Barth 1967; Bailey 1960).

I earlier mentioned yet another possible limitation of the approach when I discussed the problem of deciding how a group of actors actually perceives the alternatives and constraints in a specific context. Again, I think any champion of the decision-making scheme must acknowledge that the list of relevant constraints and alternatives in a given situation can only approximate what is going on in the actors' minds, even though there are ways of limiting the research to the situations in which there is less likely to be confusion about the major constraints. The problem is magnified by the fact that many actors are unable to articulate their perceptions in interviews or that they may articulate false ones to avoid personal embarrassment or to hide certain motives. There is, in short, an unquestionable risk of wrongly deriving existing constraints from observations of behavior. Service has stated the problem succinctly: "an inference drawn from behavior . . . if used then to explain the behavior, faces us with a classic tautology" (1971:84).

But all behavior takes place within a context, and it is possible for the anthropologist to become very familiar with some of the sociocultural and natural contexts within which the behavior of the group is placed. This familiarity in turn allows him to know something of the *major* constraints and incentives involved in activities within those contexts, although, again, the constraints in some sorts of activities—such as economics or politics—may be more readily identified than those of other activities. And, the inferences from the generally similar behavior of many individuals at different times in a given context are relatively less dangerous than those made on the basis of the behavior of one individual at a single point in time (cf. Wilson and Wilson 1945:75). Logically, then, the study that focuses upon decision-making by a single entrepreneur is more liable to distortion than one that focuses on patterns of the decision-making of a group.

Relevance to Other Approaches

Mead (1964) has already linked the decision-making approach with that of specific cultural evolution (Sahlins 1960), although her focus on the evolutionary cluster is not a tactic usually employed by others who could be labeled cultural evolutionists (see Chapter Six). It adds a more specific dimension to the understanding of evolution by documenting the steps by which and by whom a given evolutionary change is originated and institutionalized.

But as the focus shifts from the particular acts of particular entrepreneurs to the aggregate decisions of groups the similarity between what I have here called the decision-making approach and that of the most recent specific evolutionists is more apparent. In fact, the kinds of studies made of the Fur households (Barth 1967) and the farmers and ranchers of the northern plains (Bennett 1969) can be regarded as a continuation of the basic approaches of Julian Steward (1955) and Clifford Geertz (1963). All convey the notion of the sociocultural system as an adaptive system; the changes that occur are processes of adaptation. What are constraints if they are not selective pressures, after all? And certainly Barth and Bennett paid as much attention as Steward and Geertz to ecological constraints or pressures.

There are significant differences as well. The evolutionist bent for tracing a progression of forms through time, present in much of Steward's work, is missing from the decision-making studies. And what the decision-making approach adds is a sense of the role played by human choice in the pursuit of valued goals (see Erasmus 1969). But these differences are in part because of the kinds of data available to the analysts and are not entirely because of the ways in which the data are used. I join Mead in suggesting, in other words, that there seem to be no fundamental incompatibilities between the decision-making approach and that of specific evolution; and, if anything, the former could add a good deal to the study of evolutionary mechanisms.

Mead (1964) has also described at length the value of the decision-making approach to contemporary contexts of "modernization" or "development," although again her comments were largely restricted to the evolutionary cluster. After emphasizing the importance of evolutionary clusters such as that of Paliau, she discussed the ways in which evolutionary clusters can be deliberately fostered by calling together gifted persons into a setting where each can most fruitfully collaborate with his fellows, with the group's understanding that their joint efforts can be communicated to the larger population. It is assumed that the interaction will be for the good of the human race as a whole, not for purposes of discovering new and better ways to build bombs.

Charles Erasmus (1961) has drawn a large series of implications for development from the incentive-constraint approach to group decision-making. He subscribed to the view of man as a maximizing beast, arguing that humans are motivated by at least three basic kinds of requirements: that of self-preservation or survival; that of sexual gratification; and that of prestige, social status, or achievement (Erasmus 1961:12). The motivation for prestige maximization is the "stimulus to development" (Erasmus 1961:14; cf. McClelland and Winter 1969). Translated into the jargon of the present chapter, his message to development experts was that if the incentives of new behavioral alternatives are sufficiently attractive, the acceptance rate of the new alternatives by a group will tend to be rapid and portions of the preexisting system may be jettisoned or altered without major trauma (Erasmus 1961:33–34). In his words, "Given adequate opportunity to measure the advantages of a new alternative, they act to maximize their expectations." This says something important about how new alternatives should be introduced, and it calls into question the technique of the hard sell for programs that offer no real advantages to the recipients.

And Erasmus, as Mead, discussed at length a way in which an evolutionary perspective can be combined with a decision-making approach. He traced the correlations between certain methods of gaining prestige (conspicuous sharing, conspicuous consumption, and conspicuous production) and an increase in cultural complexity, from the level of peasant society to that of the developed nation.

* * *

I believe the potential of the decision-making approach in both of its aspects (i.e., the focus on entrepreneurs and the focus on group decisions) has yet to be fully realized. It cannot perform some of the tasks that will continue to involve many students of change, and it has some areas of fuzziness in documenting constraints and incentives. Yet I believe it is a rigorous approach to the understanding of dynamic processes and is one that explicitly emphasizes a central concern with the relationship between the larger sociocultural system and individual behavior, a relationship which anthropologists have been at times reluctant to consider. It permits a great deal of flexibility, and can be linked with evolutionary approaches and perhaps other approaches as well. Even with the several recent attempts, how this can profitably be accomplished remains an interesting challenge.

◫◫◫◫◫◫◫◫◫◫◫◫◫◫◫◫◫◫◫◫◫◫◫

CHAPTER NINE

SOME CONCLUDING OBSERVATIONS

◫◫◫◫◫◫◫◫◫◫◫◫◫◫◫◫◫◫◫◫◫◫◫

THERE have been two major themes running through this book. I have considered it my task to re-emphasize them and to use them as organizing vehicles in an attempt to describe several major approaches to the study of change. The first theme is that none of the approaches "just grew." Each developed out of a pre-existing social scientific *milieu*. I have tried to convey a sense of this historical continuity between the approaches, which for all their diversity still reveal some methodological and theoretical similarities to their predecessors and contemporaries.

The second theme is a repetition of the question "Given *their* data, *their* assumptions, and *their* methods, how have the several approaches documented *processes* of change?" As I said in the introduction to this book, I believe it is legitimate to ask this of any approach that purports to get at sociocultural dynamics.

I want to re-examine these themes separately as a means of making explicit the generalizations that can be drawn from the preceding chapters.

Historical Continuity

Tracing the historical development of the several approaches reveals not only the persistence of similarities in method but the changes in notions about what aspects of change are important and some of the reasons why the approaches developed as they did. The development has been as much a "reaction against" as a "building upon" predecessors, meaning that both change and continuity have been involved in the emergence of each perspective.

To call attention to continuity and similarities is not to ignore or deny the real differences between each approach. But insofar as each has shared with others a concern for certain issues—such as reconstruction of the past, functional interrelationships of system components, or the role of material factors in change—its methodology has necessarily been similar to that used by others. I have reiterated this point because the similarities have often been masked by debate over which of the several alternative schemes is the "right" or "best" one. There has at times been a preoccupation with emphasizing distinctions at the possible cost of creating valuable syntheses.

This tendency seems less marked at present than in the heyday of historicist blasts against classical evolutionists or of the haggling between twentieth-century evolutionists, historicists, and functionalists. Not that the disputes themselves are fewer or less intense now (cf. Service 1968 and Harris 1969); but there seems to be a more explicit recognition that different approaches can be used to solve different problems in the study of change (e.g., Mead 1964); and, alternatively, that the approach used in solving a particular problem cannot always be labeled *exclusively* as "acculturational" or "ecological" or "evolutionary" (Bennett 1969 is a good example) because of a degree of methodological overlap among all these alternatives.

Sources of Discontinuity Between Approaches

In the Introduction I defined "change process" as the interaction of causal factors so as to produce a transformation of one condition into another. I have wanted to know how successfully each approach has been able to identify the causal factors and have also wanted to show how the causal factors interact to produce the observed changes; in other words, I have wanted to know how each approach has documented change processes. I have not assumed the existence of a single set of causal factors or a single processual scheme against which all approaches may be compared. I have instead emphasized the obvious point that what sorts of factors are involved in "a process" and how the operation of these factors is documented depend in part of the level of analysis or abstraction the analyst selects.

If, as in Julian Steward's or Leslie White's approaches, the objective is to determine the processes by which culture or a series of cultures passed through similar stages of evolution over long periods of time, then the specifics of personalities, diffused traits, and the like need not be (and often cannot be) invoked as causal factors. White and Steward noted this repeatedly. If, however, one wishes to understand the processes involved in the transition of forms in a single sociocultural system over a limited time period, such specific factors can be crucial. Factors in general evolutionary processes, such as the harnessing of energy, may be neither necessary nor sufficient to account for, say, the emergence of the Yippie movement in modern America.

Yet, the documentation of change processes seems necessarily to involve at least some consideration of specific sociocultural systems regardless of whether the intention is to show general progression of forms through long periods of time or to show the specific effects of a given entrepreneurial cluster over a short time period. The general evolutionist can document the importance of energy control or property relations only by discussing as examples the Industrial Revolution in Great Britain or the relations between the patricians and commoners in ancient Rome. At the opposite extreme in analytical levels, individual behavioral approaches are fruitful only to the extent that the behavior can be placed in the larger context and that the effects of behavioral change are detectable in the sociocultural system—such as the effect of achievement motivation training on business enterprise in Indian or Mexican cities. An analysis of individual behavior alone can tell very little about the dynamics at the level of the larger system unless it is related to that system. Of course, general evolutionists and those using the decision-making approach have quite different requirements for data, and thus neither approach can directly address itself to the kinds of issues confronting the other (cf. Mead 1964:Chap. 2). The point is that neither the extremely specific nor the most general schemes can make much sense without at some point applying their analyses at the level of a single sociocultural system, even though they make different demands on the data at that level.

Levels of analysis are, however, only one of the major distinctions between approaches. Another is the kinds of causal factors chosen for intensive analysis. The general evolutionists have been largely concerned with immanent factors, factors within sociocultural systems, while holding individual behavior constant. For those using the innovation approach, mental processes are what matter in sociocultural change. And, two approaches may focus on different factors within a single analytical level. For example, acculturationists and historicists have studied the contact between a given group and other, "external" groups, while cultural ecologists have concentrated on the relations between a group and its "external" natural setting (although whether the natural setting is an "external" or "internal" factor is a moot point). Approaches to change in a single society may emphasize material rather than ideological factors as causal in processes, while some others may choose to operate largely in the ideological realm. And some have concentrated on identifying the stages in the evolution of sociocultural systems more than on the causal interaction of factors (e.g., Lewis Henry Morgan and E. B. Tylor); that is, they have been more concerned with classification than with process. So, while none of the approaches has totally ignored processual issues, each has limited its perspective on causal factors and in ways different from the others.

It could be argued that the factors *must* be limited if regularities and generalizations are to be determined. Steward, for example, was very concerned with this issue and offered an elaborate justification for limiting attention to the culture core. Yet there is a danger in limiting the factors too stringently, to the point where a single factor becomes deterministic. The demonstration of its effectiveness can only work at such a general level that it becomes trite or superficial to an understanding of the dynamic processes in specific cases. Another potential danger lies in taking an overly eclectic or particularistic view and in arguing that so many causal factors are involved in a given process that generalization becomes virtually impossible. I have discussed approaches that verge on both these extremes. There remains a broad middle ground on which battles over "probabilistic determinism" and "selective eclecticism" can still be waged (e.g., Service 1968 and Harris 1969).

Yet even with limitations, proponents of some of the approaches have argued explicitly or implicitly that their schemes provide both the necessary and the sufficient explanations of dynamic process. This contention is, after all, the basis for much of the debate about which approach is "best." My position has been that the claims must ultimately be resolved empirically; hence my preoccupation with detection and documentation of change processes. Those who do claim such capability must be able to demonstrate it by rigorous scientific application to a wide variety of empirical situations; and they must be able to show that alternative explanations can be ruled out.

Methodological Similarities Among Approaches

Later in this section I intend to argue in favor of linking several approaches into a multilevel, synthesizing strategy for studying sociocultural dynamics. But to strengthen the argument, I must first briefly mention the areas of methodological similarity among the various schemes.

The task of reconstruction is a feature common to all the schemes. In order to show change, there must be some temporal point of departure, some base line or zero point against which subsequent developments can be compared. As F. G. Bailey observed, change can only be identified retrospectively, regardless of how specific the level of analysis may be. How far back in time the reconstructed events are to be traced, however, imposes limitations on the approaches that can be utilized. For example, the decision-making approach cannot be used for tracing developments over long time periods, nor is the general evolutionary approach well suited for changes over a brief time span.

Also, none of the approaches has ignored the functional interrelationship of subsystem components (a mutually influencing relationship among components is implied in the concept of "system"). Some, it is true, (like several historicists) have focused on these interrelationships less than others, and some have conceived of the relationship as being largely one-way: from a material base to an ideological superstructure. Yet, as I pointed out earlier, all the scholars have been to a degree "functionalist" in their methodology, just as they have been to a degree involved in historical reconstruction.

The concept of constraints has been used particularly in the decision-making approach to change. In a broader perspective, however, all the approaches have explicitly or implicitly been concerned with the constraints operating on human behavior. A case in point is "psychic unity," which was used in the nineteenth century as an explanation for why different cultures tended to develop along similar lines. A slightly different and more modern interpretation of the concept (cf. Erasmus 1950:386) viewed it as the product of a series of constraints operating upon human behavior; in other words, there are definable limits to man's biological, sociocultural, and psychological variability, and these limits create a basic similarity in human behavior everywhere. To cite an example used earlier: there are still only four basic ways in which kinship can be traced and still only a few basic patterns of kinship terminology (Murdock 1949), for all the apparent diversity among cultures.

The historicists' "limitation of possibilities" has been applied to more specific conditions, in which the constraints operating to produce those conditions are more easily documented. But, as Erasmus (1950:386) noted, the differences between psychic unity and limitation of possibilities as causal explanations are not differences in kind but in degree. They share essentially the same reference to limitations of behavioral alternatives. Steward's ecological-evolutionary scheme was an exercise in the study of the limitation of possibilities: given certain environmental and technological conditions, further development could take place in only a limited number of ways. Whether labeled as psychic unity or limitation of possibilities, then, the notion of constraints has been clearly a part of evolutionist and historicist methodology.

It is more difficult to argue convincingly that many approaches also share some single basic notion of goal-directed behavior in change processes, that is, that they share a view of man as being a maximizing animal. Again, this is an explicit assumption in the decision-making approach. Implicitly it may be traced in some of the evolutionist schemes, both general and specific, even though the scholars involved may have ignored or even dismissed the role of goal-directed behavior as a dynamic factor (cf. Erasmus 1969). It seems a *necessary* assumption, even though for analytical reasons or for lack of data the focus of a particular approach may be on other conditions. What, after all, induces man to seek greater control over sources of energy? Why was irrigation developed in the high civilizations of Peru, Mesoamerica, China, Mesopotamia, and Egypt? And why, following the agricultural and industrial revolutions, did production eventually level off into a series of plateaus? To say that these occurrences took place because culture was ready for them or because the potential for their emergence was present may be enlightening if documented. But such explanations tend to ignore the motive force provided by humans' desire to improve their lot. They continually strive for mastery even though their efforts are successful only under certain conditions and even though the success of some may be only at the expense of others. I am not intending to preach reductionism; the urge to maximization cannot alone explain the developments that have preoccupied the evolutionists. Yet if one of the tasks of dynamic theories is to understand the constraints that operate to channel group behavior in certain directions, it seems only logical that maximization is a necessary (but not sufficient) motive factor in the movement along the directional tracks. It is all well and good for analysts to consider human behavior a "given"; but why not acknowledge more explicitly that one of the important behavioral "givens" is the human desire to maximize? This is, in fact, also a statement about another facet of psychic unity—not in its reference to limits of variation but as a motivating factor in the dynamics of group life.

Again, I emphasize these points because I wish to indicate some possible areas of complementarity among approaches whose distinctions have until recently been among the major issues in much of the change literature. And, in view of this complementarity, I join others in a belief that it is possible to construct an analytical continuum extending from the less abstract, decision-making approach, through the specific evolutionary approach, to the highest, general evolutionary level (cf. Mead 1964; Sahlins and Service 1960; Erasmus 1961).

Such a continuum would have as its theme the idea that sociocultural systems are systems of adaptation (Sahlins and Service 1960; Bennett 1969). They are ultimately man-made systems, however, that are the abstracted result of collective efforts on the part of individuals to adapt to changing constraints and incentives in their life-space. Sociocultural change processes are processes of adaptation that can be studied at three major levels of analysis, even though the distinctions between levels cannot be clearly demarcated: the level of individual behavior is one, which permits an understanding of the linkage between the actions of individuals and the larger sociocultural system as well as permits a detailed analysis of how specific changes are instigated. Analysis at this level would necessarily concentrate on a somewhat short time period. Examples of appropriate methods are provided by Barth's entrepreneurial studies (1963) and by Bailey's studies of Indian politics (1960) and decision-making patterns (1969).

At some point in the analysis, it would also be necessary to move from an individual's actions to the collective actions of a group. This merges into the second major level of analysis, a focus on the sociocultural system itself, with attention given to longer-term patterns of adaptation to constraints imposed by the local environment (including other sociocultural systems) and with attention given to management of internal tensions or conflicts. Moore's "tension management" perspective or those advocated by proponents of specific evolutionary approaches (Sahlins and Service 1960) are examples of how analyses at this second level might proceed. The third, or most general, level would involve cross-cultural comparisons of adaptive strategies over very long time periods, with the emphasis upon determining regularities of adaptive processes among a number of societies. Julian Steward's (1955; orig. 1949) work on the evolution of irrigation-based civilizations is an example of this level of analysis, as is Sahlins' (1958) study of the evolution of stratification systems in Polynesia.

At each level there would be a major concern with specifying the constraints influencing the emergence of given patterns. There also would be an assumed functional interrelationship among system components. And, to show proc-

ess through time, there would be some attempt to reconstruct past conditions—the more general the level of analysis,
the greater the time period included in the reconstructions.
And finally, I believe it would be necessary to assume a
continuity of human motivation to maximize. Without this,
something is missing from an understanding of why patterns
succeed one another in time.

How the various constraints are handled analytically will
vary, of course. A materialist strategy, for example, may
focus on a single set of constraints. And the continuum
would leave room for other ramifications as well. It would
be possible to concentrate on system components at the
various levels—such as economics or politics or kinship—
rather than on whole systems. It is unlikely, however, that
a single analyst would be able to carry analysis from one
level to the other two. The requirements for data are simply
too burdensome. Thus, for a synthesized study it would be
necessary to have a team of scholars working at the several
different levels, with the sorts of cross-fertilization of ideas
that the "team" concept implies.

The continuum or synthesizing strategy would be most
appropriate for what have been called "regional studies"
(e.g., Bennett 1969; Pelto and Poggie 1974). In such studies,
attention is focused upon groups living within a specified
geographical region (such as the central highlands of Mexico
or New Guinea or the plains of Saskatchewan) for purposes
of comparing and contrasting their adaptive strategies
through time. Within a single region it may be relatively
easy to control certain environmental and diffusion variables
and thus to study the effectiveness of other sorts of dynamic
factors (cf. Sahlins 1958). By "control" I do not mean
"ignore"; whether or not the environment is uniform in a
given region must be determined empirically.

The studies of the strategies of adaptation of each group
in the region and of how the groups have changed would
involve analysis at the first and second levels of the synthesizing approach. It would then be possible to offer some

generalizations about adaptation in the region as a whole, and, if desired, to compare and contrast the dynamics of adaptation in one region with those of others at the highest, or most general, analytical level.

Here I cannot delimit more explicitly the analytical levels, the sorts of causal factors involved, or the precise distinction between "short-term" and "longer-term" patterns of adaptation in a synthesizing approach. These are methodological decisions that are best made in the context of a given research project. My purpose here is merely to offer suggestions about what characteristics such an approach might have. However, a greater awareness of its potential for studies of sociocultural evolution or adaptation has emerged from a consideration not only of areas of disagreement among the various pre-existing strategies but of areas of their possible compatibility as well.

"Practical" and "Academic" Applications

This has obviously not been a study of approaches devoted exclusively to "applied" or "practical" issues of change confronting contemporary populations. Such a study as that must necessarily take a different tack from the one taken here, with more concern for issues like the morality of directed change, problems of dealing with various vested political interests (anthropologists lack much political clout), and the debate over what precisely the anthropologist's role should be in the change process itself (cf. Goodenough 1963).

Yet I have been anxious to suggest that none of the approaches discussed is simply an abstract academic exercise in theoretical manipulation of variables nor a narrow-minded scheme for re-examining the past—regardless of how its major champions may have applied it. To be sure, more or less modification of some of the approaches is necessary to bridge an apparent dichotomy between "academic" and "practical" application that has persisted to some extent since the nineteenth century.

Karl Marx and Friedrich Engels were not responsible for this dichotomy. Reconstruction of past development was of utmost practical significance, for it revealed to them the inevitability of events in the present and the future—and they took care to show just how circumstances in nineteenth-century Europe were related to the feudal and ancient past. Tylor also argued that an understanding of past development could help in understanding contemporary conditions. But unlike Marx and Engels, he seemed relatively unconcerned about just what that understanding should be or about what should be done once it flowered among active scholars.

Some of the applications of subsequent strategies have maintained a Tylorian preoccupation with events of the past, at the expense of tracing the significance of these events for an understanding of contemporary conditions or at the expense of developing strategies for altering such conditions. This is not to condemn scholars who follow what they consider to be important intellectual issues; nor is it to assert that the problems that they have attempted to solve are unimportant or irrelevant. It is to reassert that an emphasis on reconstruction of the past should not obscure the possibility of applying these approaches to contemporary problems—for a greater understanding of those problems, of course, but also for help in their eventual solution.

BIBLIOGRAPHY

ADAMS, R. McC.
  1966 The Evolution of Urban Society: Early Mesopo-
       tamia and Prehispanic Mexico. Chicago: Aldine-
       Atherton.
AYOUB, V.
  1968 The Study of Values. *In* Introduction to Anthro-
       pology. J. A. Clifton, Ed. Boston: Houghton
       Mifflin Co. pp. 245–272.
BAILEY, F. G.
  1960 Tribe, Caste, and Nation. Manchester: Manchester
       Univ. Press.
  1969 Stratagems and Spoils: A Social Anthropology of
       Politics. New York: Schocken Books.
BARTH, F.
  1966 Models of Social Organization. Royal Anthropo-
       logical Institute of Great Britain and Ireland Occa-
       sional Paper No. 23.
  1967 On the Study of Social Change. American Anthro-
       pologist 69 (6):661–669.
  1969 Ethnic Groups and Boundaries. Boston: Little,
       Brown and Co.
BARTH, F., Ed.
  1963 The Role of the Entrepreneur in Social Change in

Northern Norway. Bergen: Scandinavian Univ. Books.

BARNETT, H. G.
1942 Invention and Culture Change. American Anthropologist 44:14–30.
1953 Innovation: The Basis of Culture Change. New York: McGraw-Hill.
1964 The Acceptance and Rejection of Change. In Explorations in Social Change. G. K. Zollschan and W. Hirsch, Eds. Boston: Houghton Mifflin Co. pp. 345–367.

BEALS, R. L.
1932 Aboriginal Survivals in Mayo Culture. American Anthropologist 34:28–39.
1953 Acculturation. In Anthropology Today. A. L. Kroeber, Ed. Chicago: Univ. of Chicago Press. pp. 621–641.

BEE, R. L.
1965 Peyotism in North American Indian Groups. Transactions of the Kansas Academy of Science 68 (1):13–61.
1966 Potawatomi Peyotism: The Influence of Traditional Patterns. Southwestern Journal of Anthropology 22 (2):194–205.
1967 Sociocultural Change and Persistence in the Yuma Reservation Community. Ph.D. dissertation, Univ. of Kansas.
1970 "Self-help" at Fort Yuma: A Critique. Human Organization 29 (3):155–161.

BENEDICT, R. F.
1956 (Orig. 1934) Patterns of Culture. New York: Mentor Books (New American Library).

BENNETT, J. W.
1944 The Development of Ethnological Theory as Illustrated by Studies of the Plains Sun Dance. American Anthropologist 46:162–181.
1969 Northern Plainsmen: Adaptive Strategy and Agrarian Life. Chicago: Aldine-Atherton.

BERNARD, H. R., and P. PELTO, Eds.
1972   Technology and Social Change. New York: Macmillan Publishing Co.

BOAS, FRANZ
1940   Race, Language and Culture. New York: The Free Press.

BOCK, K. E.
1970   (Orig. 1963) Evolution, Function, and Change. *In* Readings in Social Evolution and Development. S. N. Eisenstadt, Ed. Elmsford, N. Y.: Pergamon Press. pp. 193–210.

BOHANNAN, P. and F. PLOG, Eds.
1967   Beyond the Frontier. Garden City, N.Y.: Natural History Press.

BOSERUP, E.
1965   The Conditions of Agricultural Growth. Chicago: Aldine-Atherton.

BOTTOMORE, T. B., Trans. and Ed.
1964   Karl Marx: Early Writings. New York: McGraw-Hill.

BOULDING, K. E.
1970   A Primer on Social Dynamics. New York: The Free Press.

BRUNER, E. M.
1956   Primary Group Experience and the Processes of Acculturation. American Anthropologist 58:605–623.

CARNEIRO, R. L.
1957   Subsistence and Social Structure: An Ecological Study of the Kuikuru Indians. Ph.D. dissertation, Univ. of Michigan.
1962   Scale Analysis as an Instrument for the Study of Cultural Evolution. Southwestern Journal of Anthropology 18:149–169.
1968   Ascertaining, Testing, and Interpreting Sequences of Cultural Development. Southwestern Journal of Anthropology 24 (4):354–374.

CARNEIRO, R. L., Ed.
1967   Herbert Spencer: The Evolution of Society. Chicago: Univ. of Chicago Press.
CLIFTON, J. A.
1965   The Southern Ute as a Fixed Membership Group. Human Organization 24 (4):319–327.
COHEN, Y. A.
1969   Social Boundary Systems. Current Anthropology 10 (1):103–126.
COMTE, A.
1961   (Orig. 1830–1842) On the Three States of Social Evolution. *In* Theories of Society. T. Parsons et al., Eds. New York: The Free Press. Vol. II, pp. 1332–1342.
CONDORCET, MARQUIS DE
1822   (Orig. 1795) Equisse d'un Tableau Historique des Progrès de l'Esprit Humain. Paris: Masson.
COON, C. S.
1948   A General Reader in Anthropology. New York: Holt, Rinehart and Winston.
COSER, L. A.
1971   Masters of Sociological Thought. New York: Harcourt Brace Jovanovich.
DALTON, G., Ed.
1971   Economic Development and Social Change. Garden City, N.Y.: Natural History Press.
DIXON, R. B.
1928   The Building of Culture. New York: Scribner's.
DOLE, G. and R. L. CARNIERO, Eds.
1960   Essays in the Science of Culture. New York: Thomas Y. Crowell Co.
DRIVER, H. E.
1961   Indians of North America. Chicago: Univ. of Chicago Press.
EICHER, C. K.
1961–1962   An Approach to Income Improvement on the Rosebud Sioux Reservation. Human Organization 20 (4):191–196.

EIDHEIM, H.
1963 Entrepreneurship in Politics. *In* The Role of the Entrepreneur in Social Change in Northern Norway. F. Barth, Ed. Bergen: Scandinavian Univ. Books. pp. 70–83.
EISENSTADT, S. N., Ed.
1968 Comparative Perspectives on Social Change. Boston: Little, Brown and Co.
EISENSTADT, S. N., Ed.
1970 Readings in Social Evolution and Development. Elmsford, N.Y.: Pergamon Press.
ELKIN, A. P.
1951 Reaction and Interaction: A Food Gathering People and European Settlement. American Anthropologist 53:164–186.
ENGELS, F.
1947 (Orig. 1888) Herr Eugen Düring's Revolution in Science. Moscow: Foreign Languages Publishing House.
1972 (Orig. 1884) Origin of the Family, Private Property, and the State. With Introduction and Notes by E. B. Leacock. New York: International Publishers.
ERASMUS, C. J.
1950 Patolli, Pachisi, and the Limitation of Possibilities. Southwestern Journal of Anthropology 6:369–387.
1961 Man Takes Control. Indianapolis: Bobbs-Merrill Co.
1969 Explanation and Reconstruction in Cultural Evolution. Sociologus 19 (1):20–38.
EVANS-PRITCHARD, E. E.
1940 The Nuer. New York: Oxford Univ. Press.
FERGUSON, A.
1819 (Orig. 1767) An Essay on the History of Civil Society. Philadelphia: A. Finley.
FEUER, L. S., Ed.
1959 Marx and Engels: Basic Writings on Politics and

240 PATTERNS AND PROCESSES

Philosophy. Garden City, N.Y.: Doubleday & Co.
FIRTH, R.
1936 We, the Tikopia. London: Allen and Unwin.
1959 Social Change in Tikopia. London: Allen and
Unwin.
1963 (Orig. 1951) Elements of Social Organization.
Boston: Beacon Press.
FOSTER, G. M.
1960 Culture and Conquest. New York: Viking Fund.
1965 Pleasant Society and the Image of the Limited
Good. American Anthropologist 67:293–315.
FRIED, M.
1952 Land Tenure, Geography, and Ecology in the Contact of Cultures. American Journal of Economics
and Sociology 11:391–412.
1967 The Evolution of Political Society. New York:
Random House.
GEERTZ, C.
1957 Ritual and Social Change: A Javanese Example.
American Anthropologist 59:32–54.
1963 Agricultural Involution. Berkeley and Los Angeles:
Univ. of California Press.
GERLACH, L. P. and V. H. HINE
1970 People, Power, Change: Movements of Social
Transformation. Indianapolis: Bobbs-Merrill Co.
GLUCKMAN, M.
1949 The Sociological Theories of Malinowski. Rhodes-
Livingstone Papers No. 16. London: Oxford Univ.
Press.
1968 The Utility of the Equilibrium Model in the Study
of Social Change. American Anthropologist 70
(2):219–237.
GOLDSCHMIDT, W. R.
1959a Man's Way. New York: Holt, Rinehart and Winston.
1959b The Anthropology of Franz Boas. American An-
thropological Association Memoir No. 89.

GOODENOUGH, W. H.
1963 Cooperation in Change. New York: Russell Sage Foundation.
GORMAN, C. F.
1969 Hoabinhian: A Pebble-Tool Complex with Early Plant Associations in Southeast Asia. Science 163:671–673.
GREENE, J. C.
1963 Darwin and the Modern World View. New York: Mentor Books (New American Library).
HALLER, J. S., JR.
1970 The Species Problem: Nineteenth Century Concepts of Racial Inferiority in the Origin of Man Controversy. American Anthropologist 72 (6):1319–1329.
HALLOWELL, A. I.
1948 Acculturation Processes and Personality Changes. *In* Personality in Nature, Society, and Culture. C. Kluckhohn and H. A. Murray, Eds. New York: Alfred A. Knopf. pp. 340–346.
HARDING, T. G.
1960 Adaptation and Stability. *In* Evolution and Culture. M. D. Sahlins and E. R. Service, Eds. Ann Arbor, Mich.: Univ. of Michigan Press. pp. 45–68.
HARRIS, M.
1968 The Rise of Anthropological Theory. New York: Thomas Y. Crowell Co.
1969 Monistic Determinism: Anti-Service. Southwestern Journal of Anthropology 25 (2):198–206.
1971 Culture, Man, and Nature. New York: Thomas Y. Crowell Co.
HARSANYI, J. C.
1968 (Orig. 1960) Explanation and Comparative Dynamics in Social Science. *In* Theory in Anthropology: A Sourcebook. R. A. Manners and D. Kaplan, Eds. Chicago: Aldine-Atherton. pp. 89–96.

HEMPEL, C. G.
   1965   Aspects of Scientific Exploration and Other Essays
          in the Philosophy of Science. New York: The Free
          Press.
HERSKOVITS, M. J.
   1941   Some Comments on the Study of Cultural Con-
          tact. American Anthropologist 43:1–10.
   1945   The Processes of Cultural Change. *In* The Science
          of Man in the World Crisis. R. Linton, Ed. New
          York: Columbia Univ. Press. pp. 143–170.
   1953   Franz Boas. New York: Scribner's.
   1966   Cultural Dynamics. (A posthumously published
          abridgment of his book Cultural Anthropology,
          originally published in 1955.) New York: Alfred
          A. Knopf.
HOEBEL, E. A.
   1960   William Robertson: An Eighteenth Century An-
          thropologist-Historian. American Anthropologist
          62:648–655.
JACOBSON, D.
   1973   Mbale, Itinerant Townsmen: Friendship and Social
          Order in Urban Uganda. Menlo Park, Calif.: Cum-
          mings Publishing Co.
KAPLAN, D.
   1960   The Law of Cultural Dominance. *In* Evolution and
          Culture. M. D. Sahlins and E. R. Service, Eds.
          Ann Arbor, Mich.: Univ. of Michigan Press. pp.
          68–92.
KATZ, E., H. HAMILTON, and M. L. LEVIN
   1963   Traditions of Research on the Diffusion of Inno-
          vation. American Sociological Review 28:237–252.
KEESING, F. M.
   1958   Cultural Anthropology. New York: Holt, Rinehart
          and Winston.
KISTE, R. C.
   1973   The Bikinians: A Study in Forced Migration.
          Menlo Park, Calif.: Cummings Publishing Co.

KROEBER, A. L.

1923 Anthropology (1st Edition). New York: Harcourt Brace Jovanovich.

1931 Historical Reconstruction of Culture Growths and Organic Evolution. American Anthropologist 33:149–156.

1944 Configurations of Cultural Growth. Berkeley: Univ. of California Press.

1948 Anthropology (Revised Edition). New York: Harcourt Brace Jovanovich.

1951a (Orig. 1923) History of Native Culture in California. *In* The California Indians. R. Heizer and M. Whipple, Eds. Berkeley and Los Angeles: Univ. of California Press. pp. 104–122.

1951b (Orig. 1922) Elements of Culture in Native California. *In* The California Indians. R. Heizer and M. Whipple, Eds. Berkeley and Los Angeles: Univ. of California Press. pp. 3–67.

1952 The Nature of Culture. Chicago: Univ. of Chicago Press.

KUNKEL, J. H.

1970 Society and Economic Growth. New York: Oxford Univ. Press.

LEACH, E. R.

1965 (Orig. 1954) Political Systems of Highland Burma. Boston: Beacon Press.

LEE, R. B.

1969 (Orig. 1966) !Kung Bushmen Subsistence: An Input-Output Analysis. *In* Environment and Cultural Behavior: Ecological Studies in Cultural Anthropology. A. P. Vayda, Ed. New York: Natural History Press. pp. 47–79.

LEE, R. B., and I. DeVore

1968 Problems in the Study of Hunters and Gatherers. *In* Man the Hunter. R. B. Lee and I. DeVore, Eds. Chicago: Aldine-Atherton. pp. 3–12.

LERNER, D.
1958 The Passing of Traditional Society. New York: The Free Press.

LESSA, W. A.
1964 The Social Effects of Typhoon Ophelia (1960) on Ulithi, Micronesia. Micronesica 1:1–47.

LINTON, R.
1943 Nativistic Movements. American Anthropologist 45:230–240.

LINTON, R., Ed.
1940 Acculturation in Seven American Indian Tribes. New York: Appleton-Century-Crofts.

LOWIE, R. H.
1920 Primitive Society. New York: Liveright.

MCCLELLAND, D.
1961 The Achieving Society. Princeton, N.J.: D. Van Nostrand Co.
1964 (Orig. 1962) Business Drive and National Achievement. *In* Social Change. A. and E. Etzioni, Eds. New York: Basic Books. pp. 165–180.

MCCLELLAND, D. and D. WINTER
1969 Motivating Economic Achievement. New York: The Free Press.

MAGUBANE, B.
1971 A Critical Look at Indices Used in the Study of Social Change in Colonial Africa. Current Anthropology 12 (4–5):419–446.

MAIR, L.
1957 Malinowski and the Study of Social Change. *In* Man and Culture. R. Firth, Ed. London: Routledge and Kegan Paul Ltd. pp. 229–244.

MALINOWSKI, B.
1929 Practical Anthropology. Africa 2:23–38.
1938 Anthropology of Changing African Cultures. *In* Methods of Study of Culture Contact in Africa. B. Malinowski, Ed. London: Oxford Univ. Press. pp. vi–xxxviii.

1945   The Dynamics of Culture Change. New Haven, Conn.: Yale Univ. Press.

MANDELBAUM, D. G.
1941   Culture Change Among the Nilgiri Tribes. American Anthropologist 43:19–26.

MANNERS, R. A.
1973   Obituary for Julian H. Steward. American Anthropologist 75 (3):886–903.

MAO TSE-TUNG
1967   On Contradiction. Peking: Foreign Languages Press.

MARCUSE, H.
1960   Reason and Revolution: Hegel and the Rise of Social Theory. Boston: Beacon Press.

MARX, K.
1963   (Orig. 1852) The Eighteenth Brumaire of Louis Bonaparte. New York: International Publishers.
1965   (Orig. 1857–1858) Pre-Capitalist Economic Formations. Introduction by E. J. Hobsbawm. New York: International Publishers.
1967   (Orig. 1867) Capital. New York: International Publishers. 2 Vols.
1970   (Orig. 1857) Introduction to a Critique of Political Economy. Edited, with Introduction, by C. J. Arthur. New York: International Publishers. Bound together with Marx and Engels 1970.

MARX, K. and F. ENGELS
1970   (Orig. 1846) The German Ideology. Edited, with Introduction, by C. J. Arthur. New York: International Publishers. Bound together with Marx 1970.

MARUYAMA, M.
1965   The Second Cybernetics: Deviation Amplifying Mutual Causal Processes. American Scientist 51 (2):164–179.

MEAD, M.
1932   The Changing Culture of an Indian Tribe. New

York: Columbia Univ. Press.

1956 New Lives for Old. New York: Mentor Books (New American Library).

1964 Continuities in Cultural Evolution. New Haven, Conn.: Yale Univ. Press.

MEGGERS, B. J.

1960 The Law of Cultural Evolution as a Practical Research Tool. *In* Essays in the Science of Culture. G. E. Dole and R. L. Carniero, Eds. New York: Thomas Y. Crowell Co. pp. 302–316.

1961 Field Testing of Cultural Law: A Reply to Morris Opler. Southwestern Journal of Anthropology 17 (4):352–354.

MILLER, F. C.

1973 Old Villages and a New Town (A Study of the Effects of Industrialization in a Mexican Village). Menlo Park, Calif.: Cummings Publishing Co.

MONTESQUIEU

1949 (Orig. 1748) The Spirit of Laws. T. Nugent, Trans. New York: Hafner.

MOONEY, J.

1892–1893 The Ghost Dance Religion. Bureau of American Ethnology Annual Report. Washington: Government Printing Office.

MOORE, W. E.

1963 Social Change. Englewood Cliffs, N.J.: Prentice-Hall.

1970 (Orig. 1960) A Reconsideration of Theories of Social Change. *In* Readings in Social Evolution and Development. S. N. Eisenstadt, Ed. Elmsford, N.Y.: Pergamon Press. pp. 123–140.

MORGAN, L. H.

1851 League of the Ho-de-no-sau-nee, or Iroquois. Rochester: Sage and Broa.

1870 Systems of Consanguinity and Affinity in the Human Family. Washington, D.C.: Smithsonian Institution.

1877 Ancient Society. New York: Holt, Rinehart and Winston.

MURDOCK, G. P.
1949 Social Structure. New York: Macmillan Publishing Co.

MURPHY, R. F. and J. H. STEWARD
1956 Tappers and Trappers: Parallel Processes in Acculturation. Economic Development and Cultural Change 4:335–355.

NAROLL, R.
1956 A Preliminary Index of Social Development. American Anthropologist 58:687–715.
1964 On Ethnic Unit Classification. Current Anthropology 5 (4):283–312.

OGBURN, W. F.
1957 Cultural Lag as Theory. Sociology and Social Research 41:167–174.

OPLER, M. E.
1961 Cultural Evolution, Southern Athapaskans, and Chronology in Theory. Southwestern Journal of Anthropology 17 (1):1–20.
1964 Cause, Process, and Dynamics in the Evolutionism of E. B. Tylor. Southwestern Journal of Anthropology 20 (2):123–44.

PARSONS, T.
1970 (Orig. 1960) Some Considerations on the Theory of Social Change. *In* Readings in Social Evolution and Development. S. N. Eisenstadt, Ed. Elmsford, N.Y.: Pergamon Press. pp. 95–122.

PELTO, P J.
1973 The Snowmobile Revolution: Technology and Social Change in the Arctic. Menlo Park, Calif.: Cummings Publishing Co.

PELTO, P. J. and J. J. POGGIE, JR.
1974 Models of Modernization: A Regional Focus. *In* Rethinking Modernization. J. J. Poggie, Jr., and R.

Lynch, Eds. Westport, Conn.: Redgrave. (In press.)

PLOTNICOV, L.
1962   Fixed Membership Groups: The Locus of Culture Processes. American Anthropologist 64:97–103.

RADCLIFFE-BROWN, A. R.
1952   Structure and Function in Primitive Society. New York: The Free Press.

RAY, V. F.
1939   Review of M. J. Herskovits' Acculturation: The Study of Culture Contact. Journal of American Folklore 52:331–334.

REDFIELD, R.
1934   Culture Changes in Yucatan. American Anthropologist 36:57–69.

REDFIELD, R., R. LINTON, and M. J. HERSKOVITS
1936   Memorandum for the Study of Acculturation. American Anthropologist 38:149–152.

RICHARDSON, J. and A. L. KROEBER
1940   Three Centuries of Women's Dress Fashions: A Quantitative Analysis. Anthropological Records 5 (2):111–154.

ROBERTSON, WILLIAM
1812   (Orig. 1777) The History of America. Philadelphia: J. Broien and T. L. Plowman.

ROGERS, E. M.
1962   Diffusion of Innovations. New York: The Free Press.
1969   Modernization Among Peasants. New York: Holt, Rinehart and Winston.

ROHNER, R. P.
1966   Franz Boas Among the Kwakiutl; and Franz Boas: Ethnographer on the Northwest Coast. In Pioneers of American Anthropology. J. Helm, Ed. Seattle: Univ. of Washington Press. pp. 149–222.

ROHNER, R. P., Ed.
1969   The Ethnography of Franz Boas. With Introduc-

tion by R. P. and E. C. Rohner. Chicago: Univ. of Chicago Press.

ROKEACH, M.
1973 The Nature of Human Values. New York: The Free Press.

SAHLINS, M. D.
1958 Social Stratification in Polynesia. Seattle: Univ. of Washington Press.
1960 Evolution: Specific and General. *In* Evolution and Culture. M. D. Sahlins and E. R. Service, Eds. Ann Arbor, Mich.: Univ. of Michigan Press. pp. 12–44

SAHLINS, M. D. and E. R. SERVICE, Eds.
1960 Evolution and Culture. Ann Arbor: Univ. of Michigan Press.

SAPIR, E.
1949 (Orig. 1916) Time Perspective in Aboriginal American Culture: A Study in Method. *In* Selected Writings of Edward Sapir. D. G. Mandelbaum, Ed. Berkeley and Los Angeles: Univ. of California Press. pp. 389–462.

SERVICE, E. R.
1960 The Law of Evolutionary Potential. *In* Evolution and Culture. M. D. Sahlins and E. R. Service, Eds. Ann Arbor, Mich.: Univ. of Michigan Press. pp. 93–122.
1962 Primitive Social Organization. New York: Random House.
1968 The Prime Mover of Cultural Evolution. Southwestern Journal of Anthropology 24 (4):396–409.
1971 Cultural Evolutionism. New York: Holt, Rinehart and Winston.

SMITH, G. E.
1928 In the Beginning: The Origin of Civilization. New York: Morrow.

SOLHEIM, W.
1970 Relics from Two Diggings Indicate Thais Were the First Agrarians. New York Times, January 12.

SOROKIN, P.
1957 (Orig. 1937-1940) Social and Cultural Dynamics (Abridged Edition). Boston: Porter Sargent.

SPENCER, H.
1876–1896 Principles of Sociology. New York: D. Appleton and Co. 3 Vols. (Portions of Vols. I [1876] and II [1882] are reprinted in Carniero 1967.)
1904 An Autobiography. New York: Appleton-Century-Crofts. 2 Vols.

SPICER, E. H.
1962 Cycles of Conquest. Tucson: Univ. of Arizona Press.

SPICER, E. H., Ed.
1961 Perspectives in American Indian Culture Change. Chicago: Univ. of Chicago Press.

SPIER, L.
1921 The Sun Dance of the Plains Indians: Its Development and Diffusion. American Museum of Natural History Anthropological Papers 16 (7).

SPINDLER, G.
1955 Sociocultural and Psychological Processes in Menomini Acculturation. Univ. of California Publications in Culture and Society No. 5. Berkeley: Univ. of California Press.

SPINDLER, G. and W. R. GOLDSCHMIDT
1952 Experimental Design in the Study of Culture Change. Southwestern Journal of Anthropology 8:68–83.

SPINDLER, L.
1962 Menomini Women and Culture Change. American Anthropological Association Memoir No. 91.

SSRC Summer Seminar on Acculturation (including H. G. Barnett, L. Broom, B. J. Siegel, E. Z. Vogt, and J. B. Watson)
1954 Acculturation: An Exploratory Formulation. American Anthropologist 56:973–1002.

Stern, B. J.
  1931 Louis Henry Morgan. Chicago: Univ. of Chicago Press.
Steward, J. H.
  1955 Theory of Culture Change. Urbana: Univ. of Illinois Press.
  1960 Review of L. White's Evolution of Culture. American Anthropologist 62:144–148.
  1968 Causal Factors and Processes in the Evolution of Pre-Farming Societies. *In* Man the Hunter. R. B. Lee and I. DeVore, Eds. Chicago: Aldine-Atherton. pp. 321–334.
Stocking, G. W., Jr.
  1963 Matthew Arnold, E. B. Tylor, and the Uses of Invention. American Anthropologist 65:783–799.
  1968 Race, Culture, and Evolution. New York: The Free Press.
Thurnwald, R. C.
  1932 The Psychology of Acculturation. American Anthropologist 34:557–569.
Turgot, A. R. J.
  1844 (Orig. 1750) Plan de Deux Discours sur l'Historie Universelle: Oeuvres de Turgot. Paris: Guillaumin.
Tylor, E. B.
  1874 (Orig. 1871) Primitive Culture. New York: Holt, Rinehart and Winston. 2 Vols.
  1879 On the Game of Patolli in Ancient Mexico, and Its Probably Asiatic Origin. Journal of the Royal Anthropological Institute of Great Britain and Ireland 8:116–131.
  1888 On a Method of Investigating the Development of Institutions; Applied to Laws of Marriage and Descent. Journal of the Royal Anthropological Institute of Great Britain and Ireland 18:245–269.
  1897 (Orig. 1881) Anthropology. New York: Appleton-Century-Crofts.
  1964 (Orig. 1865) Researches into the Early History of

Mankind. Edited and abridged, with Introduction by P. Bohannan. Chicago: Univ. of Chicago Press.

VICO, G.
1948   (Orig. 1725) The New Science. T. G. Bergin and M. H. Frisch, Trans. Ithaca, N.Y.: Cornell Univ. Press.

VIDICH, A. J.
1966   Introduction to P. Radin's The Method and Theory of Ethnology. New York: Basic Books.

VOGT, E.
1960   On the Concepts of Structure and Process in Cultural Anthropology. American Anthropologist 62 (1):18–33.

WALLACE, A. F. C.
1956   Revitalization Movements. American Anthropologist 58:264–281.
1961   Culture and Personality. New York: Random House.

WAX, M.
1956   The Limitations of Boas' Anthropology. American Anthropologist 58:63–74.

WAX, R. H. and R. K. THOMAS
1961   American Indians and White People. Phylon 22:305–317.

WHITE, L.
1945a   Diffusion Versus Evolution: An Anti-Evolutionist Fallacy. American Anthropologist 47:339–356.
1945b   History, Evolutionism, and Functionalism: Three Types of Interpretation of Culture. Southwestern Journal of Anthropology 1:221–248.
1949a   Ethnological Theory. In Philosophy for the Future. R. W. Sellars, V. J. McGill, and M. Farber, Eds. New York: Macmillan Publishing Co. pp. 357–384.
1949b   The Science of Culture. New York: Grove Press.
1957   Review of J. H. Steward's Theory of Culture Change. American Anthropologist 59:540–542.

1959   The Evolution of Culture. New York: McGraw-Hill.

1963   The Ethnography and Ethnology of Franz Boas. Texas Memorial Museum Bulletin No. 6.

1966   The Social Organization of Ethnological Theory. Rice Univ. Studies 52 (4).

WILSON, E.

1953   (Orig. 1940) To the Finland Station. Garden City, N. Y.: Doubleday and Co.

WILSON, G. and M. H. WILSON

1945   The Analysis of Social Change. Cambridge: Cambridge Univ. Press.

WISSLER, C.

1923   Man and Culture. New York: Thomas Y. Crowell Co.

1926   The Relation of Nature to Man in Aboriginal America. New York: Oxford Univ. Press.

WOLF, E. R.

1957   Closed Corporate Peasant Communities in Mesoamerica and Central Java. Southwestern Journal of Anthropology 13:1–18.

1965   (Orig. 1956) Aspects of Group Relations in a Complex Society: Mexico. *In* Contemporary Cultures and Societies of Latin America. D. B. Heath and R. N. Adams, Eds. New York: Random House. pp. 85–101.

WORSLEY, P. M.

1957   Millenarian Movements in Melanesia. Journal of the Rhodes-Livingstone Institute 21:18–31.

INDEX

PATTERNS

AND

PROCESSES

🔲🔲🔲🔲🔲🔲🔲🔲🔲🔲🔲🔲🔲🔲🔲🔲🔲🔲🔲🔲🔲🔲🔲🔲🔲🔲🔲🔲🔲🔲

AN INTRODUCTION TO
ANTHROPOLOGICAL STRATEGIES
FOR THE STUDY OF
SOCIOCULTURAL CHANGE

🔲🔲🔲🔲🔲🔲🔲🔲🔲🔲🔲🔲🔲🔲🔲🔲🔲🔲🔲🔲🔲🔲🔲🔲🔲🔲🔲🔲🔲🔲

Robert L. Bee

Fp **THE FREE PRESS**

A Division of Macmillan Publishing Co., Inc.

NEW YORK

Collier Macmillan Publishers

LONDON

The Free Press
A Division of Macmillan Publishing Co., Inc.
866 Third Avenue, New York, N.Y. 10022

Collier Macmillan Canada, Ltd.

Library of Congress Catalog Card Number: 73-10791

Printed in the United States of America

printing number
       7 8 9 10